Bridging the Fin
in Housing and Inf

Urban Management Series

Series Editor: Nick Hall

Bridging the Finance Gap
in Housing and Infrastructure

Edited by
Ruth McLeod and Kim Mullard

ITDG
PUBLISHING

Published by Intermediate Technology Publications Ltd
Schumacher Centre for Technology and Development
Bourton on Dunsmore, Rugby,
Warwickshire CV23 9QZ, UK
www.itpubs.org.uk
ISBN 1-85339-6397
ISBN 978-1-85339-6397

First published in 2006

A catalogue record for this book is available from the British Library.

Intermediate Technology Publications Ltd is the wholly-owned publishing
company of Intermediate Technology Development Group Ltd (working
name Practical Action). Our mission is to build the skills and capacity of
people in developing countries through the dissemination of information
in all forms, enabling them to improve the quality of their lives and that
of future generations.

Cover: Construction underway at Milan Nagar, the first community-led
resettlement project for pavement dwellers in Mumbai.
Source: Homeless International.

Index preparation: Indexing Specialists (UK) Ltd
Typeset in Utopia Std and Humanst521 BT
by S.J.I. Services
Printed by Replika Press

Contents

The Urban Management Series

The Urban Management Series focuses on the impacts of demographic and economic change in developing countries. The series offers a platform for practical, in-depth analysis of the complex institutional, economic and social issues that have to be addressed in an increasingly urban and globalized world. One of the UN's Millennium Development Targets calls for significant improvement in the lives of at least 100 million slum dwellers by 2020. This is a depressingly modest target as nearly 900 million people currently live in slums – that is one-sixth of the world's population.

By 2025 two-thirds of the poor in Latin America and almost half the poor in Africa and Asia will live in cities or towns. The urban poor face very different issues and livelihood choices in comparison to the rural poor. The reduction of poverty levels requires carefully designed policies and depends on the determined commitment on the part of governments, in particular. The livelihoods and rights of the poor must be at the centre of any strategy to reduce poverty and develop and inclusive society.

Cities and towns, and the industrial and commercial activities located in them, are a positive force for national economic growth. This is why cities are popular: where you find the mass of bees is where to look for honey. Urban areas provide consumer markets and services for agricultural producers. They are also gateways to larger national, regional and international markets. But the opportunities from urban development have not been maximized by poor people. Their rights are curtailed and they are often excluded from accessing secure land, shelter, services, employment and social welfare due to the discriminatory practices of government, the private sector and civil society.

This series of books addresses the many challenges facing urban management professionals. First and foremost, they aim to improve understanding of how hundreds of millions of poor people are struggling to live and earn a living in cities and towns. With better understanding the institutional and political conditions for poor people to participate and benefit from the urban development process may be improved. The lessons from research and dialogue should show how best to involve the private sector and civil society in mobilizing the necessary resources for inclusive and sustainable development; how to mitigate the impact that poor environments and natural hazards have on the poor; how to enhance the social and economic synergy between rural and urban populations; and how to strengthen efforts by the international community to co-ordinate support for a positive urbanization process.

Bridging the Finance Gap in Housing and Infrastructure concentrates on how groups of poor people – coalitions of the poor around the world have been able and been enabled to lead the process of transforming slums into vibrant and stable neighbourhoods. It showcases the strategies and the dedication, commitment and achievement of one northern NGO – Homeless International – as it has pioneered new approaches to analyzing and helping to arrange finance for community-led slum upgrading. This is a very encouraging story. It confirms that the homeless poor in the world's slums should never be dismissed as the helpless victims of urbanization. Given even half a chance they will confound their critics, forming self-help groups and catalyzing international coalitions that have been startlingly yet quietly capable of influencing both global agendas and the most hard-nosed bankers. The UN's Millennium Project has proposed that funding to finance community-based slum upgrading is one of the most promising 'quick win' interventions for achieving the Millennium Development Goals. This book shows how that proposal is being realized in a few cities and could transform the lives of hundreds of millions of people in many other cities.

Technically, this book is valuable for the explanation of how innovative financing packages can be arranged for slum upgrading programmes. But primarily, it is about human rights and how institutions and organizations respect and help people to realize their rights. The work of Nobel Laureate Amartya Sen has explained that birth endows everyone with a set of rights, and living should entitle everyone to progressively realizing those rights. This book, and Homeless International's work, begins and ends with the assertion that all people have an equal right to adequate, safe and secure shelter and that people who are unable to exercise this right are, in effect, homeless.

Nick Hall
Series Editor

Acknowledgements

First of all we would like to thank our partner organizations, and the federations and other organizations of the poor with whom they work, because without them we would have had nothing to write about. Thanks to all staff and representatives from the Asian Coalition for Housing Rights (ACHR), Centre for Community Organisation and Development, Malawi Homeless People's Federation, Dialogue on Shelter for the Homeless in Zimbabwe Trust, the Zimbabwe Homeless People's Federation, Integrated Village Development Project (IVDP), Namibia Housing Action Group (NHAG), Shack Dwellers Federation of Namibia (SDFN), Orangi Pilot Project (OPP), Pamoja Trust/Akiba Mashinani Trust, Muungano wa Wanavijiji, People's Dialogue South Africa, South African Homeless People's Federation (SAHPF), People's Dialogue Ghana, Ghana Homeless People's Federation, People's Process on Housing and Poverty (PPHP), the Zambian Homeless People's Federation, Fundación Pro Habitat, Slum/Shack Dwellers International (SDI), SPARC, Nirman, the National Slum Dwellers Federation (NSDF), Mahila Milan, Youth Charitable Organisation (YCO), Urban Poor Development Fund (UPDF), and Solidarity and Urban Poor Federation (SUPF).

We would particularly like to thank Sheela Patel, Sundar Burra, Jockin Arpurtham, Celine D'Cruz, Vijay Agarwal, Srilatha Batliwala, Mr Joshi, Mr Achrekar, Devika Mahadevan, Aditi Thorat, Gayatri Menon, Jane Weru, Jack Makau, Bob Kanyi, Joseph Muturi, Somsook Boonyabancha, Aseena Vicajee, Indu Agarwal, Subash Day, Beth Tatenda Chitekwe, Anna Muller, Joel Bolnick, Rose Molokoane, Sheila Magara, Patrick Hunsley, Edith Mbanga, Tom Kerr, Maurice Leonhardt, Mr K Francis, Arif Hasan, Aaron Wegmann, George Masimba, Ted Bauman, Sikhulile Nkhoma and Farouk Braimah.

We would also like to thank everyone who was involved in the 'Bridging the finance gap' and Urban Management Programme research projects, not already mentioned above, including Michael Mutter, Ilias Dirie, and Dr Solomon Mulugeta. Thanks to our technical advisers and friends who have generously given of their time and expertise on many occasions, including Caren Levy, John Benington, David Satterthwaite, Grahame Hindes, Virginia Grace, Derek Joseph and Andrew Cowan. Key board members (past and present) – Eric Armitage, Jon Rouse, Bob Paterson, Richard Newcombe, Martin Prater, Bill Payne, Jenny Rossiter, Malcolm Harper, Mike Dudman, and Tamsin Stirling.

Without the crucial support of the UK housing movement and their associated consultants we would never have developed our guarantee fund or been able to back new and innovative ways of doing things that no-one else would risk supporting. We are therefore particularly grateful to the National Federation of

Housing Associations, the Welsh Federation of Housing Associations, the Scottish Federation of Housing Associations, the Northern Ireland Federation of Housing Associations, the Chartered Institute of Housing, Airways Charitable Trust, ASRA Greater London Housing Association, Cambridge Housing Society, Plus Housing Group, CDS Housing, Comino Plc, East Midlands Housing Association, Family Housing Association (Birmingham), Family Housing Association (London), Horizon Housing Group, London and Quadrant Housing Trust, London Housing Foundation, New Leaf Supporting Independence, Places for People Group, Portsmouth Housing Group, Riverside Group, Servite Houses Charitable Trust, Southlands Housing Association, South London Family Housing Association, Waterloo Housing Association and Yorkshire Community Housing.

Thanks to DFID for funding the Bridging the Finance Gap research and to John Hodges in particular who backed its transformation into the CLIFF initiative. John Heptonstall from Ashridge Management College provided significant support to the research design. Pelle Persson, Sunita Chakravarty and Thomas Melin from Sida, Gavin McGillivray, Zoe Hensby and Christine Smith from DFID, Bob Buckley and Maryvonne Plessis-Frassard from the World Bank, and Billy Cobbett, Kevin Milroy, Rama Krishnan, Krishnaswamy Rajivan, and the rest of the Cities Alliance team have all made valuable inputs into our work with CLIFF. Comic Relief has provided invaluable on-going support for our work in Africa. Gratitude to the rest of the HI team, past and present, in particular Charlie Davies, David Ireland, John Walton, Rebecca Landall, Sarah Mitchell, Lucy McFarland and Jo Parish. Thanks also to all the other agencies and individuals who have provided funds to support our work and whom we may have unwittingly omitted from these acknowledgements.

We have been privileged to work with a wide range of bankers who have gently educated us along the way and are particularly grateful to Dr Nayak of UTI Bank, Anil Kumar of ICICI, Yashwant Thorat and Usha Thorat of the Reserve Bank of India and Stephanie Baeta Ansah of NHC, Ghana.

Finally, our sincere gratitude and respect to all the communities who have led the process and shared their work with us over the last 20 years.

Preface

I write this preface as a celebration of my longstanding friendship and association with Ruth McLeod and Homeless International. I am sure that I am joined in spirit by many people who have been drawn into this circle of friendship. One of them is Professor Arjun Appadurai, who in the mid 1990s joined this group as a contributor to "naming" the moments or processes that all of us experience in the deepening of friendships and relationships that are both personal and organizational. I asked him to remind me of the name of the concept that he used to describe this relationship. This is what he wrote back to me, which I have taken below as his quotations (in italics):

> *Some decades ago, social historians, particular of classical Europe made an interesting discovery. They realized that the stories of individual kings, saints and heroes were always connected to the stories of other people whom they knew, grew up with, and worked with, often during their most important adult years. This led these historians to invent a field called "prosopography" or "collective biography" which tries to tell the stories of these friendships and alliances together. In telling these stories of the relationships between important individuals, prosopography lets us see more about social change, about the nature of politics and about the power of shared visions.*

The story of the Indian Alliance of SPARC Mahila Milan and NSDF in India, Shack Dwellers International (SDI), the Asian Coalition of Housing Rights (ACHR), and Homeless International, IIED, Cordaid, Misereor, Selavip and Ford Foundation, is in many ways a perfect example of why we need to tell our stories about the friendships between special individuals as elements of a collective biography.

> *In today's world, friendships continue to be seen as one element of a traditional, personal, intimate world which has little to do with the public world of politics, money and change. As a consequence, the story of many social movements becomes mysterious and abstract, as if social movements come out of project proposals and social change comes out of a committee. The reality is that many of our best ideas and our most powerful visions come out of the accidents of history and biography, and of the luck through which we meet our closest allies.*

Jockin started the National Slum Dwellers Federation (NSDF) in 1974 at the time when he was fighting evictions in his settlement of Janata Colony, in Mumbai. Srilatha Batliwala, Rajesh Tandon, Celine D'Cruz and many others helped start SPARC in 1984, and we began to work with NSDF and Mahila Milan in 1986 as part of a collective commitment to work with the poorest communities in Bombay, the pavement dwellers, to help them to get secure homes. In 1986–

87 a grant from the IYSH Trust UK helped us to develop a strategy by which more than 500 women from eight pavements began to explore issues of habitat and shelter in the city. In 1988–89 I was in the UK on a sabbatical from SPARC and I met with Ruth who had just come from Jamaica where she had set up and worked with the Women's Construction Collective, and who had moved to Coventry as the newly appointed Director of Homeless International, the successor organization to IYSH Trust UK. I was invited to be part of the Gender and Habitat Committee of Homeless International, which met at IIED in London. It was there we developed the first transnational community exchange between Bombay and Bogotá community groups. This concept was so hard to describe in terms of what it could facilitate in knowledge creation and transfer, but it became the most well used development tool of SDI.

Two significant milestones occurred in the 1990s that can be linked directly to events described in this book.

In 1992 soon after my colleagues Celine and Jockin visited South Africa, Joel Bolnick started People's Dialogue and we helped set up the emerging South African Homeless People's Federation through exchange visits with financial help from Homeless International. It subsequently led to Homeless International (and the other northern NGOs mentioned) raising grant support for various federations that now form SDI. Around the same time, it became clear that once federations of the organized urban poor (like NSDF) negotiated for land, they wanted to undertake construction themselves. This could not be financed at scale through grants and so it became crucial to explore obtaining loans for project finance and individuals. Father Jorge Anzorena, who represented Selavip, and has been a friend and guide to all of us since 1984, helped us to get a guarantee from their bank to secure an Indian currency loan from the Housing and Urban Development Corporation (HUDCO). The Homeless International focus on finance, and on creating guarantee funds, emerged after that experience.

In 1997–98 our negotiations with Citibank for a loan to take on a community managed housing project with the Rajiv Indira Housing Cooperative, led to all of us learning to calculate financial risks and start a dialogue with bankers and financial service providers. That in turn created the basis for the 'Bridging the Finance Gap in Housing and Infrastructure' research project that led to the establishment of the Community Led Infrastructure Finance Facility (CLIFF). It was in 2000, while we were going through these experiences, that Ruth and I spent a long session with Arjun where we started looking at how community federations and their capacities to manage social and political risks actually make them very strategic trustees of venture capital to initiate housing by and for the poor themselves. Today, 5 years later, and with CLIFF operational we can see the beginnings of how communities of the urban poor, organized as federations, and we as non-profits assisting them, are beginning to adopt and appropriate practices for managing these funds and producing housing and infrastructure projects. This helps to produce the credibility that deepens dialogue with government, banks and other resource providers and encourages them to create policies and practices designed to increase direct access by the poor to land and housing. Within SDI this has triggered a reflection on how community practices for managing savings and credit can be linked to housing finance and how organized communities can connect their activism to methods for gaining resources for secure habitat.

This story, which merits a longer study in its own right, tells us many things. It tells us that friendships, especially long-term friendships, count. It tells us that new visions for change require the long-term evolution and testing of ideas and values which only deep friendships can bring. Such friendships bring each individual involved a precious resource in terms of the fortitude and courage required to hold unorthodox ideas and fight long and otherwise lonely fights. It demonstrates that the resources of a cohort of real friends make learning a dynamic, pleasurable, passionate experience in which new knowledge can be exchanged in a framework of trust. Last, but hardly least, since each individual in this story has their own changing and growing network of friends, collaborators, supporters and allies, the core group has growing access to a bigger bank of social capital.

This form of social capital, which multiplies trust and links it to risk-taking in the realm of social change, has hardly been studied. My friendship with Ruth is a privilege in itself. But it is also part of an untold story of friendships – and collective biographies – as a precious long-term asset of transnational activism and of many serious visions for social change.

– Sheela Patel, with inspired help from
Arjun Appadurai (as written in italics) 2006

List of boxes

List of figures

List of photographs

List of tables

Acronyms and abbreviations

ACHR	Asian Coalition for Housing Rights
AMT	Akiba Mashinani Trust (Grassroots Savings Trust)
BSDP	Bombay Sewerage Disposal Project
BMC	Brihanmumbai (Greater Mumbai) Municipal Corporation
CAG	CLIFF Advisory Group
CBO	Community-based organization
CCGHS	Commonwealth Consultative Group on Human Settlements
CLIFF	Community-Led Infrastructure Finance Facility
CRZ	Coastal Regulation Zone
CODI	Community Organizations Development Institute
DFID	Department for International Development (UK Government – successor to ODA)
FSI	Floor Space Index
Habitat II	Second United Nations Conference on Human Settlements (held in Istanbul, 1996)
HDFC	Housing Development Finance Corporation
HUDCO	Housing and Urban Development Corporation
IIED	International Institute for Environment and Development
IUDD	Infrastructure and Urban Development Department (former department of DFID)
IVDP	Integrated Village Development Project
IYSH	International Year of Shelter for the Homeless (1987)
KOWA	Korogocho Owners Welfare Association
KfW	Kreditanstalt für Wiederaufbau (German Development Bank)
MDG	Millennium Development Goal
MFI	Microfinance institution
MOU(s)	Memorandum (Memoranda) of Understanding
MUIP	Mumbai Urban Infrastructure Project
MUTP	Mumbai Urban Transport Project
NABARD	National Bank for Agriculture and Rural Development
NHAG	Namibia Housing Action Group
NHB	National Housing Bank
NGO	Non-Governmental Organization
NSDF	National Slum Dwellers Federation
ODA	Overseas Development Administration (UK Government – succeeded by DFID)
PMC	Pune Municipal Corporation

PRSP	Poverty Reduction Strategy Paper
ROSCAs	Rotating savings and credit associations
SDFN	Shack Dwellers Federation of Namibia
SIDBI	Small Industries Development Bank of India
SPARC	Society for the Promotion of Area Resource Centres
SDI	Shack/Slum Dwellers International
SHG	Self-help group
SUPF	Solidarity for the Urban Poor Federation
SRA	Slum Rehabilitation Authority
SSNS	SPARC Samudaya Nirman Sahayak (SPARC's assistance to collective construction)
SSP	Slum Sanitation Programme
SUF	Slum Upgrading Facility
TDR	Transferable development rights
UK	United Kingdom (of Great Britain and Northern Ireland)
UN	United Nations
UN-Habitat	United Nations Human Settlements Programme, formerly United Nations Centre for Human Settlements (UNCHS)
UNICEF	United Nations Children's Fund
UPDF	Urban Poor Development Fund (Cambodia)
UTI Bank	Unit Trust of India Bank
YCO	Youth Charitable Organization

About the authors

Ruth McLeod. Following 14 years working on urban poverty issues in Jamaica, Ruth became the Chief Executive of Homeless International in 1989. She established the Homeless International Guarantee Fund and co-ordinated the research project 'Bridging the Finance Gap in Housing and Infrastructure' which led to the creation of the Community-Led Infrastructure Finance Facility (CLIFF).

As well as overseeing Homeless International's work as a whole, Ruth has worked on a range of international research projects and produced numerous papers focused on urban poverty and financing of community-led development. She lectures at Warwick Business School and the Development Planning Unit of University College, London.

Kim Mullard. Kim is Homeless International's Policy Adviser and also co-ordinates ComHabitat, the Commonwealth network for human settlements issues. She has worked for Homeless International since 1998 and was previously responsible for the international grants portfolio. She was involved in the 'Bridging the Finance Gap in Housing and Infrastructure' research project from the beginning and edited many of the papers. She is a past Co-ordinator of the UK Urban Poverty Group (a network of NGOs, academics and consultants interested in urban poverty issues) and has represented the UK Government and the Commonwealth on delegations to UN-Habitat and Commission on Sustainable Development meetings.

Becky Telford. Becky became Homeless International's UK Activities Co-ordinator in 2001. Drawing on her background as a founder member and Secretary of Equality Housing Co-operative and an activist in housing rights in the UK, Becky has worked closely with the social housing domain to raise awareness of Homeless International's work. She has since left Homeless International and now works as a communications consultant.

Malcolm Jack. Malcolm Jack is Homeless International's International Grants Co-ordinator, having worked in the International Grants Team since 2000. In addition to co-ordinating Homeless International's grants portfolio, he has co-ordinated the UK Urban Poverty Group (a network of NGOs, academics and consultants interested in urban poverty issues) since 2003. Malcolm carried out Homeless International's 'Feasibility study for the application of Community-Led Infrastructure Finance Facility (CLIFF) operations in Ghana' with Farouk Braimah.

Dave Hughes. Dave worked as Funding and Research Officer at Homeless International between 2003 and 2006. During this time, Dave co-authored our 'Feasibility study for the application of Community-Led Infrastructure Finance Facility (CLIFF) operations in Zambia', in 2004, along with George Masimba of Dialogue on Shelter for the Homeless in Zimbabwe. He also wrote the first monitoring report for CLIFF in Kenya, in mid-2005.

Ian Morris. Ian is Homeless International's Financial Services Co-ordinator, and began working for the organization in 2002. He co-ordinates the Community-Led Infrastructure Finance Facility (CLIFF) at the international level, as well as Homeless International's Guarantee Fund. He worked for three years at GEC on the programme management of large engineering projects, and for two years in Bangladesh advising a local NGO on management issues.

CHAPTER ONE

Introduction

Ruth McLeod and Kim Mullard

We live in an urbanizing world. The urban areas of developing countries will absorb 95 per cent of the world's population growth between 2000 and 2030 (UN-Habitat 2003: 10). Evidence implies that the proportion of urban dwellers that are poor will increase at a faster rate than the urban population, resulting in an increasing prevalence of slums[1] (UN-Habitat 2003: 12). Nearly one in six of the world's population – 900 million people – are currently living in slums (UN Millennium Project 2005a: 26), in what amount to a health- and life- threatening environment, largely excluded from city life and from achieving their political, social and economic rights. Urban poverty is often underestimated, unrecognized and poorly understood. In many nations, official poverty lines define significantly fewer urban dwellers as being poor than would be suggested by an examination of nutritional levels or health outcomes in urban areas (Satterthwaite 2004: 11). As poverty becomes increasingly concentrated in urban areas of the developing world, the need to access new sources of finance for slum upgrading, resettlement and infrastructure provision becomes correspondingly acute. This is particularly so for organizations of the urban poor as they enter into collaborative arrangements with the state and with the private sector, in order to scale up settlement solutions that work for the poor as well as for urban centres as a whole. It is now widely recognized that the mobilization of local resources provides the only sustainable long-term option for the kinds of development that are needed. However the means of achieving this are considerably less clear, particularly given the complexity of economic, financial, social and political relationships involved.

This book documents some of the experimentation and developments that have taken place in this area of urban resource mobilization and management from the perspective of a northern non-governmental organization (NGO), Homeless International. Over the 20 years during which the organization has been operational it has radically changed the means by which it supports a growing, independent network of people's organizations. Starting from conventional small-scale grant giving to nascent NGOs in Asia, Africa and Latin America, the organization has broadened its methodology to include collaborative design of new financial products including an international guarantee fund and the Community-Led Infrastructure Finance Facility (CLIFF). CLIFF provides loan capital for bridge financing large-scale developments that are prioritized, designed and managed by organizations of the urban poor. Whilst these developments have largely evolved organically and in response to the growing capacity of Homeless International's long-term partners, the road has proved challenging and complex, incorporating an increasing number of actors and spanning a local to global continuum of institutional arrangements and resource bases. One of the major aims of the book is to share experiences with other agencies that may be interested in building on the lessons learnt in order to create a wider collaborative capacity to bridge the financing gaps identified.

This introductory chapter sets the wider context for Homeless International's work in financing housing and infrastructure development. It examines the challenges of urbanization and the urbanization of poverty, together with the vital issues of governance and access to land, before considering community-driven slum upgrading. A brief introduction to the structure of the book and the other chapters is provided. The chapter concludes with an explanation of how and why this book came to be written. [2]

URBANIZATION AND POVERTY

The urgent need for targeted resources to support organizations of the urban poor to demonstrate the possibilities of community-led slum upgrading is brought home by the rapid pace of urbanization across the developing world. Africa, generally viewed as an overwhelmingly rural continent, already has 37 per cent of its total population living in cities – by the year 2030 this ratio is expected to have risen to 53 per cent (UN-Habitat 2004: 1). In developing regions as a whole, a sizeable 43 per cent of the total urban population currently lives in slums, but in the least developed countries this ratio rises to a staggering 78 per cent (UN Millennium Project 2005b: 1). Old assumptions that poverty will always be worse in rural areas may no longer necessarily hold (Ravallion 2001).

Target 11 of the Millennium Development Goals (MDGs) aims for 'significant improvement in the lives of at least 100 million slum dwellers by 2020', but the scale of the challenge is emphasized by the fact that, even if this target were met, it would benefit only a little over 10 per cent of those currently living in slums. Current projections are that 1.4 billion people will live in slums by 2020 if urgent action is not taken, showing that far more needs to be done (UN Millennium Project 2005b: 21). Slum upgrading and urban planning are interventions that can contribute to all eight MDGs (UN Millennium Project 2005a: 281-293). Without addressing urban poverty, the MDGs will not be achieved because 'as the world becomes more urban, the integration and synergies emerging from the potential of comprehensively addressing the Goals in a specific, dense location are best achieved in the very settlements where slum dwellers live' (UN Millennium Project 2005b: 2).

The United Nations Millennium Project's Taskforce on Improving the Lives of Slum Dwellers took the view that a dramatic neglect of the needs of the urban poor, by their own local and national governments most immediately, but also by international donors, 'stems not from indifference but from a failure to understand the challenge of urbanization – its magnitude and unique characteristics; the connection between the lives of the urban poor and the prospects for a vibrant, equitable and productive urban system; the contribution of urban development to development as a whole; and the centrality of Target 11 to achieving the

Millennium Development Goals.' (UN Millennium Project 2005b: 10). This failure to appreciate or comprehend the challenge of urbanization may in turn be the result of the rigidity of traditional measures of poverty which, being income based and generally bereft of any meaningful adjustment for different costs in different areas, fail to take account of the far more monetized nature of the urban economy, which means that the poor are likely to have to pay for far more of their basic needs, and at a significantly higher cost than would be the case elsewhere. The result is that, while official statistics may suggest that only 1 to 15 per cent of a city's population is poor, data on housing conditions and deficiencies in infrastructure and service provision give a range of 33 to 50 per cent (Satterthwaite 2004: 2).

A key result of the underestimation of urban poverty, and a key barrier to the tackling of such poverty, is that Poverty Reduction Strategy Papers – one of the main determinants of aid spending by sector in the poorest countries – tend to pay little attention to urban poverty, with the result that efforts to tackle urban poverty are correspondingly under-resourced (Mitlin 2004a; ComHabitat 2005). Given the increasing enthusiasm of international donors for the low transaction costs implied by direct budgetary support, addressing this lack of recognition is crucial if the growing challenge of urban poverty is to be effectively addressed.

Whilst certain aspects of the challenge of urban poverty might seem rather abstract or prediction reliant, the picture in terms of health and death is stark and clear. It is estimated that in low-income nations 'infant and child mortality rates in urban areas are 15 to 20 times higher than they would be if there were provision for good-quality health care, water and sanitation, and safety nets for those lacking the means to get adequate food' (Satterthwaite 2005a: 101). The case of Nairobi – where under-five mortality rates in slums are 151 per 1000 live births, significantly higher than the average of 62 for Nairobi as a whole or of 113 for rural Kenya – gives an idea of what this means in practice (African Population and Health Research Center 2002: xvi). The World Health Organization, indeed, believes that good slum upgrading programmes can reduce infant and child mortality rates by at least 80 per cent (cited in D'Cruz and Satterthwaite 2005). The poverty experienced by slum dwellers is often hidden by statistics, as the latest United Nations (UN) report on the MDGs emphasizes:

> Sharp disparities in access to sanitation exist between urban and rural areas. Rural populations have less than half the coverage of urban areas. But statistics on coverage in urban areas mask the deprivation in urban slums. Both use of safe water and basic sanitation coverage remain extremely low in the burgeoning slums of the developing world... disease, mortality and unemployment are considerably higher in slums than in planned urban settlements. Surveys suggest that in some African cities, the death rate of children under age five who live in slums is about twice as high as that of children in other urban communities (2005: 34).

The available statistics for disease are just as shocking as those for mortality. It is estimated that nearly half of the total urban population in developing countries suffers from at least one of the major diseases resulting from deficiencies in water and sanitation provision, such as diarrhoea or worm conditions (World Health

Organization 1999). Taking a specific country example, it has been found that the prevalence of serious diarrhoea in young children is more than three times higher in slum areas of Nairobi than it is in rural areas (UN Millennium Project (2005b: 17). The risk of communicable diseases such as tuberculosis and meningitis is likewise heightened by severe overcrowding in slums, a situation compounded by the fact that resistance to disease is reduced in such areas by a combination of higher incidences of malnutrition and lower levels of vaccination. UN-Habitat's slum dweller estimations are based on a definition of a 'slum household' as lacking either: access to improved water; access to improved sanitation facilities; sufficient living area (having less than three people per habitable room); a durable dwelling (non-hazardous location, permanent structure adequate to protect from climatic extremes); or security of tenure (UN-Habitat 2003: 18). Many of these slum dwellers will be more vulnerable not only to disease but also to disasters, because of their precarious living conditions. The rapid growth of cities is likely to push the poor into more and more vulnerable areas, such as steep hillsides or flood-prone valleys and coasts, at the same time as the unpredictability of climatic events is apparently increasing.

Children can account for up to half of the residents in some poor urban communities, and living conditions can greatly affect children's welfare. As Bartlett (2005: 344) points out, 'Secure, functional housing; proper provision for water, sanitation, drainage, garbage collection and electricity; and safe, pleasant public space are all fundamental to children's health, well-being and long-term development'. For this reason, women often prioritize investment in improving living conditions above other forms of investment. Improved housing and basic services can also result in major time saving, especially for women and girls. For instance time is saved when it is no longer necessary to collect water by hand, when the house can be cleaned and maintained more easily and when it is no longer necessary to bury garbage or to carry it to distant dumps (McLeod and Satterthwaite 2000). Slum upgrading can therefore have particularly beneficial effects for women and children, and indeed well managed community-driven development processes can enable women to enhance their status within communities (see Chapter 3).

URBANIZATION AND ECONOMIC GROWTH

In general, the more rapid a country's economic growth, the faster it urbanizes – urbanization both reflects, and contributes to, economic growth and economic development patterns. The increasing numbers and proportions of the population living in urban areas in most developing countries reflects a growing concentration of people, and their families, seeking to take advantage of the increased demand for labour in the industrial and service sectors (Jack 2006). Overman and Venables argue that rates of urbanization are 'strongly correlated with per capita income, productivity tends to be high in cities, and urban job creation is an important driver of economic growth... The performance of the urban sector bears on overall economic growth' (2005:1). However, the linkages between urbanization and economic development present a major paradox. The urban poor provide many of the basic services and pool of labour that keep towns and cities running, but struggle to find adequate, affordable places to live. A recent study of Asian cities by the Asian Coalition for Housing Rights (2005a: 10) contends that:

> Cities grow as private investment concentrates there. But there is no automatic development of any capacity to govern the city and ensure that growing populations and economic activities can get the land, infrastructure and services they need. Cities may concentrate wealth, both in terms of new investment and of high-income residents, but there is no automatic process by which this contributes to the costs of needed infrastructure and services... All cities and most smaller urban centres face a contradiction between what drives their economic development (and the in-migration this generates) and what contributes to adequate accommodation for the workforce on which they depend.

LAND, TENURE AND GOVERNANCE

Sustainable urbanization strategies – which plans for and manage service provision and affordable shelter – can promote economic growth and help tackle urban poverty. Investment in low-income housing and settlement development is vital if cities are to promote sustainable, equitable economic development. Sustainable city development cannot be separated from slum upgrading when so many people live in such health and life-threatening environments. Slums are the result of a lack of affordable housing and land.

Many countries are in the process of decentralizing responsibilities to local government, particularly in relation to land, housing and infrastructure development. However, the decentralization of responsibilities is rarely matched by decentralization of resources or investment in local capacity to deliver. At the same time, effective local government, and effective local governance, are key to ensuring that economic growth contributes effectively to poverty reduction. 'There are hundreds of millions of urban dwellers whose unmet needs for water, sanitation, health care, schools will have to be addressed if the MDG targets are to be achieved. . . These needs will not be met without changes in local governments and in other local organizations' (Hasan *et al.* 2005: 3). The situation described by the Sri Lankan Government illustrates the challenges faced by many countries attempting to promote sustainable urbanization:

> Urbanization in Sri Lanka has proceeded largely in an unplanned manner, with peri-urban sprawl imposing strains on municipal services and adding to congestion. Urban management by local government has been weakened by a neglect of the way in which urban and town boundaries have been defined. A combination of an underestimation of the urban problem with obsolete settlement regulations has prevented municipal authorities from playing an effective role in urban development' (Government of Sri Lanka 2002: 83-4).

Insecure tenure exacerbates urban poverty. Improving security of tenure is central to improving the lives of slum dwellers (UN Millennium Project 2005a: 73). Security of tenure enables slum dwellers to invest in the improvement of their own homes and living conditions and to access essential services, whereas the threat of forced eviction inhibits investment and places people in constant fear that their homes may be demolished. The precise strategies and policies for ensuring security of tenure will vary between countries and cities. In Nairobi, for instance, pressure on land – largely from commercial interests – has led to a situation where 55 per cent of the city's total population is crammed onto a mere 1.5 per cent of the total land area (Alder 1995: 99). Housing for these 1.5 million or so people typically consists of shanties made of mud, wattle and iron sheets, with densities of up to 250 units per hectare. Access to water, electricity, basic services and infrastructure tends to be minimal or non-existent, with an estimated 94 per cent lacking access to adequate sanitation (Alder 1995: 98, 103). Most structures are let on a room-by-room basis with most households, averaging 5.8 people, occupying just a single room and lacking any security of tenure (Pamoja Trust 2005: 15).

COMMUNITY-DRIVEN SLUM UPGRADING

Although other aspects of housing and infrastructure development are touched upon, the major concern of this book is how to finance community-driven slum upgrading. It might be helpful therefore, to define what we mean by community-driven slum upgrading. The definition in the 'Cities without slums action plan' provides a comprehensive overview of the potential activities involved in slum upgrading (see Box 1.1). In the main, this book uses the term 'community-driven' rather than 'community-based' to reflect Homeless International's belief that sustainable solutions can be created only if people have an opportunity to play a lead role in designing and managing the development of housing and infrastructure in their community.

The Sachs report identifies funding to finance community-based slum upgrading as one of the 'quick win' interventions for achieving the MDGs (UN Millennium Project 2005a: 66). A paper initially developed as a background paper for the Millennium Project's Task Force on 'Improving the Lives of Slum Dwellers' outlines the many advantages that community-driven upgrading can offer in meeting the MDGs, including reaching poorer groups and lower costs compared to government or donor-led programmes (D'Cruz and Satterthwaite 2005).

THE CHAPTERS

The book comprises three main sections – an introduction that outlines the major contextual factors; a section on the development and implementation of specific financial products needed by the urban poor; and a final section reflecting on the experience of working with federations of the urban poor, their support NGOs, the state, various aspects of the private sector, donors and multi-lateral agencies. We have drawn heavily on the work carried out during a research project called 'Bridging the finance gap in housing and infrastructure' co-ordinated

Box 1.1 Cities Alliance definition of slum upgrading

'Slum upgrading consists of physical, social, economic, organizational and environmental improvements undertaken co-operatively and locally among citizens, community groups, businesses and local authorities. Activities include:

- installing or improving basic infrastructure – for example water supply and storage, sanitation/waste collection, rehabilitation of circulation, storm drainage and flood prevention, electricity, security lighting and public telephones;
- removing or mitigating environmental hazards;
- providing incentives for community management and maintenance;
- constructing or rehabilitating community facilities, such as nurseries, health posts and community open space;
- regularizing security of tenure;
- home improvement;
- relocating/compensating the small number of residents dislocated by improvements;
- improving access to health care and education, as well as to social support programmes in order to address issues of security, violence, substance abuse etc.;
- enhancing income-earning opportunities through training and micro-credit;
- building social capital and the institutional framework to sustain improvements.'

(World Bank and UNCHS 1999: 2)

by Homeless International and involving most of our partner organizations.[3] The Department for International Development's (DFID's) Knowledge and Research Programme funded the 'Bridging the finance gap' research.[4] However the views expressed here are not necessarily those of the Department for International Development.

The first four chapters set the scene for Homeless International's involvement in financing urban development. In Chapter 2, Kim Mullard outlines the development of Homeless International, its working practices and the philosophy behind them. This chapter also provides a brief historical overview of the organization's involvement in urban finance. Becky Telford begins Chapter 3 by defining the concept of small-scale capacity building, what it is, and why it is crucial to community-led slum upgrading. With this in place, she explores the range of ways in which community capacity can be developed, and the financial mechanisms needed for this, with a focus on the work undertaken by Homeless International and our partners. Finally, her chapter looks at the future of such mechanisms and their role within sustainable urban development. In Chapter 4, Ruth McLeod looks at specific areas of risk, particularly those that must be managed by organizations of the urban poor and their support NGOs when they enter into collaborative relationships with government and formal financial institutions. Chapter 5 considers a continuum of financial services that is needed in order to support the development and scaling up of community-driven processes in settlement development.

The second section of the book, comprising Chapters 6 and 7, examines two financing mechanisms through which Homeless International has supported its partners' work, the Homeless International Guarantee Fund and the Community-Led Infrastructure Finance Facility (CLIFF). Malcolm Jack's chapter examines Homeless International's experiences and achievements in developing the guarantee fund, before examining the limitations of the mechanism and how these influenced the development of the Community-Led Infrastructure Finance Facility (CLIFF). Ian Morris's chapter sets out the background to CLIFF, how it is designed and how it operates. He goes on to analyse the implementation of CLIFF in Kenya and India and outline the emerging learning.

The financing mechanisms that support the involvement of the urban poor in urban development, discussed in Chapters 6 and 7, have the potential to catalyse changes in urban development; however, achieving change at scale involves engaging with government and the private sector. In the third section, comprising Chapters 8 to 10 we reflect on the experience of Homeless International and our partners. In Chapter 8, Ruth McLeod and Dave Hughes address the development of relationships with the private sector. In Chapter 9, Kim Mullard summarizes the complex inter-relationship between government policy and practice and the financing of urban development, before examining Homeless International's experiences of engaging with local and national government, and with intergovernmental agencies and donors, in the area of financing urban development. Finally, in Chapter 10, Malcolm Jack attempts to bring together some of the lessons so far from Homeless International's experiences in exploring how to bridge the finance gap in housing and infrastructure. It includes perceptions about the key features of Homeless International's operational structure and processes that have enabled it to carry out the work described in Chapters 2 to 9, as well as an analysis of how Homeless International, as a United Kingdom-based NGO, has positioned itself internationally to carry out this work most effectively.

WHY HAS HOMELESS INTERNATIONAL WRITTEN THIS BOOK?

Homeless International decided to write this book because, in spite of the huge challenges posed by the urbanization of poverty, there are few agencies specifically addressing the issue and we think that more people ought to get involved. Urbanization is increasing and poverty will be highly concentrated in urban areas of developing countries within the next 20 years. However the major bi-lateral donors have largely dismantled any focused internal capacity to address the issue. 'Urban' is off the political agenda and, while there will be a significant increase in funding for international development as a whole, the majority of funding will be channelled to direct budgetary support or channelled through multi-lateral donors able to administer large-scale programmes. There are only a handful of NGOs that have consistently funded the organizations and urban development processes that Homeless International has supported, notably Cordaid, Misereor, Ford Foundation, IIED, and SELAVIP. Homeless International would like to see many more NGOs and donors focusing on housing, infrastructure and urban development, because of the considerable opportunities we believe exist within urban areas for addressing poverty, reaching the MDGs and building a foundation for long-term economic growth and sustainable development.

Another reason for writing the book is that the role of northern NGOs is changing. As southern NGOs and their international umbrella organizations are growing in strength and capacity, their need for the services of northern NGOs will reduce unless northern agencies, because of their location, specific skills, personnel, connections or influence, are able to clearly demonstrate that they can provide specific added value. We wanted to be able to show how we have been able to add value, specifically in the design and management of initiatives that provide broader financial services for the poor.

Our final reason for writing the book is to draw attention to a huge gap in the provision of financial services to the poor. The exploration of potential linkages between community or informal finance systems and formal financial markets has been on the development agenda for many years. The evolution of the microfinance sector over the last 20 years has also led to extensive documentation on the constraints that formal finance institutions face in lending to the poor: high transaction costs, little if any conventional collateral and small returns. To some extent these constraints have been overcome with the emergence of microfinance products characterized by high interest rates that arguably compensate for the costs and risks of lending to the poor. However serious gaps in financial service delivery to the poor still remain, particularly in the areas of medium and long-term finance delivery to organizations of the poor rather than to individuals. Whilst microfinance has become mainstream in the delivery of financial services especially for microenterprise, access to medium and long-term financing for infrastructure and housing development, including slum-upgrading remains extremely limited. Provision in this area arguably provides an important 'missing link' in the broader development of financial markets in developing countries. An additional complexity in financing housing and infrastructure results from the challenges of the decentralization of responsibilities without the commensurate financial or human resource capacity of local bodies to deliver basic services related to settlement development. This book is the story of how we have worked with our partner organizations to both support and develop mechanisms for the medium- and long-term financing of infrastructure and housing development.

This book is not therefore a neutral, objective examination of financing urban development, but rather a book written by an organization with a clear set of values and an activist mindset, located in UK civil society. We have been privileged to be a part of a much larger process, and the book could not have been written without the many hours spent with our partner organizations and the communities that they have worked with. Many of the examples and stories in this book come from India, because it is in India that we have our longest standing partnerships, and in India that our work on financing urban development has been broadest and deepest, particularly with the development of CLIFF. However we hope and believe that the examples we have chosen have a broader resonance. While acknowledging Homeless International's debt to our partner organizations, we must emphasize that this book is our take on our history.

CHAPTER TWO

Homeless International's involvement in urban development finance

Kim Mullard

INTRODUCTION – WHAT IS HOMELESS INTERNATIONAL?

Homeless International was initially established as the International Year of Shelter for the Homeless Trust (IYSH Trust UK) in 1984. The Trust was founded by a group of individuals and organizations within UK civil society who, because the then government was not planning any activities for the 1987 International Year of Shelter for the Homeless, decided to do something themselves. There was a dynamic and successful fundraising campaign involving many people and organizations and, as a result, grants were given to over one hundred shelter-related projects. Half of the projects were in the UK and half in developing countries. By the end of the International Year it had become clear that there was a strong and unmet demand from non-governmental organizations in developing countries, for shelter-related international assistance. Organizations requested grants for regularizing land tenure, for establishing funds so that loans could be extended to build houses, and for improving infrastructure such as sanitation and water supplies. Some organizations were working to help protect communities from the impact of natural disasters, others were working to ensure that women got a say in housing developments, others still were engaged in fighting evictions. At the end of the International Year the trustees of the organization were expected to close the organization down. However, around £200,000 remained in the accounts and a small number of trustees felt that they should use the funds to try to establish a permanent organization, which could respond to the demand that had been so clearly demonstrated by organizations in Asia, Africa, Latin America and the Caribbean. As a result, a Director, Ruth McLeod was appointed, the Trust was renamed Homeless International, and the organization began operating from Coventry in 1989.

Homeless International is now a membership organization, registered as a Charity and Company Limited by guarantee[1] under UK law. It has a membership base composed of individuals and organizations, including a long-standing core support base within the UK social housing sector. The organization has become known as a niche charity supporting organizations in developing countries that are working with poor communities to alleviate poverty and improve living conditions. Over the years Homeless International has increasingly focused on providing assistance to organizations addressing urban poverty, which use methods that enable communities to take a lead in the developments that make sense to them. Most of the initiatives and projects supported are community-led and seek to facilitate slum upgrading, resettlement and infrastructure improvements.

Homeless International's work is guided by a set of core beliefs that were agreed in 1990. The beliefs are that:

- All people have an equal right to adequate, safe and secure shelter and that people who are unable to exercise this right are, in effect, homeless.
- Shelter is more than a house – it is a space for privacy, economic activity, social care and personal fulfilment.
- Shelter development is more than the building of houses – it is the development of neighbourhoods and communities that provide opportunities for social and cultural expression.
- Homelessness is a characteristic feature of poverty and the eradication of poverty requires investment in the development of shelter that is economically, socially and environmentally sustainable.
- Sustainable solutions to homelessness can be created only if people have access to appropriate land, finance, information, organization and technology, and also have an opportunity to play a lead role in designing solutions that work for them.
- Sharing information about creating solutions to homelessness allows people to learn from, and support, each other.

Homeless International's trustees felt strongly that, in order for the right to safe, secure and adequate shelter to be meaningful, it could not simply exist in the legislative realm but must be realized in practice. An emphasis was therefore placed on supporting organizations that were working towards the realization of this right and it was agreed that, as far as possible, we would seek to work in long-term relationships rather than simply providing grants for short-term projects.

As Homeless International has grown from having one member of staff to a dozen, and from an annual income of less than a hundred thousand pounds to several million, its core working practices have remained the same. It supports work that is designed and implemented at the local level by indigenous partner organizations; it does not have field staff and does not implement projects directly. Homeless International has managed to establish long-term partnerships with its partner organizations, and invests considerable time in doing so. It is not an endowed charity, but raises funding for the work it supports from a multitude of sources, including its support base within the UK social housing sector. Finally, recognizing the limitations of its funds, it seeks to use them in a way that will have the largest impact, through either: supporting initiatives that have the potential to scale up, attract other funding and influence policy; or supporting and developing financial mechanisms that make the money go further.

HOMELESS INTERNATIONAL'S HISTORICAL AND INSTITUTIONAL POSITION

Homeless International's development cannot be understood without examining its institutional location within UK civil society and its historical positioning as an organization established in the late 1980s. It began as a fairly conventional, albeit niche, grant-giving agency and initially continued the work of its predecessor the IYSH Trust, working with a range of organizations that had received grants during the international year.

The International Year of Shelter for the Homeless was in 1987. Neo-liberal economic orthodoxy was at its height: Margaret Thatcher and Ronald Reagan were in power and the prevailing development paradigm preached that the market would deliver, if barriers to its operation were removed. Structural adjustment still dominated discussions of economic development, although the human impact of adjustment policies was beginning to be recognized with the publication of UNICEF's report on adjustment with a human face (Cornia *et al.* 1987). Within the UK, responsibility for management of social housing was gradually being shifted away from local government to non-governmental organizations called housing associations. Some associations had been established for many years, but the vast majority had grown up as voluntary organizations in the 1970s. By the mid-1980s they had become significant players in the development and maintenance of housing in the UK and their asset base was large and growing.[2]

Homeless International was established with close links to the UK social housing movement and construction sector and the majority of Homeless International's trustees have always come from these fields, as has the bulk of our voluntary fundraising income. It is therefore scarcely surprising that developments within the UK housing sector have had an important influence on the way in which the organization has evolved. In 1990, when the belief statement was drafted to guide the organization's development, a decision was also made to change the constitutional base of the organization in order to formalize its location within the UK social housing and construction sector. Consequently, Homeless International became a membership organization and was incorporated as a Company Limited by guarantee in 1992, in addition to its charitable status. Its largest corporate members were the national federations of housing associations in England, Scotland, Wales and Northern Ireland and a range of national professional associations with a major interest in the sector, such as the Chartered Institute of Housing and the Royal Institution of Chartered Surveyors. This change in structure was part of a strategy to position Homeless International as the international charity of the UK housing and construction sector, and to ensure high-level representation from the sector on our board of Directors.

As Homeless International developed, changes in the paradigms dominating international development assistance and, more domestically, our membership base in the UK housing sector influenced our direction. Internationally, it soon became clear that the market alone could not deliver poverty reduction and more subtle approaches involving public, private and civil society sector were needed. In response to structural adjustment programmes, the state in most developing countries was withdrawing from direct provision of housing, often rhetorically taking on a facilitative role but increasingly faced by an economic inability to deliver the shelter and services required in urban centres with rapidly escalating populations. At the Second United Nations Conference on Human Settlements

(Habitat II) held in Istanbul in 1996, governments adopted the 'Habitat Agenda', which emphasized the need to implement national enabling strategies.

In the early 1990s, one of the patterns that began to emerge among Homeless International's partner organizations was a demand for grants to capitalize small-scale revolving loan funds. It became clear that poor people were saving and managing small-scale loans, but the big constraint was access to land and to capital. Partners argued that if loan funds were available people could construct affordable housing themselves. This housing might be on land where communities had *de facto* tenure rather than *de jure* title. The housing might therefore be technically illegal, but it provided a means for people to begin seriously improving their settlements. Homeless International was able to raise funds to start and support a range of funds, which were generally very successful, at least in the rural areas. People took loans, built houses and then repaid the loans. The problem was that there was not enough capital to finance the houses needed in the rural areas, and in the urban areas access to land proved highly problematic. Homeless International was beginning to recognize that conventional small-scale grant giving was likely to have little impact, given the scale of the shelter problems being faced by its partner organizations. Other mechanisms were clearly needed if solutions were to be scaled up.

Meanwhile in the UK, government was slowly reducing the grant-funding available for new construction of social housing, and housing associations were being expected to raise funds from the commercial banking sector. As Homeless International began exploring financial mechanisms other than grant giving, key advisers who were designing the private lending initiatives for UK housing associations joined us as volunteers. The idea of a guarantee fund that could be used to encourage banks to lend to the poor for housing had already been mooted, but now people began to work on it seriously. By the mid-1990s, the Homeless International Guarantee Fund had become a reality, operating with deposits largely raised from housing associations in the UK. The development of the guarantee fund is described in more detail in Chapter 6.

Over the next decade Homeless International's work increasingly focused on the problems being faced by the urban poor. Just prior to Nelson Mandela's release, Homeless International's Indian partners – SPARC (Society for the Promotion of Area Resource Centres), the National Slum Dweller's Federation (NSDF) and Mahila Milan – had formed a partnership with a network of South Africans living in informal settlements. The South African Homeless People's Federation rapidly emerged, influenced by the Indians and replicating many of their methods. The approach spread to Zimbabwe, then Namibia, then Kenya and it became clear that the fastest growing area of Homeless International's work lay with networked organizations of the urban poor who worked collaboratively, sharing skills, experience and support through an ongoing process of community-to-community exchanges. As their membership grew and their organizational strength increased, groups began to negotiate with the state for access to land. The success of this movement only heightened the challenge. Where was the capital going to come from for members of this movement to build the homes they needed? Clearly the funds could not all be provided by northern NGOs but how could local funding be mobilized for long-term development at scale? We had to find a way to help partner organizations to access funds locally, from government where this was feasible, but also from local commercial financial markets.

LONG-TERM PARTNERSHIPS

We have already noted that Homeless International decided at an early stage to support local partner organizations on a long-term basis. There was no interest in developing 'exit strategies'. However there was a clear recognition that we had to keep adapting to the changing demands of our partners by finding new sources and mechanisms for providing support from Europe. It is significant that Homeless International is still supporting two organizations that first received funding from the IYSH Trust. The Integrated Village Development Project (IVDP) received an initial grant in 1987 for re-roofing rural homes in Tamil Nadu. When IVDP completed its work in a large remote area, it moved to another area, building on the same approach of supporting networks of women's savings groups. Homeless International continued to provide grant funding and in recent years we have jointly negotiated several guarantee arrangements with local banks using our guarantee fund (see Chapter 6).

Another organization that received an IYSH grant was SPARC, a Mumbai-based NGO that has become not only Homeless International's largest grant recipient, but also a collaborative partner across all our areas of work, including research and advocacy. SPARC works together with two organizations of the urban poor, the National Slum Dweller's Federation and Mahila Milan; this grouping is described in more detail in Box 2 below and is referred to as the Indian Alliance throughout this book. The 1987 grant was for the first model house exhibition organized by women pavement dwellers, an initiative that has since influenced the development practice of federations throughout India and in many other countries.

Homeless International has worked together with SPARC on many areas beyond the grant-giving relationship. At an early stage, Homeless International's Chief Executive, Ruth McLeod, and SPARC's Director, Sheela Patel, made a decision to broaden the institutional relationship between the two organizations by ensuring that their staff built relationships with their counterparts in the other organization. As both organizations have grown and developed, their learning has been reciprocal. For example, SPARC and Homeless International collaborated on the development not only of research into capital financing requirements but also the design of database systems, documentation, and strategies for international advocacy.

Homeless International's relationship with SPARC has been central to the development of our work on financial mechanisms. In 1989, when Sheela Patel spent a year in the UK, Ruth and Sheela had their first discussions about loan guarantees. Three years later Homeless International's Guarantee Fund was launched. In 1997/98, the Indian Alliance initiated its first slum redevelopment

Box 2.1   The Indian Alliance

The National Slum Dweller's Federation (NSDF) is a network of slum communities set up in 1974 in order to challenge polices affecting the urban poor. They saw the work of SPARC and Mahila Milan and sought an alliance with these organizations in 1986. NSDF members are all slum dwellers and the Federation operates throughout India.

SPARC. The Society for the Promotion of Area Resource Centres is an Indian NGO that provides professional support to the National Slum Dwellers Federation and Mahila Milan in their organizational work in over 70 cities in India.

Mahila Milan is a network of women's collectives, which began in 1986 when the first group of women pavement dwellers began to work with SPARC on housing. Mahila Milan creates space to enable large numbers of women in communities and networks to link up and work together to obtain skills and training. Membership of Mahila Milan includes membership of NSDF; as a result more than 50 per cent of the leadership of NSDF, which was a male organization in 1974, are now women.

SPARC Samudaya Nirman Sahayak – known as Nirman (SSNS) – is a non-profit company set up by SPARC, NSDF and Mahila Milan to support the housing and infrastructure initiatives developed by communities.

scheme under the new Mumbai slum rehabilitation rules – the Rajiv Indira[3] project. Homeless International and SPARC began exploring the possibility of Homeless International providing a hard currency guarantee for a bank loan for the project, which eventually came through (see Chapter 6). However, it was apparent that for the Indian Alliance to meet the Federation demand for large-scale slum upgrading projects, other sources of finance would be needed. This realization led to the development of the collaborative research project 'Bridging the finance gap in housing and infrastructure', which not only involved SPARC, but many other Homeless International partner organizations (see Chapter 5). The 'Bridging the finance gap' research articulated the need for capital funds that could be directly accessed by organizations of the urban poor to enable them to scale-up approaches that had worked well as smaller pilots. Eventually, the 'Bridging the finance gap' project gave rise to the development of a new financing mechanism, the Community-Led Infrastructure Finance Facility (CLIFF), which was piloted in India with the Indian Alliance (see Chapter 7).

In addition to IVDP and SPARC, Homeless International has funded other partner organizations for long periods. Many of these organizations support federations that are members of the Shack/Slum Dwellers International (SDI) network (see section below) or are linked to the Asian Coalition for Housing Rights (ACHR). Although Homeless International aims to work with partner organizations on a long-term basis, not all of the relationships that we have had have lasted the course of time. Fundamental differences in approach have sometimes emerged, which have made it problematic to continue a relationship, and there are organizations from which we have withdrawn funding. In the beginning, Homeless International invited project proposals from any non-governmental organization in a developing country that was active in the area of shelter improvement. Nearly 20 years later, projects are developed collaboratively with a network of inter-related organizations and new relationships evolve largely from the expansion of that network.

As Homeless International has grown, we have also developed ideas about scaling up housing and infrastructure development through the work we have funded, and have become more realistic about the kinds of support that we can provide with our organizational structure and methodology. Homeless International's emphasis on long-term in-depth relationships with partner organizations limits the number of organizations we can work with, whilst our lack of field staff means we can only support organizations that have reached a certain level of development. The following statements from Homeless International's 2003 International Grants Policy illustrate the outlook we have developed.

- Homeless International will make grants to its international partner organizations for initiatives that have the potential to scale up, attract other funding and influence policy.
- Homeless International will make grants to its international partner organizations for initiatives within the context of a broader strategic partnership between Homeless International and the partner.
- Homeless International will only make grants to new international partner organizations that have basic management systems in place and where existing partners (or networks of partners) can provide support.

Homeless International has also developed long-term partnerships with its funders and supporters, particularly within the UK social housing sector. For example one organization, Waterloo Housing Association, has consistently supported every major organizational development since 1987. They provided funds for the first pavement dwellers' house model exhibition, they supported the first Indian–South African exchanges, they contributed to the first toilet blocks, they gave a significant deposit to the guarantee fund and they have supported the development of new Federations, most recently in Ghana. Other housing associations, such as Portsmouth Housing Association, have a similar record of ongoing support, particularly in areas that other funders consider too high risk.

FEDERATION PROCESS

As we have already noted, Homeless International's work has become increasingly focused on supporting federations of the urban poor that are part of the Shack/ Slum Dwellers International (SDI) network, although other organizations such as ACHR and the Orangi Pilot Project have also remained important partners. Homeless International's design of new financial mechanisms has been integrally linked to the development of the federations, their housing and infrastructure projects and their loan funds (McLeod 2005b). The development processes that are characteristic of the different federations that belong to SDI are covered in more detail in Chapter 3. However it might be useful to identify here key elements of the federations' processes:

- The formation of saving and credit groups creates a basis for collecting money, people and information resulting in collective capital and basic organizational capacity.
- Enumerations and settlement mapping, carried out by the urban poor themselves, enable the collection of settlement-based information – particularly relating to housing, land and infrastructure – which is owned by the poor rather than by outsiders.
- Housing and toilet exhibitions and festivals demonstrate the possible in a manner that enables fundamental choices to be made about allocation of collective assets – particularly land and infrastructure – provided through local or national state agencies. Exhibitions also create a space for policy makers, politicians and the urban poor to explore alternative options for investment and new options for planning and building standards. Life-sized models act as a mobilizing tool in communities, enabling people to get a feel for the space created and to enhance communities' aspirations about what is possible.
- Learning and mutual support are nurtured through a process of exchanges: visits to each other's communities so that experiences can be shared. Increasingly such exchanges also include public officials and other professionals, encouraging their exposure to the way in which organizations of the urban poor perceive, analyse and respond to the issues that they prioritize within their local contexts.
- The implementation of small pilot projects which demonstrate how a community can design and implement solutions that make sense to them, and which act as precedents for larger-scale development.
- The creation and management of urban poor funds,[4] which provide access to capital for larger-scale housing and infrastructure developments led by communities in partnership with local authorities and Municipalities.
- The creation of city–community–state agreements facilitating the development of long-term strategies for tackling slum upgrading, resettlement and infrastructure provision.

TIMELINE OF HOMELESS INTERNATIONAL'S INVOLVEMENT IN URBAN DEVELOPMENT FINANCE

From its very beginnings, Homeless International has been involved in financing urban development. With Homeless International's initial grant-giving work including support for revolving loan funds and the establishment of savings groups, there was an early recognition that such community-level financial mechanisms needed to be locally designed and socially and economically appropriate to the local context (Homeless International 1992). Homeless International also began giving capital grants for demonstration projects – for example, supporting community-designed toilet blocks in India – that we hoped would be both replicable

Box 2.2   Milestones in Homeless International's development

1984	International Year of Shelter for the Homeless (IYSH) Trust registered.
1987	IYSH projects with SPARC and IVDP funded.
1989	Homeless International established as a permanent organization.
1989	Ruth McLeod (Homeless International) and Sheela Patel (SPARC) first discuss guarantees.
1992	Homeless International becomes a membership organization, incorporated as a Company Limited by guarantee.
1992	Homeless International's Guarantee Fund established.
1995	International Meeting on housing finance in Mumbai
1995	The first guarantee arrangement with the Housing Development Finance Corporation (HDFC) was finalized, to support the Youth Charitable Organization's (YCO's) work in Andhra Pradesh.
1996	Homeless International and partners organize a workshop on the guarantee fund at Habitat II in Istanbul.
1996–1997	The Indian Alliance initiates the Rajiv Indira–Suryodaya project. Discussions begin with Citibank.
1997–1999	Discussions about Rajiv Indira, the Indian Alliance's growing construction portfolio and other SDI members financing needs result in the design of the 'Bridging the finance gap in housing and infrastructure' research project.
1999	'Bridging the finance gap' research project begins, the first phase involves six country studies. Citibank releases 3 million Rupees for Rajiv Indira–Suryodaya as a sign of commitment to financing the project after the Indian Alliance threaten to boycott a press conference for the project if no finance is released.
1999–2000	Ruth McLeod contracted by DFID as part of design team for the C3 Challenge fund.
2000	International workshop on 'Bridging the finance gap' held in London to review first phase.
	Second phase of 'Bridging the finance gap' begins, involving more detailed studies of partners' project portfolios in India, South Africa and Kenya. The first guarantee arrangement outside India was finalized, after several years of discussion and negotiation, releasing a US$48,000 loan (£33,500) to Fundación Pro Hábitat, our partner organization in Bolivia.
	Indian Alliance begins preparing for implementing CLIFF, scaling up project implementation.
2000–2001	CLIFF explored by DFID and the World Bank. DFID develops CLIFF as an internal proposal to Cities Alliance.
2001	First guarantee arrangement to support IVDP agreed.
	Final phase of 'Bridging the finance gap' begins, with a more detailed examination of risk and forms of financing needed for community-led slum upgrading.

	Homeless International Letter of comfort issued to Unit Trust of India Bank (UTI Bank) to secure bid deposit for Bombay Sewerage Disposal Project (BSDP).
	Cities Alliance approves the CLIFF proposal.
2002	Homeless International provides £60,000 in bridge finance to the Rajiv Indira–Suryodaya project whilst there are delays in receiving Citibank loan disbursement and CLIFF funds.
	First call on Homeless International's Guarantee Fund, when, after seven years, YCO fails to meet repayments.
	CLIFF officially begins with a commitment of funds to March 2008, Homeless International receives capital funding several months later.
2003	CLIFF funds eventually reach India to support projects.
	Second guarantee arrangement with IVDP agreed.
	Work begins on an implementation plan for a second CLIFF pilot in Kenya.
	Final 'Bridging the finance gap' workshop held in Coventry.
2003–2004	Homeless International carries out research work on the feasibility of establishing CLIFF-like facilities in Ethiopia, Ghana, Uganda and Zambia, commissioned by the Urban Management Programme of UN-Habitat (see McLeod 2004, Jack and Braimah 2004, and Hughes and Masimba 2004).
2004	National Housing Bank in India approves a loan, guaranteed by Homeless International, to the Indian Alliance's Bharat Janata project (see Chapters 6 and 7).
	First guarantee to support IVDP released following full repayment of the associated loan. Loan term was four years and repaid almost two years ahead of schedule.
2005	ICICI approve a loan, guaranteed in part by Homeless International, to the Indian Alliance's Oshiwara II project (see Chapter 7).
	CLIFF Kenya implementation plan approved and first CLIFF funds disbursed to Kenya.

and have policy impact (Homeless International 1992: 173). Chapter 3 describes the importance of such pioneering projects in building community capacity to take the lead in urban development.

The establishment of the guarantee fund was an important development in that it enabled Homeless International and some of its partner organizations to begin discussions with banks. The fund did not by any means provide an easy fix, but it led us into a recognition that we needed to strengthen our skills in financial analysis. Homeless International needed to understand what bankers were talking about, and it needed to develop the systems and procedures that would support scaling up at local level. As the limitations of guarantees became clearer, Homeless International and its partners then moved into a new area – that of raising capital funds in volume that could be used as bridge finance for projects, while local bank loans and government subsidies were negotiated. CLIFF was then developed.

Homeless International continued to raise funding for grants to support the development of federations and basic community capacity building from a variety of sources. However by 2006 the broader challenge had been recognized as that of ensuring that our partner organizations and the federations with whom they work have access to a continuum of financial services that can be accessed as and when federations develop the capacity to use these facilities effectively. Box 2.2 above gives a brief overview of how far Homeless International has come along that path.

CHAPTER THREE

Building community foundations

Becky Telford

INTRODUCTION

This chapter begins by defining the concept of small-scale capacity building, what it is, and why it is crucial to community-led slum upgrading. With this in place, it then explores the range of ways in which capacity can be developed, and the financial mechanisms needed for this, with a focus on the work undertaken by Homeless International and our partners. Finally, this chapter looks at the future of such mechanisms and their role within sustainable urban development.

Small-scale capacity building – what and why?

It is commonly recognized that more can be achieved by people who work as a group: if two heads are better than one, what about a whole crowd of people? This is particularly relevant to the millions of 'invisible' slum and shack dwellers who suffer daily from having their needs and desires ignored. But how can divergent groups of people come together to have an impact against the odds? Many of the traditional definitions of community have to be re-examined when used to talk about such large and heterogeneous groups, who usually come together in closely affiliated local groups, and loose, wider networks. Small-scale capacity building covers a range of mechanisms and tools that are designed to build up the ability of these groups of the urban poor to work together to design and manage their own development.

Capacity building is crucial because of the huge impact it has on communities' ability to take part in, and lead, negotiations around a range of issues that affect them. By utilizing a range of tools, communities are also able to develop their asset base, in terms of money and knowledge, and work to have these assets recognized and their ideas taken seriously. This basic capacity building has to come first, giving communities a space to develop the skills, relationships and asset base they need to take their place effectively at the negotiating table. Homeless International's partners all undertake small-scale capacity building as the first step, a lesson which became clear during the early days of the Asian Coalition for Housing Rights (ACHR) as described by Patel, outlining the growth of Asian federations and alliances:

> The emerging network of community-based organizations [that became Slum/shack Dwellers International (SDI)] was resolute in its insistence that local capabilities had to be built within the leadership of the urban poor. What was unconventional about the strategy was that the aim was to make community-based organizations the leading force in the struggle against

*poverty, with NGOs playing a supportive role, helping link people's organizations with mainstream governmental or private institutions, and acting as researchers and fundraisers....
This involvement of people's organizations meant that the analysis of problems and emerging solutions reflected the needs and aspirations of the urban poor (Patel et al. 2001: 48).*

Supporting the urban poor to build their capacity to engage with the development of the areas in which they live, is also crucial to creating good urban governance. The World Bank defines participation as the 'process through which stakeholders influence and share control over priority setting, policy-making, resource allocations and access to public goods and services.'[1] In his foreword to 'The World Bank and Participation' paper, Lewis Preston, the then President, notes that the Bank's 'operational experience suggests that projects can be more efficient and sustainable when they involve those they are intended to help. Participation can also be complex and time-consuming...but I believe that increased participation will increase the effectiveness of development' (World Bank 1994). This illustrates one of the key reasons participation is important. Projects which have communities on board from the outset – where the issues have been identified by them, and a solution is one which they want – tend to be more successful, and continue to be successful in the long term. In many ways this is because the buy-in creates a sense of community ownership, and therefore a pride in something and a desire to make it work. As well as meaning that the end product is more appropriate for the community, the project becomes more cost-effective for the donor, and the process builds up the capacity of the community to be recognized as a crucial partner within urban development.

Through international networks such as SDI, federations of the urban poor have been able to explore a menu of tools, adapting and developing them to fit their own circumstances. They include:

- partnerships between federations of the urban poor and NGOs;
- creating and managing saving and loan facilities;
- enumerating and mapping informal settlements;
- developing and managing urban poor funds; and
- horizontal exchanges, sharing ideas, knowledge and experiences.

Homeless International has worked to support the use and development of these tools, and the particular forms of financing needed for this work (see Chapter 5 for more on forms of financing). The tools, lessons learned from examples of how they have been used successfully, and how they have been financed, are explored in this chapter.

TOOLS USED AND LESSONS LEARNED

Partnerships between federations of the urban poor and NGOs, financed by grants

The development processes used by the federations with whom Homeless International works were briefly outlined in Chapter 2. The member federations of SDI usually work in partnership with a support NGO, as described above. In

Photo 3.1 The strength of community organizations, and the central role of women, has been crucial to the achievements of the Indian Alliance
Source: Homeless International

some cases, as their work has grown, these federation–NGO partnerships have established another institution to manage the financing of large-scale housing and infrastructure projects; for example Nirman (SSNS) in India, the Akiba Mashinani Trust in Kenya and the uTshani Fund in South Africa. The legal form and governance of these institutions varies according to the national context and needs of the particular federation.

The core costs of the federations and their support NGOs are relatively small given their well-documented achievements.[2] However they do have to be met, and grants for this purpose will continue to be necessary for the foreseeable future. The role of a local support NGO, and the 'community-first' relationship between them and the federation they are working with, has been crucial to the success, particularly the scaling-up, of many of Homeless International's partners' work.

This relationship framework is central to the work of all of Homeless International's partners. As one of the leading proponents of this way of working, the Indian Alliance provides an excellent example of how the different groups work together. The structure of the Indian Alliance is outlined in Box 2.1, Box 3.1 explains the Indian Alliance's philosophy and collaborative processes in more detail.

Creating and managing saving and loan facilities, financed by immediate short-term loans to individuals

Saving and credit groups have been recognized as a way of providing an important basis for the accumulation and circulation of capital within local communities. In the early stages, collective savings are used for emergency, consumption and

Box 3.1 Complementary partnerships within the Indian Alliance

'In 1984, when SPARC was formed, it began working with the most vulnerable and invisible of Mumbai's urban poor, the pavement dwellers. SPARC's philosophy is that if we can develop solutions that work for the poorest and most marginalized in the city, then these solutions can be scaled up to work for other groups of the urban poor across the country and internationally. . . [NSDF's] main aim is to mobilize the urban poor to come together, articulate their concerns and find solutions to the problems they face. . . Mahila Milan aims to provide a space for women to take on important decision-making roles and be recognized for their critical contributions towards improving the lives of their communities. The roles of each member of the Indian Alliance are clearly defined. The NSDF organizes and mobilizes the urban poor and negotiates with resource-providing institutions, Mahila Milan supports and trains women's collectives to administer and manage their community's resources and participate in NSDF activities, and SPARC provides the administrative, financial, policy, documentation and other support necessary for these processes to be successful on the ground.' (www.sparcindia.org)

Together with Nirman (SSNS), the not-for-profit company established by SPARC, NSDF and Mahila Milan to support their housing and infrastructure projects, the Indian Alliance works towards the following goals:

'The immediate aim of the Indian Alliance is to create the institutional arrangements that are necessary for large numbers of the poor to access land housing and infrastructure. Our long-term vision is to support a process where organized groups of the urban poor can participate in making decisions about how their cities are developed and managed.' (www.sparcindia.org).

A crucial aspect of how the Indian Alliance of SPARC–Mahila Milan–NSDF operates is the strength and scale of community organizations and their Federations which underpin all of the initiatives and which make possible the setting of such ambitious goals for community-led urban development. The Indian Alliance focuses on building strong and large-scale federations of the urban poor. The federations are usually organized around their land tenure. For example, the Railway Slum Dwellers Federation is made up of people living on land owned by the Railway Authority, the Airport Slum Dwellers live on land owned by the Airways Authority, and so on. Linkages between federations within and between cities make it possible for the alliance as a whole to take on ambitious goals for community-led urban development. Each partner is able to use their particular skills and abilities, whilst leaving breathing and growing space for the urban poor themselves.

business purposes, often helping families to avoid falling into debt traps in order to cover their basic needs. Housing savings are more specialized – these help to build the deposits that many longer-term housing loans require. Within the federation model typified by the Indian Alliance, groups manage finances themselves and determine the interest rates at which they lend their own money to each other. However patterns of consistency develop over time as the groups learn through experience and share this learning with other groups through

Box 3.2 People Square Saving Scheme, Windhoek, Namibia

The Shack Dwellers Federation of Namibia is a network of housing saving schemes that aims to improve the living conditions of low-income people living in shacks, rented rooms and those without any accommodation. The Federation is supported by the non-governmental organization Namibia Housing Action Group (NHAG). In the experience of the majority of Homeless International's partners and the communities they support, saving has been the starting point of organizing for development. Edith Mbanga, a member of the People Square Saving Scheme explains the role of savings and the developments of the Federation:

'We from People Square Saving Scheme started in 1989 as poor women without houses, to organize ourselves to work together to solve our housing problems. We were mostly domestic workers living in backyard shacks and rented rooms, which cost often half of our small incomes of about N$400 (around £35) per month. As poor people we could get assistance for housing. We had regular meetings to discuss what steps to take. Because we were poor, we decided to save together, and with these savings we could show the government that we are serious to do things for ourselves.

'In the beginning our main objective was to get our own land. We as members negotiated with the municipality to obtain land with the assistance of our NGO [NHAG]. The municipality is recovering the service costs when buying land. Therefore the individual plots were too expensive for us, and we proposed to the municipality to buy a block of land, which we will service ourselves. We bought the land in 1992 and we moved immediately to the plot. It was very important to live together. We could work more easily together to make bricks and building the houses and use the money we used to pay for renting rooms and backyard shacks, to pay for the land and save for security for our loans. In the beginning we saved monthly for this security money, but when we learned from the Indians and South Africans about daily savings, we started to do daily savings for all our needs' (Homeless International 2001: 12).

federation networks. Savings and credit activities establish a credit management record and can facilitate mobilization of additional external capital provision for loan funds. Saving also operates as one of the fundamental means through which people learn to organize effectively as a group and to manage increasingly large amounts of money.

In South Africa, the Homeless People's Federation has a slogan: 'Amandla! Imali! Nolwazi!' which is Zulu for 'Power! Money! Knowledge!' When communities control their own money and information, they gain the power over their own development processes. The concept of 'empowerment' assumes that power is being 'given' from the powerful to the powerless. Recognition of the assets of poor communities shifts the focus to one where the poor can create their *own* power by mobilizing their *own* resources to play a key role in their own development. The communities supported by Homeless International's partner organizations in

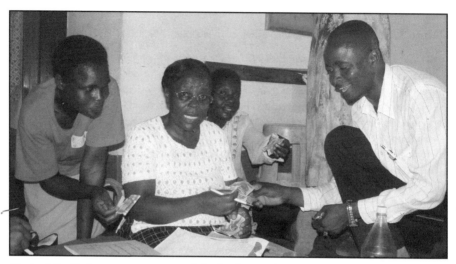

Photo 3.2   Savings operate as one of the fundamental means through which people learn to organize effectively as a group and to manage increasingly large amounts of money. The Victoria Falls Federation in Zimbabwe, shown here, has enabled large numbers of poor people to save together and discuss development options. Having negotiated for land from the city authorities, this group has been installing infrastructure and building houses for more than 500 families in spite of Zimbabwe's economic meltdown.
Source: Homeless International

Asia and Africa are all involved in a number of activities that enhance community participation.

The process of forming saving and credit groups creates a basis for collecting money, people and information, resulting in collective capital and basic organizational capacity. As saving groups mature and move into credit activities, the ability of their leaders, mainly women, to manage collective finances develops. At the same time, as saving groups become federated locally at first, then nationally, the options to leverage this capital expand at the same time as organizational capacity increases. Local and national federations create a critical mass of poor people with shared priorities and principles, to which policy makers are increasingly obliged to listen. These advantages are explored further by Boonyabancha (2001:11):

> First, [community saving and loan activities] draw people together on a regular and continuous basis. They offer opportunities for members of low-income communities to develop their strengths gradually through making collective decisions about concrete activities that affect the community. Second, the financial mechanisms are grounded in daily activities; saving and lending are quick, simple, and related to the real daily needs of the urban poor, as defined by the poor themselves. Third, saving and loan activities provide the urban poor with their own resource base to answer to their basic needs. Fourth, as importantly, the process creates an on-going learning within the community about each other's lives, about how to manage together and how to relate to external systems with greater financial strength in order to achieve more than day-to-day needs. It is a process that every community member can relate

to and which everyone can be involved in controlling. It is a gradual process that provides the community with the capacity and confidence needed for a true and comprehensive self-development process.

Boonyabancha emphasizes that community saving and loan activities are not merely an end, but rather a means to strengthen communities, enabling them to work together to meet their needs, including secure housing.

Savings form the backbone for community organization. By creating a financial base, communities begin to demonstrate their ability to bring their own assets to the table, and their ability to take the lead in their own development (see Box 3.2). The process of collecting and recording savings, and managing loans and repayments, brings community members closer together. Information is shared at the same time as money and both resources can then be used strategically to engage with other external actors and institutions with influence and power.

Enumerating and mapping informal settlements, financed by external grants for basic capacity- building

Grant funding has supported the development of strong community organizations anchored in women-led saving and loan groups. Community-led mapping of settlements and enumerations to gather information about the number of families and services in an area is a crucial federation tool, and one of the areas that requires some level of grant funding.

Enumerations and settlement mapping, carried out by the urban poor themselves, enable the collection of settlement-based information, particularly relating to housing, land and infrastructure, which is owned by the poor rather than outsiders. Enumeration exercises usually involve a number of processes as described in Patel *et al.* (2002) and Burra *et al.* (2005):[2]

■ hut/shack counting;
■ house numbering;
■ mapping and survey of the settlement, including detailed cadastral surveys;
■ settlement profiles describing infrastructure and services;
■ household surveys, involving detailed interviews with each family, conducted by fellow community members;
■ taking family photographs and producing family identification cards;
■ data verification.

As Cornelia Lungu, an enumeration leader from the Zimbabwe Homeless People's Federation notes: 'There is such mystery about information gathering that I had never thought that I, an uneducated person, could actually collect information that is useful to myself and others in my situation. Moving around talking to people also enabled me to understand my settlement better and I found out that there was so much I shared with people in my community' (DFID 2001: 43).

When this information is shared and collaboratively checked and analysed, it provides the basis for collective knowledge, owned by organizations of the poor, which can be used to strategically negotiate with, and frequently to assist, local

Photo 3.3   Family photos and house numbering, like those used here in the Muria Mbogo settlement in Nairobi (Kenya), are used to produce family ID cards and to verify who lives where.
Source: Homeless International

and national authorities. This process is particularly effective when local government does not have the resources, capacity or inclination to gather accurate information about informal settlements. As Jane Weru, the Director of Pamoja Trust in Kenya, notes: 'Enumerations represent the first part of the process through which informal settlements become "regularized" with secure tenure, house construction to improve conditions and infrastructure built or negotiated from local authorities... Enumerations provide the means by which data are gathered to allow for local planning but also the process by which consensus is built and the inclusion of all residents are negotiated.' (2004: 50)

There is usually very little reliable information about those who live in low-income areas, holding camps and squatter settlements. Statistics are generally unavailable on, for example, the number of residents, number of people sharing rooms, toilets or water taps, number of years people have been on municipal waiting lists, income levels. Government agencies often do not have the resources or inclination to gather accurate data about poor communities. During enumerations, community members gather valuable information about their community members and local politicians about their housing needs. Federation members from other areas train one another to develop questionnaires, conduct interviews, compile and analyse the results and feed this information back to their communities and local officials. These community surveys have been an effective tool in initiating relationships with local government.

Weru (2004) argues that enumerating and mapping settlements is not the simple job it may first appear to be. Many settlements have grown very rapidly, and contain great numbers of people with different interests and agendas. As such, however, the benefits and rewards of a successful enumeration are also wide-ranging and crucial to negotiating for security of tenure, appropriate infrastructure and services, and fighting against evictions (see Box 3.3).

Undertaking small-scale precedent setting projects, financed by grants and revolving loan funds

'Precedent-setting activities are those that demonstrate better development alternatives for the poor, perhaps on a small scale in the initial process' (Patel *et al.* 2001: 51). With basic organizational capacity at community level, organizations of the urban poor are able to take on small-scale investment projects in slum rehabilitation, resettlement and/or infrastructure provision: toilets, sanitation, water, solid waste management, access roads and drainage. These projects demonstrate how designs and ideas developed at community level can work in practice. They provide an opportunity to develop and test new skills, not least within the relationships that need to be negotiated as a project is implemented. Perhaps most importantly they provide a chance for people to learn from their own collective initiative.

Setting precedents within relationships is a key part of why these small-scale projects are so crucial. By having a specific programme to work together on, it is a test of the communities' negotiation skills writ small. All the obstacles and interactions with other stakeholders will need to be dealt with, however small the project, and valuable lessons can be learned. Federations also find themselves in a position to challenge the status quo, and, once given a chance to explore how they would do things differently, have some astonishing successes. 'The South African Homeless People's Federation demanded a pilot initiative with the state so they could have direct access to housing subsidies and build their own houses... [They] found that communities could build their core houses entirely with the subsidy money and at a cost that was 40 per cent lower than that of private developers.' (Patel *et al.* 2001: 50).

The South African communities involved in that initiative were able to expand it, and to keep building on the relationship with the state to negotiate to work on more programmes and increase the voice of the urban poor in city life.

House modelling

Another tool used to mobilize communities and involve everyone in the process of settlement development is the house model where communities demonstrate

Box 3.3 Fighting evictions in Nairobi

In December 2001 in Nairobi, the government issued a directive that the 10 000 inhabitants of the Korogocho slum should be given the municipal land they lived on and in situ development should be undertaken. As is the situation in the majority of slums in Kenya, there are a number of structure owners in Korogocho who make a living from renting out the shacks that they own: the Korogocho Owners Welfare Organization (KOWA) has 2460 members. Because of this, the directive caused huge tension between the structure owners and the tenants, particularly because the structure owners stood to make a lot of money if they were granted tenure of the land their shacks stood upon. As such, the well-organized KOWA had lobbied the government to grant the directive and anticipated benefiting greatly from it.

Pamoja Trust and other groups in Nairobi sought for a fairer process, and an end result that would benefit the tenants also. During an exchange visit from the Indian Alliance, Jockin Arpurtham, the President of the Indian National Slum Dwellers Federation, suggested that one of their first steps in negotiating the case of Korogocho would be to gather the data and detailed maps needed through enumerating the settlement. Because of the size and levels of tension in Korogocho, it was decided to undertake the first enumeration in Huruma, a much smaller settlement. The involvement of the Indian Alliance, with their broad experience of undertaking enumerations, was crucial to this process. But even that was not enough to get the enumeration running smoothly first time.

'It took ten days to complete this first enumeration. A first draft of questions for the enumeration was prepared and discussed between Pamoja Trust and SDI, and then the enumeration began, undertaken by community residents. Numbers were given to each house and each household was interviewed. As work got underway, the difficulties became apparent, as did many inhabitants' anxiety about the process. In some house structures, there were both structure owners and tenants; in others, only tenants, with the structure owner living elsewhere in the settlement; in others, only tenants with the structure owner living outside Huruma. Some tenants would not talk (or told the enumerators that the landlord had said they should not be enumerated), whilst others gave false information (for instance putting down their children as separate households or claiming that their kitchens were in separate housing units in the hope that they would get two plots)' (Weru, 2004: 51).

After a lot of work between the organizations and federations involved, continued negotiations with structure owners, the local authorities and police, Korogocho enumerations eventually took place. The process was not finished there though, as KOWA took the case to court. However, in 2002 the information had been correlated and was taken back to the residents for verification. As Weru notes:

'With a strong verification process, people realize that it is not in their interests to cheat. In recent exchanges between community members [from Huruma and another settlement in Nairobi, Soweto-Kahawa] Huruma residents said that it did not pay to cheat and you would be found out and embarrassed. Compare this with the non-negotiating stance of any official data collection undertaken by state agencies, where, in the absence of clarifications and internal dialogue, some people get away with many houses or if caught are humiliated and punished' (2004: 54).

The strong position that the Federation and Pamoja Trust held after these enumerations – and the enumerations that followed – has been key to their success in negotiating with the state for access to land and services. Recognition of the added value of community involvement has formed a keystone of community-led development in Nairobi, and further afield.

Box 3.4   Using house modelling to plan improvements

Edith Mbanga's experiences highlight the power of house modelling, used by the Shack Dwellers Federation of Namibia.

'To prepare for the plan, we made small models of the houses and looked at possible layouts. First we planned semi-detached houses, with open communal space in between for children to play. The Directorate of Housing and the NGO, NHAG helped to draw the municipal approval plans for us. We had no funds to build houses, but applied for house loans from the government's Build Together Programme. Each person borrowed N$7,500 (about £650) for a 25 square meter house. We started to measure the houses with the support of a volunteer architect from the Ministry of Regions, Local Government and Housing, and the NGO's building technicians. In 1993 we started with 21 houses and completed them in March 1994 when the first group moved into their houses. The women and our sons were trained by the building technician to build houses. We have one semi-skilled woman builder. In 1996 we started to build the other 24 houses, each person borrowing N$12,000 (about £1,000) to build 31 square meters. After seeing the finished houses, we decided to change the plans. We then drew the new house plan on the ground and the NGO finalized and submitted our plans to the municipality. We have learned from that lesson, that it is difficult for us poor women to read plans and nowadays we built life-size house models of cloth. We completed the last houses in August 1997. Now everyone has a house.

We work well together; everyone felt this is her project. We planned together, took decisions together, when we have our weekly meetings. Drain stoppages until now occurred only in the main municipal sewer and not in our sewer therefore, they will come and fix it. If something goes wrong with our own water pipes or sewer line we will have to get a plumber to come and help us...

...We have become aware that we should not only work on a few projects like we did in the past and now we are linked through our own Shack Dwellers Federation of Namibia. Although we started out by aiming for a house, we are not concentrating on houses alone any longer, but we are serious to improve our lives. Our Federation has grown to include 110 saving schemes, involving about 3500 households. The groups in informal settlements have also started to do their own mapping and layout planning, with the intention to develop the land they are staying on.' (Homeless International 2001: 13) their ability to design and cost out their own houses (see Box 3.4). Housing and toilet exhibitions and festivals demonstrate what is possible in a manner that enables fundamental choices to be made about the allocation of collective assets – particularly land and infrastructure – provided through local or national state agencies. Exhibitions also create the space for policy makers, politicians and the urban poor to explore alternative options for investment and new options for planning and building standards. The life-size models act as a mobilizing tool in communities, enabling people to get a feel for the space created and to enhance communities' aspirations about what is possible.

Developing and managing urban poor funds, financed by grants

Who decides how development resources are used? In many conventional development approaches, communities are allowed to 'participate' as far as contributing labour and ideas, or perhaps cost-sharing, but they are almost never allowed to manage the money, or even touch it. In the name of accountability it's kept firmly in the hands of the professionals and project managers, who dole it out in little bits, like feeding a baby who you imagine can't hold a spoon yet. This is not only disempowering, it works to further entrench the poor's age-old position as beggars, petitioners and recipients of somebody else's idea of what they need. (Asian Coalition for Housing Rights 2002: 4)

Over the last decade a range of urban poor funds (also known as community development funds) have been established in Asia and Africa. Some of these have been initiated by the state, some by NGOs and federations of slum dwellers and some by partnerships formed by Municipalities, NGOs and slum dwellers' federations. The funds are used to finance development projects that have a strong precedent-setting role, demonstrating how alternative community-led approaches with high levels of local participation can be implemented affordably, and with high levels of acceptance by the urban poor often working in partnership with city authorities. The Community Organizations Development Institute (CODI) in Thailand is the best known of the funds initiated by a central government. CODI provides a range of credit and grant facilities to organized communities seeking to drive their own development, and is governed by a Board that has strong representation from networks of community saving groups from across the country. The Gungano Fund in Zimbabwe is a fund initiated by a national federation of slum dwellers working in partnership with a local NGO, and Nirman in India is a non-profit company set up by the Society for the Promotion of Area Resource Centres (SPARC) and the National Slum Dwellers Federation (NSDF) that holds and helps manage similar funds. The Urban Poor Development Fund (UPDF) in Cambodia is an example of a fund established by a partnership that includes a local slum federation, a municipality and local NGOs.

In many cases the funds play a catalytic role, providing seed capital to demonstrate the practicality of an approach which can later be scaled up with additional finance from the public sector and, in some cases, from the commercial banking sector and from commercial contractors and land owners. However the most important role that the funds play is that of providing a practical means for the urban poor to design long-term solutions that work for them and to develop the capacity they need to implement those solutions in partnership with others. Without this capacity the urban poor have little chance of real involvement in urban development, and are more likely to remain, at best, victims of the cyclical interest of politicians that court them with empty pre-election promises.

One of the reasons that urban poor funds have proved so successful is that they do not function as isolated financial mechanisms but are embedded in a larger process of community mobilization and capacity building. Srilatha Batliwala, from the Kennedy School at Harvard, has explored the degree to which the poor are able to access and influence the global development debate and emphasized how important it is for the urban poor to develop collective skills in four areas:

■ Conducting and applying research, for example the community enumeration and mapping exercises that have become a central feature of the work of members of SDI.
■ Understanding legal, technical and economic documentation and training relevant professionals to work with them as allies.
■ Communication and advocacy, not just between the urban poor themselves but also with the whole gamut of other players with a stake in urban development at local, national and international levels. The growth of trans-national networks such as SDI and their increasing engagement with multi-lateral development institutions is particularly significant.
■ Relationship building and negotiation, such as the skills demonstrated in the development of community–city partnerships for slum upgrading and infrastructure provision in cities such as Pune, Mumbai and Durban.

Urban poor funds play a critical role in enabling the development of these collective skills.

At the time of writing, the Indian Alliance is in the midst of one of the most innovative projects they have taken on. Slum dwellers in Mumbai are advocating for a more collaborative approach to delivering infrastructure, and are competing for, and winning, contracts to provide sanitation to their settlements. Other approaches to sanitation have failed because facilities have not been maintained, but the Indian Alliance is demonstrating a sustainable alternative approach (see Box 3.6)

This Indian project has been about more than the provision of toilet blocks, however. It has set a precedent for developing community-led infrastructure initiatives which are beneficial to both the city and communities, and which are sustainable in the long term. By designing and constructing toilet blocks for their own community, users have developed a sense of ownership of the assets and taken full charge of their management. Since the communities are involved in, and retain control of, the whole process, from planning to construction, to maintenance and management, they can easily decide to add extra facilities to their community toilet blocks by contributing the extra funds. So far, numerous community toilet blocks have been equipped with community centres, crèches, playgrounds, caretakers' rooms and so on. They have become financially self sufficient through monthly fees paid by each family that uses the toilet.

Box 3.5 The Urban Poor Development Fund, UPDF

The UPDF was launched in Phnom Penh, Cambodia, in 1998. ACHR (a network of professionals and communities across the region) worked closely with the Solidarity for the Urban Poor Federation (SUPF, a network of poor communities) to establish the fund. It provides loan finance and small-scale grants for community-led housing, infrastructure and collective enterprise development schemes. However, because it has been set up with representatives from organized poor communities, NGOs and the Municipality of Phnom Penh on its governing board, it is also an innovative mechanism to promote collaborative decision-making, joint strategic planning and shared 'visioning' of how city development should take place. Community involvement and prioritization is embedded in the mutual support networks created through SUPF. The UPDF is also closely linked to other development activities, such as community-led mapping and surveying, land searches, exchanges and pilot schemes, which reinforce in practice the new collaborative relationships built at board level.

In a context where civil war and uncoordinated donor interventions have resulted in minimal capacity within government, the UPDF has pioneered an innovative approach to urban poverty reduction in tandem with reconfiguring governance relationships, such that poor communities are increasingly viewed as credible and essential actors in city development strategies. At the same time, the UPDF has provided a forum through which the Municipality has been able to deliver to its poorest citizens, by combining government's skills and assets with those of poor communities, and changing development policies that previously curtailed progress. The UPDF experience offers lessons in developing financial mechanisms that bring together urban development and good governance processes:

- Providing a forum for engagement – decisions about resources and priorities are made collaboratively.
- The UPDF process is built upon, and reinforces, a network of organized poor communities, which provides a core of experience and capacity to influence the decision-making process. SUPF carries out sophisticated processes of prioritization amongst communities that underlie requests for funds, rather than decisions simply being made by a detached committee based on uncoordinated community applications for funds.
- Providing a mechanism through which large-scale donor funds can be channelled effectively to schemes prioritized jointly by local communities and local authorities.
- Supporting schemes that test, challenge and offer workable alternatives to existing policies and practice.

'This city doesn't only belong to the rich. It belongs to all of us, so we should all be involved in improving it. ... We have to sit down and set concrete plans for this upgrading programme together.' Mr Chev Kim Heng, Vice Governor of Phnom Penh (www.achr.net).

Horizontal exchanges, sharing ideas, knowledge and experiences, financed by grants

Learning and mutual support are shared through a process of exchange visits to each other's communities so that experiences can be shared. It is through exchanges

Box 3.6 Setting sustainable precedents: the Bombay Sewerage Disposal Project

'If you want to mobilize people, go to the public toilets' – Jockin Arpurtham, President of NSDF and SDI.

In 1995, the World Bank approved a seven-year loan for the Bombay Sewerage Disposal Project (BSDP) to strengthen the capacity of the Municipal Corporation to provide sewerage services. One of the objectives within the project was specifically aimed at 'improving the health and environmental conditions in Greater Mumbai, including slum dwellers', and it was with this in mind that the Slum Sanitation Program (SSP) was developed by the Mumbai Municipality.

Historically in Mumbai, the provision of toilet blocks has been through public agencies without any involvement of communities in the designing, planning, building and maintenance of these facilities. However, publicly managed toilet blocks are usually poorly managed and maintained, and the service rapidly becomes defunct. Up to 900 people use a single toilet and surveys suggest that up to 75 per cent of existing facilities are not functioning. As a result, people are forced to defecate in the open, which is a particularly difficult situation for women and results in dangers to public health. The Indian Alliance offered an alternative arrangement.

The Indian Alliance's formula for the division of roles suggested that the city should pay for the capital cost of toilet construction (which would be no more than the cost of contractor-built toilets that the municipality was used to funding), and the communities would manage and maintain the toilets themselves and generate the funds to do so. Thus, the sanitation programme would be implemented through NGOs and community-based organizations (CBOs) already active in those slums. The relationships involved in the construction of toilets challenged all the institutions concerned, particularly as, for an initial project, the scale was huge.

Although the construction of the toilets is the output focus of this project, in reality it covers a host of other issues:

- All the communities involved in toilet-building projects have to first form societies and plan for the maintenance of the toilet block. The Indian Alliance supports the creation of these new CBOs to ensure that they are not taken over by individuals who will dominate the democratic management process.
- Many politicians in Mumbai have opposed community control of building and maintaining toilet blocks, and dealing with this hostility has been a constant challenge.
- Building toilets is not complex technology, and the federations are deeply committed to building up communities' capacity by creating opportunities for slum-based contractors.
- Technical issues must be dealt with, such as linking up to electricity, water, drainage and sewage.

The programme required 45 per cent investment in advance, and the bridge funds that SPARC uses to ensure the smooth running of projects, despite financial hold-ups, have become increasingly scarce since the Indian Alliance's activity has begun to really scale up. CLIFF has played a crucial part in providing the necessary bridging funds in order that slum communities, in partnership with SPARC, can design and construct toilet blocks. The approach has been extremely successful and, with technical help from SPARC, communities have already completed over 150 toilet blocks, with the remainder being at different stages of completion.

that people are exposed to new ways of doing things, and are able to develop new relationships that can evolve into effective and long-lasting alliances. Increasingly such exchanges also include public officials and other professionals, encouraging their exposure to the way in which organizations of the urban poor perceive, analyse and respond to the issues that they prioritize within their local contexts. So, as knowledge has emerged from the work that we have supported in Africa, Asia, Latin America and the Caribbean, much of it has 'travelled' through south–south community exchanges and been transformed into practices that have begun to change the way that development in informal settlements takes place. People, who were previously seen as a 'problem' to be got rid of through evictions and forced resettlement, are increasingly being recognized as providing a huge resource; 'enemies' who were previously seen as being completely antagonistic to the poor, find a means to share their concerns and perspectives. Dialogue begins and it becomes possible to consider new and collaborative approaches in which everyone wins. Over time new partnerships between organizations of the poor and official bodies such as Municipal Authorities and Regional Government are created and these new partnerships in turn become a resource from which others can learn.

CONCLUSIONS

The various tools, mechanisms and facilities discussed in this chapter provide the backbone of community-led urban development. As organizations of the urban poor walk through these new experiences and link up with others their ability to take on the challenge of larger scale interventions grows; but it does take time. There are no quick fix or overnight solutions to the evolution of real organizational capacity and it is vital that this is in place before groups are expected to successfully handle significant levels of external financing.

As McLeod notes in her feasibility study for the expansion of CLIFF, there are a range of things that need to be in place for areas to be able to take on a large finance facility (2005b: 28). These are:

- 'An established saving and loan system managed by the community.
- Linkages and exchanges with other settlements facing similar problems and trying to build similar capacities. (Ideally representatives of different settlements come together over time to form a network generally known as a federation).
- The capacity to generate comprehensive and reliable settlement-level data.
- Experience with implementing pilot schemes.
- Prior engagement and negotiation with local authorities.
- Well-developed community organization able to implement community-led developments.'

Financial mechanisms cannot work on their own. However, if they are appropriate to the capacity of communities and their ability to create, manage and develop relationships between the different actors in the city, they can become a vital aspect of urban development.

CHAPTER FOUR

Taking risks

Ruth McLeod

INTRODUCTION

The word 'risk' derives from the early Italian risicare, which means 'to dare'. In this sense risk is a choice rather than a fate. The actions that we dare to take, which depend on how free we are to make choices, are what the story of risk is all about. And that story helps to define what it means to be a human being. (Bernstein 1998: 8)

This chapter examines how risk is perceived, analysed, managed and mitigated by a range of actors involved in community-led slum upgrading, resettlement and infrastructure provision. In particular the chapter focuses on how differing understandings of risk impinge on the negotiation and implementation of financial agreements between organizations of the urban poor, local NGOs, public sector agencies, commercial businesses such as banks and contractors, and both governmental and non-governmental donors. Basic questions such as what constitutes a risk, why specific risks are worth taking and how risk burdens are shouldered and by whom, arise throughout the discussion. The backdrop to the discussion arises from findings of the 'Bridging the finance gap in housing and infrastructure' research project which demonstrated that the urban poor, and the NGOs that seek to support them, take substantial risks when they enter into relationships with the formal financial sector in order to access development finance. They also take risks when they proactively enter into collaborative relationships with the state. Unfortunately, this risk-taking has remained largely invisible and unacknowledged in development theory. This chapter seeks to redress that omission. Much of the discussion within this chapter focuses on the experiences Homeless International has shared with the Indian Alliance of the National Slum Dwellers Federation, SPARC and Mahila Milan. This is because of the long-term mutual exploration that we have gone through in building relationships with Indian banks and our collaboration in finding ways to manage the risks associated with that exploration.

The chapter begins with a general discussion of risk. The reasons why formal financial institutions perceive lending to the poor to be high risk are then explored, before considering the specific risks that organizations of the urban poor take when they collectively initiate development projects that challenge inadequate approaches to city development and service provision in urban areas. We then look at specific experiences where bank loans or guarantees have been negotiated and at how the banks involved viewed and assessed risk in the projects in question, tracking how this has begun to change as bankers have become more familiar with how community-led processes work. The use of guarantees is explored and other steps to reduce risk are briefly discussed. The chapter ends with a series of reflections on learning about risk.

ASSUMPTIONS ABOUT RISK

As Homeless International's thinking around options for housing and infrastructure finance have developed, we have made a number of important assumptions about the nature of risk. We believe that risk is about what can go wrong, how badly it can go wrong, and what may happen as a result, when attempts are made to try and do something differently. Risk analysis involves judgement about the likelihood or probability that something will go wrong, how severe the consequences will be and what the potential benefits will be if things work out. Perhaps most importantly risk is about choice and the ability to choose. It is, as Bernstein has pointed out, 'a set of opportunities open to choice' – ' the actions that we dare to take, which depend on how free we are to make choices' (1998: 8). Where there is no choice, risk taking is not an option, and impediments and problems that exist remain just that, challenges that must be faced whether you like it or not. It follows that one's circumstances can determine whether or not one's actions constitute risk-taking behaviour. Sleeping on the streets to find out what it feels like and to assess one's reactions might be considered risk-taking behaviour. Sleeping on the streets because you have no alternative constitutes an attempt to survive. As Jockin Arpurtham, President of the National Slum Dwellers Federation puts it 'We don't think about risks when we think about problems. A problem is something you can do nothing about. We don't focus on what can go wrong. We know this is where we are and this is where we want to go. To get from point A to point B we have to go through all these things, and each one is a milestone, and when we cover one milestone we automatically move onto the next. It's a question of time, commitment and conviction – to make people see that this is the way to move ahead'. However, when the National Slum Dwellers Federation and their support NGO SPARC enter into discussions with bankers to obtain financing for the schemes that they initiate, bankers will apply risk analysis with considerable care in order to reduce the possibility of things going wrong from their own perspective, and ensure a margin of profit that makes their lending worthwhile.

We have made some further assumptions that have been well articulated by Beck (quoted in Lupton 1999). He argues that:

> *Risks only exist in terms of the.... knowledge about them. They can be changed, magnified, dramatized or minimized within knowledge, and to that extent they are particularly open to social definition and construction. Furthermore some people are more affected by the distribution and growth of risks and there are winners and losers in risk definitions. Power and access to and control of knowledge thus becomes paramount in a risk society.*

In other words, risk is socially defined and constructed, people from different contexts define risk differently, and people's access to, and control of knowledge, affects whether or not their definition of risk is accepted by others. It is therefore not a surprise that one of the biggest challenges in negotiating risk is that of language. People have very different conceptual understandings of the same words. In negotiations, it can all too often be assumed that words, and concepts, are being used by everyone in the same way. We have found that terms such as security, leverage, asset and guarantees, to name but a few, in fact mean very different things to different people depending on their experience and backgrounds. One of the biggest challenges is therefore to create a process of dialogue so that these differences can be recognized, explored and sometimes challenged. In our experience, the best context for this to happen is on site – physically where the project is – so that the discussion is rooted in the practical rather than relying on theoretical imaginings.

Risk measurement presents particular challenges when the activities that are being undertaken are unprecedented. Risk can be relatively easily measured in retrospect. However when new approaches and methods are being tried, within the context of new relationships where there is a lack of perceptive consensus, risk measurement can become contentious. Perhaps more importantly, until the new approach is tried in practice, the pitfalls and barriers remain unknown in any detail. There is no objective data about cost variations, time frames, payment delays and all the other factors that can turn a project that initially looks viable into a loss-making venture.

WHY ARE FORMAL FINANCIAL INSTITUTIONS SO RELUCTANT TO LEND TO THE POOR?

Scaling up precedent-setting projects for city-wide application requires an engagement with the formal development process and the building of working relationships with formal sector institutions. This constantly proves financially problematic, largely because public sector financing is severely constrained, but also because the most obvious local sources for financing – banks and other formal financial institutions – have generally proved reluctant to lend to the poor and to adapt their systems to accommodate non-formal investment processes. Explanations of this reluctance have engaged a plethora of development theorists. Our own limited findings suggest the following possible reasons.

In some cases local financial markets are relatively underdeveloped and medium and long-term financing is not yet being offered at all by banks. Where the financial markets have developed further, existing demand from the commercial sector and from higher income consumers may absorb all the available financing. Crowding out commercial loans also occurs in cases where governments borrow extensively on the domestic market, typically by issuing Treasury Bills. For example, in Uganda, when Homeless International carried out research for UN-Habitat's Urban Management Programme, banks were investing in treasury bills rather than lending to anyone because the rates on treasury bills were so favourable.

Banks may also consider the margins on lending for community-driven urban development to be uncompetitive, particularly where significant investment is required in developing new mechanisms and systems for credit delivery.

In many cases banks have never been asked to deliver this form of financing either by local government or NGOs, and therefore have not considered the options or explored how viable such lending might be. NGOs may also not have developed the capacity to articulate such a request in a form that can be implemented by banks and local governments, and may need technical assistance to achieve this.

Banks, with few exceptions, are established to make profits, and their business models emerge from this fundamental purpose. As a result they have a strong aversion to risk. Their assessment of risk is based on judgements that revolve around the notion of asymmetric information: in layman's terms, the chances that, as a potential lender, their knowledge of the likelihood of a borrower repaying a loan differs from that of the borrower. In our many discussions with bankers during the research, it was interesting that only one mentioned the concept of asymmetric information directly. Their conversations however were frequently punctuated with the term 'comfort'. The need for 'comfort', the search for an elusive 'comfort factor', and the acknowledgement that frequently the criteria for determining how 'comfortable' a lending arrangement might be resided in the intuitive judgement of a credit manager with a 'nose for the business'. This confirmed our own guess: if the banks don't understand the context of the borrower they will entertain her with a polite conversation, and then either shut the door firmly behind her or string out negotiations for so long that the effort to obtain the loan becomes more costly than the value of the loan that is being sought. In particular, banks may fail to grasp the form in which security is symbolized within the borrower's reality and the nature of the borrower's asset base.

The investment strategies of the poor nearly always begin as survival strategies that reverse the logic of the formal planning and approval process that operates in most countries. While the formal process begins with an assumption of a 'legal' route, the informal process is often forced to assume that legality is non-achievable, at least in the short term. Banks create investment profiles that assume the legal or formal route (obtain tenure, install infrastructure, build a house, move onto land); the poor require investment profiles that can deal with the likely route of their investments based upon their survival strategies (move onto land, build shelter, negotiate for infrastructure, negotiate for tenure). McLeod (2001c) explains the conundrum in more depth.

Box 4.1 below provides a story that illustrates how difficult it can be for the urban poor to obtain loans for housing and how important these loans can be in providing a means of withstanding unpredictable changes in government policy.

The real reason that organizations of the urban poor have so much difficulty in obtaining loans for housing and infrastructure from banks, and from other formal financial institutions, is that they have difficulty in demonstrating effective demand to the banks. Officials in the institutions involved simply do not believe that the urban poor can lead and manage complex housing and infrastructure projects, nor that they can mobilize savings and repayments in order to repay medium and long-term loans. As a result, the urban poor remain unable to

Box 4.1 Persuading the banks – the Philippines

'My name is Sonia – a community leader under the Homeless Peoples Federation in the Philippines and the SDI network. I want to share our experiences of evictions in my country – particularly in my community. We live on five hectares of privately owned land. According to my grandparents the community has been there for almost a hundred years with more or less 600 families. Eviction threats started when the owner of the land wanted us to leave his property so he could use it for his own purposes. The community people said 'No'. So the owner went to court. We went to seek assistance from the local government but nothing happened.

'The demolition team came and started dismantling the house of one of the community leaders. And because people were resisting and fighting back one of the members of the demolition team died and many of the community were injured. The most ironic part was that the Mayor was watching and said he could not do anything because the order of the court is final and executory.

'Before that we had already been saving. We had a community savings programme in the area and had tried to engage in some of the government's land and housing programmes through the National Housing Authority's resettlement schemes. We tried to comply with all the requirements and process all the necessary documents and other requirements like the 10 per cent equity payment for the cost of the land. But when we reached the final stage of completion with our documents the President changed. With the new President there began a totally new set of policies and guidelines. And the new President ordered a moratorium on all the soon-to-be-realized projects of the National Housing Authority. And because of that we began to lose hope. Then we decided to use our savings to negotiate for a piece of land close by – land owned by the bank that is near our settlement.

'At first the bank did not believe we had the capacity to buy. They didn't believe that our community, we dirty people, would have that much money. We handed in three million pesos. We carried it in plastic bags, coming from our savings and from our urban poor development fund in payment for the property we bought. After that purchase the bank opened its doors for us community people, and offered more foreclosed land that they could sell at a lower market price because they now believed that we dirty people had the capacity to do it.' (Homeless International 2002b)

develop solutions that are legal, affordable and acceptable to their own communities, and financial institutions fail to diversify their lending base to a new and rapidly growing potential market. Supply and demand are, in effect, isolated from each other, and neither is fully effective.

In theory the provision of guarantees, particularly hard currency guarantees, should help to alleviate the nervousness that banks and other financial institutions display in lending to organizations of the poor. In practice guarantees are difficult and expensive to negotiate (see Chapter 6). Even when negotiations are successful, two-year delays in delivery of contractually agreed financing following the completion of guarantee agreements are not unusual, leading to an enforced use of scarce bridging finance. This is often because banks will not lend if full compliance with planning and building regulations[1] has not been certified by the authorities. In addition, guarantees and other security requirements from formal lenders continue to be onerous. Homeless International has managed to achieve significant gearing in some cases, for example 25 per cent guarantees with the Housing and Urban Development Corporation (HUDCO) and the Indian Bank, but other institutions have required 100 per cent hard currency equivalent guarantees and HDFC in India insisted on 109 per cent to ensure that interest on a wholesale loan would also be secured. This begs the question 'why continue to negotiate guarantees?' The answer comes back to the need to create space for the development of new relationships that can potentially benefit the urban poor. Once a guarantee negotiation begins, an important new space is created: for learning and understanding how the processes of informal and formal credit allocation differ, for exposure to new terminologies, and for engagement in dialogue that sometimes leads to accommodation and compromise. However, the guarantee path is not for the faint-hearted or impatient.

While guarantees can create space, it is important to acknowledge that the basis on which they are usually negotiated relies on demonstrations of the achievable. These demonstrations themselves have to be financed and, at least in their early stages, invariably require bridge financing. For large-scale investments that can provide a basis for scaling up, the lack of access to bridge financing is a serious impediment that cannot be overcome with the relatively slim resource base of NGO funders.

An additional complication arises from the fact that most bank lending for low-income housing in developing countries, where it exists, is not asset- but income- or revenue-based, even where reserve banks stipulate clear title as a requirement. So guarantees are not necessarily required to replace conventional mortgage security in the form of clear land title, which allows foreclosure and seizure of a house in the case of default. Banks know that extended legal processes make this an expensive and administratively tortuous process. Guarantees are more likely to be required to cover potential shortfalls in revenue streams, be they from project or individual income sources. Confidence by the lender that revenue or repayments will be forthcoming, in turn relies on accurate information concerning the security of household income or project revenues, and the support that others will provide to ensure that repayment takes place. In short, asymmetry of information needs to be minimized – the banker wants to know as much as the borrower about the chances of repayment so that the bank can have an adequate level of 'comfort' about lending – and security needs to be maximized through organized support systems. However this information is frequently not available in a form that bankers recognize as being legitimate. Communities may be creating a significant organizational base by establishing saving and loan systems, building up databases of information that can be used to negotiate with local authorities and developing pilot approaches that can be tested and refined, but bankers are not necessarily aware of these dynamics. Their lack of familiarity and understanding means that the comfort factor remains elusive.

RISK AS ENCOUNTERED BY ORGANIZATIONS OF THE URBAN POOR

The urban poor face a multitude of problems on a daily basis ranging from the lack of adequate food, right through to the danger of forced eviction and the destruction of the shelter that they have manage to create. For some, short-term risk management dominates their daily lives. For others a longer-term perspective is possible, as is the potential to develop strategies to manage risk that can be combined with investments aimed at escaping poverty altogether. This longer term potential arises most often when the urban poor are organized, and have an institutional base with associated allies, which provides a means to engage in pro-active negotiations with the state and financial institutions (McLeod and Satterthwaite 2000). This section explores the risks that the urban poor take when they begin to engage collectively in creating new approaches to slum upgrading, negotiated resettlement and the provision of urban infrastructure and services. Homeless International's research in the 'Bridging the finance gap' project has shown clearly that organizations of the urban poor, and the NGOs with whom they work, are managing significant and substantial levels of risk in order to finance demonstration projects and to set the basis for scaling up (McLeod, 2001b). Indeed, Homeless International's Guarantee Fund and the CLIFF initiative were developed to ensure that some of this risk taking could be shared and not left completely on the shoulders of the poor.

Political risk

Policies that are antagonistic to the urban poor, such as those that support forced evictions without negotiated resettlement, can provoke actions that exacerbate poverty. Recent forced evictions in Zimbabwe testify to the impact of policies that can rapidly undermine previous development investments. For example the Zimbabwe Homeless People's Federation, prior to the evictions, had worked for many years to build collaborative relationships with local government in order to create new planned settlements as alternatives to the terrible conditions of hostel and shack living. Changes in national-level policy and the implementation of a national clearance strategy led to massive displacement, including evictions where local government and local federations had signed land development agreements.

One of the hallmarks of the national NGO-Federation alliances with whom Homeless International works is that they design and implement projects intended to create policy changes. These policy changes can lead to breakthroughs that can, in turn, result in a transformation in the living conditions of the urban poor on a significant scale. Each project has the potential to become an exemplar, a practical means of demonstrating how things could be done differently and more effectively. However, the choices that the poor have in making these interventions are limited by policy constraints applicable in particular places at particular times. It is only by building a critical mass of organized citizens able to demonstrate alternatives in practice, that new precedents are likely to seriously impact on city-, sub-national- and national-level policies. When new precedents work and large numbers of people, who are organized around the same issues, form a critical mass, it sometimes becomes possible for the poor to take a place at the policy formulation table. For example, the Indian Alliance has resettled more than 20,000 families under the Municipal Urban Transport Project (see Burra 2005: 72) and has worked with different cities to provide access to sanitation to more than 200,000 people (see Chapter 7 on CLIFF), leading to a situation where both state and central governments regularly consult them on matters concerning slum policy and programmes, including housing finance for the urban poor. Federations of the urban poor have also been included as advisers on governmental bodies in a number of other countries: South Africa, Kenya, Namibia and Thailand, to name but a few.

One of the factors that makes management of political risk particularly complex is that its location is extremely varied. Within a globalized world, policy influence comes from a range of different institutional arrangements, including local government, regional government, parastatals (particularly those controlling utilities and transport), central government, private and public financial institutions, bi-lateral and multi-lateral organizations such as the World Bank, the regional development banks, the United Nations Human Settlements Programme (UN-Habitat), Cities Alliance and so on. In short, local alliances have to explore dialogue with many, if not all of these institutions, in order to create space for the poor to present their solutions. The most effective means of doing this is by sharing practical experience on the ground of projects in which a range of these agencies, by necessity, must be involved. As Sheela Patel from SPARC has put it, 'For the federations, the *doing* demonstrates their power and gives them both voice and choice.'

So what are the policy areas that have been prioritized by local alliances? Primarily they have been around land allocation, resettlement, upgrading, building standards, sanitation and access to finance, with a particular emphasis on creating alternatives to forced evictions. A focus on accessing subsidies, where these exist, has also been important. Once a precedent has been demonstrated and supported within policy, however, there remains a risk that the policy will be reversed or significantly changed to the detriment of the poor. In Andhra Pradesh, for example, the long-term sustainability of housing loans was ruined when the state government and HUDCO began to offer highly subsidized housing loans, undercutting the arrangements that HUDCO had previously made with a local NGO. This would have been acceptable if the new state programme had had the capacity to meet the housing needs of the poor. However it did not, so the conditions of the poor worsened and the painfully built institutional arrangements, developed to create a financially viable housing loan system, were destroyed.[2]

Initial engagement with policy makers also carries the risk of communities, and support NGOs, being co-opted and drawn into processes of political patronage. When governments change or individual politicians are displaced or move on, this can lead to official abandonment of schemes. This has required a strong stance that, again, is a characteristic of most of the organizations with whom Homeless International works. At the institutional level none of the NGO-Federation alliances offer allegiance to local political parties or individuals. This is important not only for ensuring that the membership of a federation bridges ethnic, religious and political differences, but also for ensuring continuity in approach and commitment whichever government is in power. At the same time, wherever possible, local, national and international politicians have been invited to visit projects and to participate in ceremonies concerning those projects (such as inaugurations), as a means of encouraging their support for approaches and methods prioritized by the poor.

Perhaps the most intractable political risk is that of initiating a project either to test or to change a policy and then facing the complexity of delays and difficulties in gaining the permissions and authority to proceed at all the different stages of construction. Delays and prevarication can result from genuine confusion about both how a project can be implemented within a particular policy framework, and during construction, how the project is proceeding. However, delays can also be created when officials expect pay-offs prior to planning and building approvals being issued. It is difficult to rapidly change historically embedded practices and it is often necessary to work with government officials and politicians over an extended time until they can see, and to some extent 'own', the benefits that finally accrue to a community. This is helped when communities identify the benefits that result from interventions. For example, when representatives from one community visit a settlement where community toilets have been constructed, they frequently return to their own community and ask their local politicians to provide the same support. Over time local electorates develop new expectations of their politicians, changing the nature of political demand.

One of the ways in which the Indian Alliance has been able to create change in the ways that policies are implemented, or catalyse the development of new and more appropriate policies, has been to work closely with technocrats within the Indian civil service. When professionals working within government are exposed to alternative ways of doing things and become champions of new approaches as a result, new options can open up. However, it is often only after a project has been completed that the way in which a policy needs to be interpreted, modified or replaced altogether becomes clear, so maintaining relationships over a long period of time is important. It is interesting in this respect that some of the relationships that the Indian Alliance has with government officials go back over 15 years.

Financial risks

As soon as a project relies on a loan for its implementation, it becomes subject to financial risk. Loans cost money in the form of interest and, sometimes, in the form of penalties that have to be paid if repayments do not go according to plan. At the same time it is important that adequate financing is in place to ensure that cash-flow inadequacies do not result in major construction delays and an inability to pay suppliers. It is therefore not surprising that bankers assessing potential loans want to see information regarding exactly how the project's finances will be managed, and to see detailed cash-flow projections. The reality is that these projections are often extremely difficult to provide in a consistent and reliable format when projects are being implemented for the first time. For example, as projects are submitted for planning and building approval, design changes may be required that not only change the entire project cost but also the sequencing of construction. A project may begin within one policy context and find that the whole situation has changed as a result of policy changes further down the line. For example, the Rajiv Indira–Suryodaya scheme was planned on the basis of agreed assumptions that had to be significantly changed once the project was well underway. Several years after the project had been planned and initiated the state government was pressurized by national government to implement a previously dormant policy for regulating construction near waterways. This immediately reduced the number of apartments that could be constructed for sale and meant that the project, instead of realizing a modest surplus, would experience a significant loss. Several years later, the precise way in which the policy would be applied was clarified, and the construction of more 'for sale' apartments was authorized. By that time the price for apartments in the specific area had also increased; as a result the project is now expected to realize a significant surplus.

Where project loans are needed, much of the negotiation regarding the loan will be based around the bank's understanding and judgement of the likelihood of the loan being repaid on time. The bank will carry out a credit risk assessment. If the borrowing agency has no previous track record the bank will have to base its judgement on factors that lie outside its immediate experience. In conventional credit risk assessment, the bank will look at a borrower's balance sheet and their track record of performance in the activity for which they are requesting a loan. The bank may also seek collateral to serve as a security against default. However, this methodology presents considerable challenges when a bank considers extending a loan to a local alliance, albeit one such as the Indian Alliance that has a specialist finance and construction management company to administer such arrangements. The problem for the bank is that most such organizations do not have the level of assets that banks expect to see on a potential borrower's balance sheet. A regular developer would normally be able to show significant reserves that could be used as working capital and many would also be able to show land reserves. With a not-for-profit organization such as SPARC, the bank's judgement rather than being based on an assessment of the balance sheet must be based on an assessment of previous projects and on the reputation of the organization's leadership (see the interview with Anil Kumar in Chapter 8).

Market or commercial risk

All projects are vulnerable to escalations in material and construction costs, with increases in the cost of some materials, usually cement and steel, being particularly important. However when projects are developed that rely for their viability on a level of cross subsidy from commercial sales, market risk can be even more complex, playing a particularly important part in the assessment of a project's potential success. The prices of land and real estate in specific locations will determine the project income that sales will generate. In Mumbai, the price of transferable development rights[3] (TDR) has been especially significant in determining project viability (see Chapter 6 for an explanation of TDR). One of the major challenges in planning community-led projects at scale is cash-flow budgeting and monitoring. The systems required not only rely on considerable technical fluency with the building process but also an intimate understanding of how the basic cost of the project has been estimated. Projecting costs is much easier where considerable experience exists. However, when projects are setting new precedents, cost projections can be very difficult, especially when the assessments and views of several parties have to be accommodated.

A case in point is that of the Rajiv Indira–Suryodaya project, which was the first community-led slum upgrading project in Dharavi, Mumbai. Jockin, the President of the National Slum Dwellers' Federation, projected construction costs, the sale price of TDR and the sale price of apartments (that were to be constructed for sale in order to provide an internal subsidy for the project) per square foot. However, when negotiations began with banks in order to secure a loan for the project, no one could produce evidence regarding these projections that the banks felt was objectively verifiable. Interestingly, nearly seven years down the road, Jockin's projections proved considerably more accurate than those of the bank, but even he could not have predicted that the price of TDR would have risen from 400 Rupees to 1600 Rupees per square foot over a period of four years.

Investment risk

It is frequently assumed that clear land title and clear ownership rights are a fundamental requirement in upgrading programmes, not only as a means of ensuring long-term security but also for securing finance for construction and other purposes. We will not go into issues of tenure in detail here, but it is perhaps salient to note that clear title does not necessarily function as a magic bullet in ensuring access to bank loans. An earlier section of this chapter alludes to the fact that most bank lending for low-income housing in developing countries, where it exists, is not asset- but income- or revenue-based, even where reserve banks stipulate clear title as a requirement. This contradicts a prevalent notion, currently being promoted by Hernando de Soto (de Soto 2000), that the allocation of clear land title is necessary to catalyse investment in improved housing and that it also, almost automatically, confers credit worthiness. We urge caution regarding this conclusion, for a number of reasons:

- It has been amply demonstrated that the poor invest in permanent housing when they perceive themselves to have *de facto* tenure security, not necessarily *de jure* secure tenure.
- The costs of obtaining clear land title can equal or exceed the costs of housing construction, making such an approach unaffordable for the poor.
- Banks frequently refuse credit to households with clear land title if they depend on uncertified incomes generated in the informal economy.
- Credit applications from households living in settlements considered 'no-go' areas by banks are refused, even where they have clear land title, because foreclosure in the case of default is considered either politically impossible or legally tortuous and expensive.

In short, it is arguable that the collective knowledge and experience base of the poor is far more important than clear land title in ensuring 'comfort' for the lender. It is also apparent that it is the social safety nets, provided by the infrastructure of federated savings schemes, which provide people with the political confidence to invest in housing and settlement upgrading on a collective basis.

Foreign exchange rate risk

Local partner organizations of Homeless International have not been subject to significant foreign exchange rate risk because where foreign exchange loans or local guarantee deposits have been provided Homeless International has assumed this particular risk. Homeless International's work has emphasized the catalysing of local lending by local financial institutions, rather than encouraging international lending. However foreign exchange risk remains a factor where building costs are sensitive to the devaluation of local currency. Cement costs are particularly sensitive to foreign exchange rates, either because cement has to be imported or when cement is locally produced, the significant energy component of its manufacturing costs has to be paid for in foreign exchange.

Interest rate risk

Where bank interest rates are volatile, interest rate risk can be a significant factor in assessing the viability of a project. Fortunately, in recent years, there have been significant reductions in interest rates in countries where Homeless International has entered into agreements with banks: India and Bolivia. One means to protect against sudden changes in interest rates is to agree a fixed rate in advance. It is also possible to negotiate interest rates in other ways. For example when interest rates fell in Bolivia, Homeless International agreed a 4 per cent reduction in the interest due on a US dollar deposit being held as a guarantee by a local financial institution, in return for a 4.5 per cent reduction in the interest charged by the bank on a loan to Homeless International's local partner. As a result, the local partner was able to on-lend to communities at a much lower, and more competitive, rate.

Fraud and financial mismanagement risk

One of the major financial risks associated with any project is the potential for fraud and financial mismanagement. Developing accounting and reporting systems that translate the informal accountability practices of federations into the formal audited reporting requirements expected of support NGOs can be extremely challenging. The first danger is that systems become over-formalized and that the NGO systems become a serious bottleneck, limiting the flow of financial resources needed on the ground and causing distrust and confusion regarding the moral 'ownership' of resources that may be held by the NGO for legal purposes. On the other hand, if accountable systems are developed that are not transparent this can lead to abuse and the undermining of organizational credibility together with, in a worse case scenario, significant financial losses.

Affordability

The final area of financial risk is affordability. If the housing units and infrastructure services that result from a project are unaffordable to the users, the scheme will inevitably fail. People may be forced to sell to better-off families, infrastructure may not be adequately maintained and services cut off. Affordability is one of the biggest challenges when people move from informal settlements into 'formal' housing. Their living conditions may have been greatly improved, but their shelter costs may have significantly increased: water bills, electricity bills, property taxes and so on can all have a significant impact on a fragile economic balancing act. For this reason the Indian Alliance places a major emphasis on building up the capacity of local savings groups and their related organizational structures. Local savings groups do not just deal with daily savings; they provide an organizational means for people to plan for future change, and to mobilize savings in advance to cover collective expenses. Savings groups also provide an information, financial and social safety net so that people do not have to struggle with vulnerability and change on their own.

Project management risk

There is a range of factors associated with project management risk. Poorly managed projects can result in major cost escalation, poor quality construction, implementation delays, confusion and contention. Officials may also delay approvals unless bribes are paid. It would be tempting to assume that the only way that these complex managerial risks could be managed is to professionalize them – in other words to employ professional managers to monitor and control the process. However, community-led processes that, by definition, seek to retain maximum control of building processes at the local level, challenge this assumption. Certainly in India, a new relationship is being developed between professionals, such as architects and engineers, who are working side by side with contractors and communities with a commitment to sharing decision-making and learning. For instance, one of the major criteria for awarding contracts with larger builders is their willingness to engage with communities and to subcontract work to local community members. Community members who have developed experience in project implementation as small contractors are now taking on larger contracts and responsibilities. The ongoing exchange process, which facilitates learning between different groups, has also helped develop new management processes, with teams from different areas of the city and different cities visiting to share how new management arrangements work in practice.

Social risk

Historically, communities living in informal settlements and in slums have had a contentious relationship with the state. However, as informal settlements become increasingly consolidated and as the critical mass of people living in such settlements, and their commensurate political power, grows, repeated and forced evictions have become less favoured as a state intervention. This is not to say that massive evictions are no longer taking place in many parts of the world. Nonetheless an increasing number of city and state authorities are realizing that exploring options for negotiated resettlements and slum upgrading offer far greater social, economic and political returns in the long term. They are also beginning to recognize that the urban poor take considerable personal risks when engaging in new approaches to resettlement and slum upgrading. When slum dwellers in Dharavi either broke their houses down and moved into transit accommodation or doubled up in the housing of their neighbours and friends so that a new community-led slum-upgrading scheme could start, they had no guarantees of how and when the project would be completed. They took a huge risk in dislocating their families in the hope that their Federation would be able to mobilize the necessary resources and successfully complete the project.

Community leadership also involves considerable risk. The responsibility and workload of community leaders who emerge through the federation process is considerable and constant. It is difficult to maintain a family, particularly a harmonious one, if you work long hours and travel frequently. The stress that high-level professionals face in their work life is widely recognized, but the stress managed by slum dwellers leading slum upgrading, resettlement and infrastructure provision processes also needs recognition and support. This is particularly so where individuals provide leadership not only at the local level but also nationally and internationally. The only long-term answer is to ensure that new leaders are constantly being developed so that the burden can be shared and the long-term continuity of the movement ensured.

One of the greatest risks, when families move from informal shelter to permanent and safe housing, is that they will be economically pressurized to sell out to better-off families. The Indian Alliance has tried to preclude this by providing collective leasehold tenure rather than clear land title. If and when families move it is the local housing society or co-operative who decides on who the unit will be transferred to and under what conditions. This approach has also been taken by federations in many other countries. In contexts where there have been high mortality rates due to AIDS this collective management of inheritance and transfer has become particularly important. For example, in South Africa children whose parent or parents die while they are still repaying housing loans, are looked after by others while the house is rented out. The rent is used to repay the loan and the children reclaim the house when they are old enough.

Institutional risk

As has emerged clearly in the section on financial risk, the reputation and credibility of a borrowing institution is of critical importance in enhancing lenders' sense of 'comfort'. The reputation and credibility of lending institutions also needs to be developed and maintained. Failure to deliver on commitments, prevarication in decision making, and an unwillingness to invest in serious institutional learning about new approaches and methods can undermine the trust that the urban poor are expected to have in banks and other financial institutions. There are three major factors that can affect both sides of this relationship between borrower and lender. The first is the challenge of being able to recruit and retain personnel with the appropriate skills, experience and attitudes. The second is ensuring continuity and consistency in leadership. The third challenge is developing the systems and procedures necessary to ensure that the learning that emerges from the planning and implementation of projects is institutional, and not limited to the experience of a few individuals. Strengthening capacity in these three areas can be problematic for both banks and support NGOs.

Personnel recruitment and retention is particularly difficult for NGOs because of the high levels of demand from the commercial sector for staff with financial skills and qualifications. It can also be extremely difficult to recruit personnel with these skills who also have the ability and inclination to work with slum dwellers as partners rather than supervisors. The mobility of highly qualified staff within both financial institutions and NGOs can be extremely high, leading to dislocation in the wider organization. One of the long-term answers for the Indian Alliance has been to invest in training and support for members of the federations, so that functions currently carried out by NGO professionals can be carried out within the federation structure itself. However this takes time, and in the interim managing rapidly expanding programmes with limited personnel capacity can produce significant institutional strain within NGOs and the federations that they support.

Clearly leadership is one of the most important elements contributing to institutional reputation and credibility. Within the Indian Alliance, the longevity of the leadership both individually and collectively is impressive. A core group of more than 50 people spanning the NGO, the federation and Mahila Milan have worked together for more than 20 years. In the case of the federation, some of the leaders have worked together for more than 30 years. This pattern of continuity is reflected in many of the other national NGO–federation alliances that Homeless International supports. The other side of the continuity coin is the challenge of managing succession. Supporting the emergence of new leaders, helping them to take over increasing levels of responsibility and building mutual support systems between them are crucial. Many of the original leaders are highly charismatic and the second generation replacing them will not necessarily have the same personalities or standing. Tackling succession remains vital if the initial successes of the federations in scaling-up their approaches and methods is to be maintained and developed.

Natural hazards risk

Informal settlements, slums and squatter camps are frequently located in hazardous locations: on low-lying land subject to flooding, on steep slopes subject to land slides, by railway tracks and roads where accidents are inevitable. Poor people are forced to take land where they can get it, and these are the areas that other people are usually least interested in, at least until they are improved and developed.

When disasters occur, such as the 2004 *tsunami*, it is usually the poor who suffer most. The difficulties are compounded when displacement as a result of natural disasters is used to remove people permanently from land where their communities may have lived for many years. It is only when communities come together to fight for alternative processes in post-disaster reconstruction that they have much chance to retain their land, or obtain acceptable new land (Asian Coalition for Housing Rights 2005b)

MANAGING RISK

The discussion so far has mentioned some ways in which the risks that the poor take are being effectively mitigated and managed. It might be useful, however, to outline some of the general patterns that have emerged. The formation of national NGO–Federation alliances of the kind that have been described elsewhere in this book (see Chapter 3) has allowed thousands of people to take risks collectively, which it would have been impossible for poor families to take on an individual basis. Large numbers of people, organized around money and information, have been able to support specific communities when they need to break rules, to demonstrate new ways of doing things and to withstand the pressures to give up when obstacles arise and setbacks occur. Communities have been able to do this because they can rely on local, national and international support from the networks in which they operate.

The leaders of national alliances have been clear from the beginning that the development process will take time and require stamina. They have provided a level of long-term consistency and continuity in organizational processes, which provides the confidence that this scale of movement requires to be successful. Inevitably there have been problems, but overall the central principles that have been applied have worked in practice and enabled a high level of collective risk taking. As the federation model has spread, a critical mass of organized people living in slums and informal settlements is beginning to develop, with a voice that is becoming more and more articulate at local, national and international levels. This has meant that an alliance taking a risk in one country may do so confident that organizations in other countries will support it by contributing information, expertise and knowledge, and sometimes funds[4]. The exchange process provides a means to share learning but also a method of sharing risk-taking and management. It helps that a lesson learned in one location rapidly spreads to another. Within this context the development of urban poor funds has been particularly important. The funds help people to demonstrate the possible by providing a mixture of loans and grants for projects on the ground. In effect the funds shoulder some of the financial risks. However, scaling up can present significant challenges, especially where there is a lack of adequate capital.

WHAT HAS PERSUADED SOME BANKS TO BECOME INVOLVED?

The initial difficulties experienced in getting banks to lend for rural housing in Andhra Pradesh, and the eagerness of banks in Tamil Nadu to become involved in lending to a local NGO known as IVDP, are discussed in Chapter 6, which looks at how guarantees have been used in India and Bolivia. This chapter focuses more on what has happened in urban areas – specifically in Mumbai – with bank responses to requests for loans by the Indian Alliance.

Over a considerable period of time the Indian Alliance has gone to great lengths to help bankers to understand how they work. Bankers have visited sites, investigated internal management systems, talked with slum dwellers and contractors and gradually become familiar with the process involved in community-led initiatives. They have also been able to visit projects that have been completed, and to talk to officials who have been part of authorizing those projects. However, this exposure process has taken many years to achieve successful results, largely because of the high turnover of senior staff within the banking sector. When discussions first began between the Indian Alliance, Homeless International and Citibank, 15 senior officials from Citibank were involved and became familiar with the work. After one year, all 15 were transferred outside of Mumbai during a period of less than two weeks, so training and exposure of bank staff had to begin again from scratch. Similar staffing changes happened at least three times. It is significant that part of the success of the agreements now being negotiated with ICICI Bank has resulted from the presence (and hence continuity) of one banker who had worked with the Indian Alliance in his previous post at UTI Bank. For further information on his experience refer to Chapter 8.

But what exactly helps bankers to feel comfortable about lending to organizations of the urban poor and their members? The first factor, relevant to individual loans, is an understanding of household financial management, with savings records providing a particularly effective means of tracking levels of disposable income available for investment in housing. The mechanisms used to accumulate savings can also provide important evidence of *backative* (a Jamaican patois term meaning back up or support) – the organizational safety nets that are constituted by social networks where community-based savings and loan systems provide a means of covering crises that may delay and prevent repayment. The savings and loan systems characteristic of federations of the urban poor belonging to Shack Dwellers International are illustrative of this 'social' or 'institutional' capital. The second factor relates to wholesale lending, either for on-lending to individuals or for collective investment by the poor in large-scale projects such as sanitation or slum upgrading (which may also entail financing by the state). In these circumstances, it is the track record and the credibility of the intermediary organizations (such as an NGO) that become important. The Indian Alliance, for example, has been able to negotiate significant guarantees and credit from both public and commercial institutions for urban development initiatives led by the federations (see Chapters 6 and 7, also McLeod 2002b).

The Indian Alliance established a track record and credibility by starting out with small-scale projects. These tested the systems and capacities of the Indian Alliance as a whole as well as the way in which state policies were being implemented. The Indian Alliance formed strategic alliances with key government officials who shared a concern that policies needed to be effectively applied on the ground, and they generated publicity and media attention when those initiatives proved successful. At the same time they strategically converted grant funds into bridge financing capital and began to engage with the Slum Rehabilitation Act in a way that allowed the development rights of slum dwellers to be leveraged in a manner that the banks could recognize and respond to. Once additional capital funding was made available through the CLIFF mechanism it became possible to broaden the range of projects that could be supported and to take on larger and more complex initiatives. Banks were invited to visit these once they were underway so they could understand the logic behind each project.

It is difficult to overestimate the importance of bridge financing in persuading banks to lend to the urban poor. Without up-front bridge financing, for example, the resettlement of over 20,000 households (as part of the World Bank-funded MUTP II project –see Burra 2005: 72) from alongside the railway tracks of Mumbai into accommodation with secure tenure would not have been possible, even though there were state funds allocated for reimbursement of project costs[5]. It was the availability of bridging finance that led to the federations being able to take control of their own resettlement and that ultimately led to secure tenure for the participating families. This achievement in turn strengthened the credibility of the Indian Alliance and made discussions with banks easier.

SOME GENERAL COMMENTS ABOUT RISK TAKING

It is important to note that the relationship between security and risk is dialectic. By this we mean, 'security at one level allows risks to be taken at a higher order, in good faith.'[6] So as federations succeed in setting new precedents in one area of work or in one city, it becomes possible to take on higher levels of risk with potentially greater returns. Development means one step at a time, but each successful step means that the next can be larger. Our ability to take risks is also strengthened when we can rely on others. It helps to have access to independent resources – both financial and human – that are not dependent on those with whom we are negotiating. It also helps to have strong alliances with others that have been tried and tested over time so that it is possible to tolerate considerable debate and disagreement without the relationship itself becoming vulnerable or compromised.

Entering into relationships with the commercial and public sectors is like swimming with alligators. It is only when you try it that you find out just how fast you have to swim, at what depth and in which direction. Asking people to plan in advance for all the consequences of such bravery is unrealistic. It is more pragmatic to try and construct that story once the process is well underway. Three years into the implementation of the CLIFF project, which is described in detail in Chapter 7, it has become possible to reconstruct the risk taking that was involved in particular projects by analysing their performance retrospectively. Delays in implementation, variations in cost, the detailed actual financial flows, and the constraints that had to be dealt with when specific policies were tested can now be tracked. To some degree the impact of managing these factors can also be costed. All of this means that the lessons learned can be applied in new projects as they are designed and the ability to manage and mitigate risk across a whole portfolio of projects is gradually becoming more refined. It is important to remember, however, that the aim of doing this is not to 'squeeze out' risk, as I recently heard one microfinance expert express it. It is to understand the level of risk that has to be undertaken to achieve the advances we hope for in creating safe and secure settlements with the urban poor.

CHAPTER FIVE

A continuum of financial services

Ruth McLeod

INTRODUCTION

In Chapter 2 we identified a number of key principles that have emerged from the work that we have supported with partner organizations in Asia and Africa. This chapter examines how these principles have been reflected in the mechanisms for accumulating and accessing financial capital that have been developed by the groups with whom Homeless International works. It looks at how the principles are reflected in the financial products and services that have emerged as the projects taken on by organizations of the urban poor have become more ambitious, both in terms of scale and in terms of the manner in which 'business as usual' is challenged.

The chapter begins with a brief overview of the history of financing for community-led development in urban areas and the manner in which such development has been treated within national and international shelter policies and strategies. The development of urban poor funds is described, and their characteristics are analysed in contrast to microfinance institutions. The findings of a research study, 'Bridging the finance gap in housing and infrastructure', are discussed in order to clarify the nature of the gap that exists in the provision of financial services that can support and build on community-led initiatives. A more precise description of the forms of financing required for such development is then provided, together with information on sources of such financing and a range of examples of each form. A case is made regarding the importance of supporting the creation of effective demand from a community perspective and in order to redress a historical focus on supply factors within financial services initiatives intended to benefit the poor. Finally the importance of subsidies is recognized and options for blending different forms of finance so that subsidies can be used optimally to the advantage of the poor are discussed.

A GLIMPSE BACK IN HISTORY

John Turner's work in the early 1970s highlighted the urgency of removing regulatory impediments that constrained poor people's capacity to build their own homes (Turner and Fichter 1972). His insights emerged from the survival dynamics of pioneer settlers on the outskirts of some of Latin America's largest urban centres. However, by the end of the 1990s the increasing commercial demand for land within large cities in the developing world was creating a crisis of major proportions for urban planners and managers, as well as for the urban poor. With inner city land at a premium and high densities precluding the kind of peri-urban development that Turner had described so well, it became clear that in many of the world's mega cities the only feasible solution was building upwards – high-rise residential development. This form of construction is not conducive to self-help, household-based initiative. At the same time it was increasingly being recognized that simply turning a blind eye to the 'illegal' development that poor households invested in could not be conceived of as a long-term solution. Planned high-density developments had to be incorporated into policy, necessitating reconsideration not only of land allocation practices but also of access to the financial capital that would be required for such developments.

During the 1980s, international interest in urban development had begun to focus on housing finance and the lack of access that the urban poor had to formal financial markets. However, by the mid-1990s it was widely acknowledged that the housing finance institutions that had been set up to meet this need had largely been subverted towards serving the requirements of middle-income groups[1] (Datta and Jones 1998). International policy makers subsequently promoted an active engagement with the private sector, assuming that the formal commercial banking sector could, and would, play a key role in the delivery of finance for urban shelter and infrastructure provision. This assumption coincided with the increasing international influence of neo-liberal economic development policies and became embedded in assumptions underlying the 'enabling strategy' promoted by UN-Habitat at Habitat II, the 'City Summit', held in Istanbul in 1996. Donors began to work with banks and other financial institutions to support their entry into housing finance and broader urban investment. Capital funds, usually in the form of soft loans, were made available to finance institutions by agencies such as the German Development Bank (KfW), the World Bank and the regional development banks. In some cases start-up capital was provided to establish mortgage finance institutions, for example, the Housing Development Finance Corporation in India. In other cases special funds allocated for low-income housing were provided.

The assumption was that banks and other private sector financial institutions would provide an efficient means of delivery for housing loans. It was assumed that they would be less susceptible to the political interference and patronage that had characterized many of the public housing finance institutions that, with a few notable exceptions, had proved so ineffective in reaching the poor, particularly in urban areas. However the new arrangements proved little more successful than their predecessors. The formal financial institutions proved highly risk averse, even when managing soft funds specifically aimed at developing a new market for housing finance among low-income earners. The reasons for this have been explored in more detail in the chapter on risk. The reality was that attempts to address the provision of housing finance to low-income groups living in the informal sector through existing formal institutions were frustratingly ineffective. A huge gap existed between the supply systems of the banking sector and the effective demands of the poor.

While all this was going on, microfinance – characterized by short-term retail lending, at relatively high interest rates, to individuals and small groups – became a popular trend within development practice. As its use spread rapidly, especially as a means of supporting the development of small businesses and microenterprises, it began to emerge that microfinance borrowers, mainly women, were frequently taking out loans, ostensibly for business purposes, but actually spending them on home improvements and extension (Harvard University School of Graduate Design 2000; CGAP 2004). Given that many homes within the informal sector have a dual function, providing shelter and a base for economic activity, this was not particularly surprising. However, it has become increasingly clear that this trend represented a major demand for housing finance and that a significant proportion of the loan portfolios of microfinance institutions (MFIs) in Asia, Africa and Latin America were being 'diverted' for use in housing development and improvement. In response to this apparent 'demand', a range of MFIs have now developed special housing finance products.[2] However these products have significant limitations. They tend to be short term, relatively expensive, provided to individuals rather than groups and largely available in rural as opposed to urban areas. There is little evidence, as yet, that they can address the kinds of financing required for large-scale slum upgrading and infrastructure provision which, by definition, requires collective action, relatively high levels of project financing and significant technical inputs.

As microfinance institutions proliferated in many different national contexts, a new form of financial institution, the urban poor fund, was slowly emerging in a small number of countries (see Chapter 3 for more information on urban poor funds). In most cases federations of the urban poor initiated these funds with their support agencies, starting with grants from northern NGOs and, in some cases, pooled savings from the federations themselves. Over time some of the federations were able to negotiate capital allocations to their funds from central government. In Thailand a national fund designed to provide loans to the urban poor was capitalized from the beginning by central government. Boonyabancha (2004) describes how the Urban Community Development Organization (UCDO) proved so successful over its first decade in operation that it was broadened to provide national credit extension in rural as well as urban areas and is now known as the Community Organizations Development Institute (CODI). In Cambodia, the Urban Poor Development Fund received substantial funding from government and is run on a partnership basis, chaired by the Municipality with representation on the Board from communities, NGOs and the government. Government has also provided funding to urban poor funds in South Africa, the Philippines and Namibia. All the funds associated with the ACHR and SDI networks have received NGO grants, in the main from Misereor, Cordaid, Homeless International, SELAVIP and the Sigrid Rausing Trust. Some of the funds have also received funds from bi-lateral donors, notably in India, South Africa, Kenya, Namibia and Vietnam.

So how do the services and products provided by urban poor funds compare with those provided by the conventional banking systems and the microfinance institutions?

■ The funds have grown in response to the effective demand of the organizations who needed them rather than being supply driven. Indeed it is arguable that the funds have had a major catalytic role in developing the effective demand of the poor by providing a means to develop new methods and approaches that suit their capacity both organizationally and financially.

■ The funds make medium- and sometimes long-term loans available, enabling groups to plan and implement collective land development strategies including housing and infrastructure provision. MFI loans tend to be short-term.

■ The loans provided by the funds are to groups rather than to individuals, supporting collective action to tackle a specific shelter or infrastructure need and thereby supporting the development of collective financial management systems. MFI housing loans tend to be to individuals rather than to groups, especially in urban areas.

■ The funds generally seek to finance projects that will include the poorest people, albeit by means of cross subsidies within or between specific schemes, rather than focusing on each family's ability to pay.

■ The funds provide a range of financial mechanisms to address access by the poor to land, housing, infrastructure and other services but these mechanisms are embedded in wider processes and 'rituals' that are also recognized as necessary in addressing the broader structural issues of poverty (see Chapter 3 on capacity building for more details). MFI and standard bank loans tend to consciously avoid these additional areas of technical and social support.

■ Information about how the loans are used is systematically shared with other groups in the wider network of organizations of the urban poor so that learning can be used to maximum effect.

■ The funds provide loans to projects that are high risk because they are experimental and often designed to challenge existing legislative and planning frameworks. This provides a buffer that enables groups to challenge vested interests and embedded processes that constrain their development efforts. MFI and conventional bank lending tends to be guided by more restricted means of risk management.

■ The funds are managed on the basis of effectiveness rather than efficiency. Notions of full cost recovery and long-term financial sustainability are treated with scepticism.[3] Indeed interest rates on loans are often consciously skewed to ensure that lending for basic needs, including housing, will be prioritized.

Urban poor funds now exist in countries as diverse as India, the Philippines, Cambodia, Kenya and Zimbabwe. In all, within the Shack Dwellers International and Asian Coalition for Housing Rights networks, there are now at least 12 such funds. They are at very different stages of development, vary in their governance structures and have differing approaches to engagement with local and national government and with the commercial banking sector. However they do have one thing in common in that they have been locally designed to provide for the broad financial service needs of people living in low-income and informal settlements. The funds place a specific emphasis on facilitating collective access to land and on supporting the efforts of the urban poor to spearhead new approaches to slum upgrading, resettlement and infrastructure provision.

Identifying key questions to ask has been an important part of Homeless International's research process. There are so many variables that could be considered, given the diversity of the countries where funds have been established. In looking at the range of funds and facilities that have been developed to support community-driven slum upgrading, and in trying to understand how they have evolved within specific contexts, we have found it useful to ask 15 key questions.

- What are the sources of capital and the conditions of provision?
- How are the activities of the fund constrained or helped by local regulatory legislation?
- Who designs the products and what are they used for?
- Who controls the loan allocation process and using which criteria?
- What is the cost of administering loans and how much does it cost groups to access them?
- What are the procurement[4] rules and whom do they benefit?
- How/where does the capital circulate and where does it end up?
- Who takes the major risk? How, if at all, is risk shared?
- Whose institutional capacity, political influence and knowledge base is strengthened by use of the fund?
- What broader impact does the capital provision have on further access by the poor to local capital?
- What broader impact does the capital provision have on the capacity of organizations of the poor to take an active role in urban governance?
- How does the fund assist the urban poor to influence national, sub-national and city policy on land allocation, and building and planning regulation?
- To what degree are the funds seen as a strategic component of broader city or state slum upgrading strategies?
- How is the effectiveness of the fund judged and assessed by its users?
- How is the learning that emerges from use of the fund captured and shared?

These questions are important because they enable an exploration of the critical areas in which the provision of capital funds to the urban poor can have a catalytic impact. They also allow a broader exploration of the impact of applying an approach based on efficacy in addressing basic structural issues of poverty, rather than merely efficiency in delivery of a restricted range of financial services. The lack of access by the poor to finance is not simply a reflection of market inefficiency or market failure. It is also a reflection of real poverty in terms of a lack of access to a complexity of resources that compose the elements required for urban regeneration – land, infrastructure, community mobilization, enterprise and employment generation, transport and housing.

WHAT FORMS OF FINANCE ARE NEEDED FOR COMMUNITY-LED INITIATIVES?

When Homeless International and its partner agencies began to explore the lack of access to the kind of finance that was required to scale up the work of organizations of the urban poor, a number of factors stood out starkly. It was clear that there was a serious dislocation between the demand from organizations of the poor for medium- and long-term finance and the supply priorities and systems of microfinance institutions and the formal financial and banking sector. It was also clear that donor efforts to widen the local investment base in infrastructure and settlement development had not been particularly successful. There were a complexity of reasons for this, but one of the most important was that in most cases the urban poor were unable to express effective demand in a form that was recognized as legitimate and feasible by donors and by local, regional and national governments. Not surprisingly, the formal banking sector had little knowledge of the potential lending market within informal settlements and even less idea of how, if at all, this kind of market might fit into their core business models. It all added up to a huge gap in provision characterized by financial ignorance on all sides despite a growing awareness that the problems of poor urban infrastructure and housing were going to become increasingly serious impediments to long-term sustainable development.

The research project 'Bridging the finance gap in housing and infrastructure' was designed to explore the nature of the gap in the provision of finance needed by the urban poor with particular reference to housing and infrastructure. When the research began, Homeless International's partners were almost entirely dependent on grants from northern NGOs to provide the working capital for demonstration projects that could show how business could be done differently. The quantum of these funds was limited and constrained. It was clear that new sources of finance would need to be located but less clear how this could be achieved without jeopardizing the leadership that communities themselves were taking in developing new approaches and initiatives. There were a number of very basic challenges.

- The existing urban poor funds lacked sufficient capital to scale up operations.
- There was contention over the degree to which funds should engage with the commercial banking sector.
- There was contention over the use of subsidies. For example, some people felt that in South Africa too much emphasis had been placed on pursuing government subsidies, to the cost of those without land who did not qualify for subsidies.
- There was contention over the degree of collaboration with government at national regional and local levels.
- The capacity to mange the funds was, and still is, stretched. Retaining finance staff of the calibre needed is difficult, particularly staff who can work comfortably with a community-led development process that doesn't meet standard procurement and reporting requirements.
- There was some confusion about who 'owned' the funds, given that their legal ownership inevitably differed from the wider moral ownership by a people's movement.
- It was not clear whether utilizing federation savings as a stakeholding in the funds was necessarily legal under different national legislations.

The research identified 10 forms of finance that are necessary if community-driven processes are to become truly effective in the development and delivery of improved housing and infrastructure in urban areas. These forms of finance are described below.

FORMS OF FINANCE REQUIRED FOR COMMUNITY-LED DEVELOPMENTS

In the 'Bridging the finance gap in housing and infrastructure' study, 10 forms of finance, categorized by their use, were identified as being important for community-led settlement upgrading. Each of these forms of finance is examined in more detail below, with an indication of the possible sources for the financing involved, the kinds of products associated with such financing and the mechanisms by which these products or services are delivered in practice. Not all these forms of finance are available in every national context. The local financial market may not have developed sufficiently to offer the financial services in question or such services may not be viable given the costs of borrowing and lending. Some of the financial services and products have been created by civil society, designed around clearly identified community needs. Such a process takes time and experience and is more likely to be evident where civil society has organized over a relatively long period of time. Others have emerged from the commercial sector having been built around conventional models of lending and borrowing. Yet others have emerged from the microfinance sector. The categories of finance that we have identified are not comprehensive. They do, however, constitute a continuum of financial building blocks that provide options for blending different kinds of resources in ways that allow the urban poor to make, and follow through on, strategic planning decisions that reflect their priorities and chosen approaches. In other words, the range of financial products provides a means for the organized urban poor to implement projects in ways that make sense to them.

Financing immediate short-term credit requirements for individuals

Saving and credit groups provide an important basis for the accumulation and circulation of capital within local communities. Collective savings are used for emergency, consumption and business purposes. Housing savings help to build the deposits that many longer-term housing loans require. Within the federation process typified by the Indian Alliance's activities, groups manage finances themselves and determine the interest rates at which they lend their own money to each other. However, patterns of consistency develop over time as the groups learn through experience and share this learning with other groups through federation networks. Savings and lending of this kind establishes a credit management record and can facilitate mobilization of additional external capital provision for loan funds. Savings also operate as one of the fundamental means through which people learn to organize effectively as a group and to manage increasingly large amounts of money.

Sources. People's own earnings, which are often daily and earned in the informal sector. Savings are usually made from the money that's left at the end of the day when necessities have been covered.

Products. Regular savings, and loans for a variety of purposes (emergency, consumption and income generation or enterprise).

Mechanisms. Community 'bankers' collect the savings, usually on a daily basis but in any case in line with the general pattern of earnings within the community. Loan repayments are collected at the same time as savings. Records of all funds are generally centralized at least at settlement level and often at town or city level. Depending on the maturity of the group, records may be computerized. Information about cumulative collective savings is posted on walls in community resource centres to ensure that everyone knows how things are going.

Management. Managed entirely at community level with no direct NGO involvement.

Examples. In all countries where there are federations of the urban poor. Other related systems are evident in many different countries in the form of informal savings groups, often referred to as Rotating Savings and Credit Associations (ROSCAs); for example, *sou sou* in West Africa and Trinidad, 'merry-go-rounds' in East Africa and 'box' in Barbados and 'partners' in Jamaica. The main difference between most ROSCAs and the savings of the federations is that there are systematic attempts to use the collective savings of the federations to 'leverage' additional lines of credit from external sources. For example, in India Mahila Milan savings have been used to negotiate for a line of credit from Rashtriya Mahila Kosh, which is an Indian Government programme which provides capital for on-lending through women's savings groups.

External grants for financing basic capacity – building the economic and social base

Grant funding has enabled the creation of strong community organizations anchored in women-led savings and loan groups. Savings processes collect people and information as well as money. Mapping and enumeration also require grant funding and are crucial in the creation of settlement databases that can be used to negotiate with the state. Representatives of established groups spread the word and help others to begin the federation process, supported by exchanges that span cities, countries and continents. In doing so they create a network of linked communities. The Indian Alliance estimates that it takes about two years of basic mobilization of this kind before a local federation emerges that shares common objectives and principles. The use of this kind of funding is described in more detail in Chapter 3.

Sources. Northern NGOs, trusts, foundations and other charitable givers. In a few cases bi-lateral donors, for example, Sida in India.

Products. Community capacity to organize savings, carry out enumerations, house modelling, etc.

Mechanisms. Usually catalysed by exposure to the work of another federation through exchanges. The wider network provides support while new groups and their support NGOs learn how to use the 'tools' of the federation process, which are also sometimes referred to as rituals. For more detail see Chapter 3.

Management. Grants are usually managed by local support NGOs. In some cases where a federation has begun to form but there is no obvious support NGO, SDI or ACHR or an alliance in another country will manage the accountability and reporting for grant funds.

Examples. All the partner organizations with whom Homeless International works. Even mature alliances require these funds to enable their work to expand into new cities and towns.

Grants and revolving loan funds for financing development of small-scale pilot and demonstration projects

With basic organizational capacity at community level, organizations of the urban poor are able to take on small-scale investment projects in slum rehabilitation, resettlement or infrastructure provision (toilets, sanitation, water, solid-waste management, access roads and drainage). These projects demonstrate how designs and ideas developed at community level can work in practice. They provide an opportunity to develop and test new skills, not least within the relationships that must be negotiated as a project is implemented. Perhaps most importantly they provide a chance for people to learn from their own collective initiative. The use of this kind of funding is described in more detail in Chapter 3.

Sources. Grants from Northern NGOs, trusts and foundations and sometimes grants from government or bi-lateral donors. Grants are often delivered as time bound 'project' funds. Occasionally pooled savings, for example, federation members in Cambodia contribute $1 per year.

Products. Capitalized revolving loan funds offering grants or loans to community groups to implement prioritized projects that everyone can learn from.

Mechanisms. Most loans are extended to groups and are usually for specific projects. There has also been experience of allocating funds to communities and requiring them to develop criteria and decide on priorities for use of the funds. In this case, once the first round of funds has been successfully used, a second, usually larger amount is provided, sometimes on the basis of matching the community savings that have been mobilized in that particular area.

Management. Usually managed by local NGOs. Over time and with sufficient volume this function may be allocated to a more specialist institution such as an urban poor fund.

Examples. All the partner organizations with whom Homeless International works.

Grants for core administration and operations

The core costs of the federations and their support NGOs are relatively small given their well-documented achievements. However they do have to be met and grants for this purpose will continue to be necessary for the foreseeable future.

Sources. Northern NGOs, governments, bi-lateral and multi-lateral donors.

Mechanisms. Project grant agreements either directly or via an umbrella mechanism such as Shack/Slum Dwellers International (SDI). In some rare cases endowment or general grants with no project-specific requirements.

Grants for financing learning, knowledge creation and capacity building

It has already been pointed out in Chapter 3 that as communities and NGOs invest in demonstration projects and in scaling-up, their learning is rapid and dramatic. Sharing the learning that takes place (and the knowledge that is created) is vital. Teams made up of representatives from municipal authorities, organizations of the urban poor, NGOs and private sector interests have successfully used funding in this area to share experiences with others. Sometimes politicians and representatives from national government have also become involved. The learning is often of most benefit when it focuses on a specific issue or area of development.

Sources. Grants from northern NGOs, bi-lateral and multi-lateral grant allocations as a component of specific projects, people's own savings and funds when the exchange is local.

Products. These vary in terms of specific objectives, time frame and participation. For example, SDI has been sending teams to Uganda regularly over a four-year period to help with the development of a local federation and a more effective governmental strategy for slum upgrading. However slum dwellers, NGO professionals and bishops from Southern Africa took just two weeks to visit Thailand and India to investigate how church land could be effectively used to provide long-term secure housing to the poor.

Mechanisms. Vary from simple 'get on a bus and go to a neighbouring community to see what they have done' to the complex logistics involved in getting large numbers of people from many different countries to meet and carry out collaborative work.

Management. Local exchanges organized directly by communities with support from their NGOs, which provide more detailed support for international exchanges.

Examples. Many exchanges take place. Perhaps one of the most impressive has been that between Kenya and India that enabled Kenyan officials to consider alternatives to forced eviction in the context of their attempts to upgrade the railway system. Officials, slum dwellers and their support NGO were able to meet with their peers in India to see how negotiated resettlement could be made to work in practice to everyone's benefit (Makau 2005).

Financing risk management and mitigation

The risks undertaken by the poor when engaging with the state and with the formal financial sector have been discussed in more detail in Chapter 4. Suffice it here to say that the risks are diverse and the costs of managing and mitigating them can be considerable, especially when new approaches are being tried. Many projects require seed capital so that potential lenders can see practical evidence that a project is feasible. Guarantee funds are also often required to cover the risks that banks associate with lending to the urban poor. Funds are also required to help organizations of the urban poor and banks to develop collaborative approaches to assessing risk.

Sources. Various organizations provide guarantees, including northern NGOs, bi-lateral donors such as the United States Agency for International Development, Sida and DFID, and multi-lateral facilities such as regional development banks and so on. However very few of them have practical experience of providing guarantees for loans to projects led by the urban poor. Most of their guarantees are used to underwrite investment projects, for example in utilities. Organizations may use their own reserves and place them under lien to provide a guarantee. Banks can also provide guarantees, for example to cover contract performance risk, but will do so under negotiated arrangements that will include a percentage fee. At the moment funding for wider areas of risk mitigation and the development of a greater understanding of differing risk perceptions and management options appears limited. Costs have to be covered from existing project funding.

Products. Guarantees can be offered in a range of ways and these are discussed in more detail in Chapter 6. Some guarantees are provided in hard currency providing a degree of safeguard against local inflation or currency devaluation. Others are provided in local currency. In all the guarantee arrangements with which we have been involved, the aim has been to release local currency loans from banks and other financial institutions.

Mechanisms. The creation and use of guarantee funds is discussed in Chapter 6. All guarantee agreements require carefully worded legal documentation, which may involve several parties. Banks offering guarantees may require a letter of comfort[5]. Each loan agreement tends to have special features that need to be addressed within the legal documentation.

Management. Risk analysis, management and mitigation is primarily the responsibility of the organization implementing any project but those involved in providing support or guarantees can usefully be involved in collaborative planning, monitoring and reporting.

Examples. Homeless International guarantees have secured lending for slum upgrading in rural and urban India and in Bolivia. Our more recent work in this area focuses on how portfolio guarantees, which provide security for a group of projects rather than individual projects, can be developed.

Financing advocacy and the creation of new alliances with public and private sector agencies

Urban slum rehabilitation, resettlement and infrastructure provision is of interest to many different stakeholders. Too often, however, the learning that is emerging from cutting edge community-driven processes is restricted to a network that is already part of the process. Funding is needed so that the lessons learned can be shared more widely. Documentation targeted at specific audiences ranging from government training colleges to business schools could usefully be developed. Funding is also needed to support exposure programmes for banking staff so that they can understand the investment processes of the poor and develop the internal mechanisms within their own institutions that are required if intermediation between informal and formal systems is to occur. The use of funding to finance advocacy and the creation of new alliances, with particular reference to CLIFF, is described in more detail in Chapter 7.

Sources. Grant funds from various donors.

Products. Informational material specifically geared to new audiences and groups.

Mechanisms. Vary depending on donor requirements.

Management. Depends on the mechanisms used and who is responsible for the funds.

Examples. Ford Foundation has provided grant funds to SDI to help them to influence policy at national and international levels.

Loans, contract fees and subsidies providing working capital for large-scale pilot projects

Once an approach has been tried and tested it may be refined so that it is then ready for scaling-up. This is a stage when the financing gap becomes very apparent. Initial attempts at scaling-up are themselves considered pilots and demonstrations but the size of the projects means that, with very few exceptions, lack of access to working capital is a prohibitive constraint. The funding required is usually too large (and sometimes too complicated) to be covered by standard NGO project financing. However, once working capital is made available, at least as bridge finance, it becomes possible, at least in theory, to draw down subsidies where these exist. Project loans, fees generated as a result of development contracts with local government, and subsidies made available through government channels all provide a source of revenue for projects. The problem is in the timing. If these revenues can only be relied on in the later stages of a project's implementation, start-up capital of some kind will certainly be required. The use of start-up project loans to finance large-scale pilot projects, with particular reference CLIFF, is described in more detail in Chapter 7.

Sources. The most obvious option for loans is to borrow from banks and other financial institutions. However we have already acknowledged that negotiating this on an affordable basis takes time. Northern NGOs have also, in recent years, been looking at the provision of loan finance. However this can be problematic if the loan is in hard currency as local banking regulation may preclude local NGOs from accepting such loans and, unless the lender is prepared to assume the foreign exchange risk, the potential costs of inflation and local currency devaluation may be too great. Ideally donors would make available additional funds to establish CLIFF facilities that could be hosted in existing urban poor funds and other facilities to ensure that larger-scale projects can be undertaken. In the interim, with no other donor funding immediately on the horizon, Homeless International is exploring issuing a bond to raise funds in the UK to lend in India and elsewhere without asking local communities to assume the foreign exchange risk.

Products. Project loans, loan agreements and monitoring systems. Associated budgeting, viability assessment and financial tracking systems.

Management. Dependent on the specific agreement but projects will often be 'packaged' as a specific initiative so that the broader portfolio of work taken on by an agency is protected from potential failure in a single project.

Examples. CLIFF has been designed to provide local loan finance and technical assistance of the kind required in India, with a small fund also being allocated to Kenya.

Commercial sales and cross subsidies

In order to ensure that the poorest are included in upgrading, resettlement and infrastructure initiatives it is often necessary to incorporate internal subsidies within a project. This is particularly so where no external subsidies are made available by the state or by donors. Experience throughout the SDI network has shown that project finance that relies purely on loans to poor households and communities, however sensitively managed, can place an unfair and unrealistic burden on those least able to deal with it. One way to address this is to incorporate a commercial component into a project, facilitating the development of property or services that can be sold to better-off households. In India the development of 'for sale' units and the sale of Transferable Development Rights provide one means of accomplishing this (see Chapter 6 for an explanation of Transferable Development Rights).

Sources. Land allocation by the state, or through collective purchase, that allows additional development.

Products. Residential and commercial real estate for sale or rent. Extra plots for sale or rent.

Mechanisms. Integrated into project planning from the beginning.

Management. Requires marketing capacity and accurate costing. Legality of local NGO doing this needs to be checked as a special institutional form may be needed.

Examples. Nirman in India. Greenfield developments in South Africa.

Mortgage financing and refinancing

Refinancing is needed to release the bridge financing that is used to cover working capital invested in rehabilitation, resettlement and infrastructure projects, so that it can be re-used on other schemes. Refinancing may come in the form of bank loans or subsidies, which we have already covered above. However, for housing, longer-term financing is usually required, which can provide mortgage financing covering a single, or group, of individual loans. For example, where a slum-upgrading scheme has units for sale, arranging loan finance so a group with common interest can access long-term mortgages for the units makes management considerably easier. Refinancing from local financial institutions, however, requires that negotiators are well prepared and appropriate technical assistance in this area, that is sensitive to the processes of organizations of the urban poor, is hard to come by.

Sources. Formal finance institutions backed by investments from pension and insurance funds.

Products. Medium and long-term loans to groups and individuals.

Mechanisms. If mortgage financing for potential purchasers of apartments, for example, can be guaranteed in advance, it makes marketing of units that are for sale considerably easier.

Management. By lenders, with support from borrowers' collectives.

Examples. None as yet, although discussions have taken place between the Indian Alliance and various workers' groups.

It can be seen from the analysis provided above that the requirement for capital financing is concentrated in the following areas:

- Capital funds for initial small-scale pilot and demonstration projects.
- Capital funds to expand the base of community emergency, consumption and income-generating loan schemes.
- Capital deposits/guarantees to secure loans from formal financial institutions or contracts from public sector bodies.
- Capital funds for initiating, and bridge financing projects, where government subsidies and/or commercial loans are being sought.
- Capital funds for loan financing for scaling-up tested approaches, where there are no current options for loans from other sources or for accessing subsidies.

THE IMPACT OF BROADENING FINANCIAL SERVICES TO THE URBAN POOR

The forms of finance discussed above are not all currently available to organizations of the urban poor. It is therefore inevitable that part of the work of supporting such organizations is to ensure that over time, and as the requirements and capacities of the organizations grow, the full range of financial services is made available. The most fundamental requirement, in all the organizations with whom Homeless International currently works, has proved to be an investment in the creation of a strong community savings and loan system. It is this system that enables groups to develop basic financial management skills, to develop priorities for use of collective financial resources and to manage the inevitable difficulties that emerge when people take on new responsibilities and accountabilities. Once this system has been developed, tried and tested it becomes possible to use it as an important collective asset. It can be used to establish track record and credibility in negotiations to obtain additional capital from donors and the state, and to initiate dialogue with financial institutions that can potentially offer access to much larger sources of longer term capital.

As urban poor funds are established and developed they face a range of issues that we have already identified. It takes time to resolve these issues and, along the way, some mistakes will inevitably be made. However it is important to support the development of these facilities because they offer many advantages in creating new development options for the poor. Some of the areas in which they can have an important impact are shown schematically in Figure 5.1.

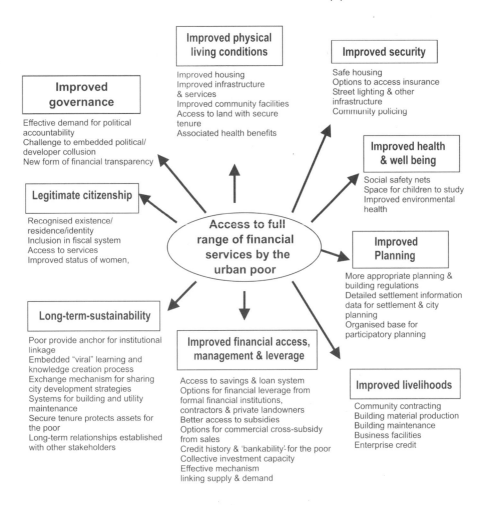

Figure 5.1 The potential impact of provision of a full range of financial services to organizations of the urban poor and their members

MIXING DIFFERENT FINANCIAL STREAMS

Working with mixed finance

When slum-upgrading initiatives are designed at scale it is unlikely that there will be a sole source of finance. Mixed financing is far more likely and, while complex to arrange, has important advantages in terms of spreading risk and in ensuring that a wide range of resource bases can be accessed. Finance sources that may be mixed, within the Indian context, which is the context where we have most experience, include:

■ government subsidies;

- bank loans;
- deposits from beneficiaries;
- up-front financial investment by contractors;
- bridge loans from urban poor funds;
- delayed payment terms from building material suppliers;
- income from sale of commercial and residential units;
- sale of development rights, where these exist;
- income generated from developments resulting from land-sharing agreements with private landowners;
- refinancing from housing finance institutions;
- loans from multi-lateral and bi-lateral agencies, usually channelled through state agencies.

Given that these revenue streams come from varying sources it is clear that managing them presents a complex challenge.

ACCESSING SUBSIDIES

The debate about subsidies has been on going for many years. It is clear, however, that if poverty is to be addressed, and the targets outlined in international agreements such as that of the Habitat Agenda and the Millennium Development Goals realized, subsidies will continue to play an important role in the distribution of public investment funds. The critical challenges in this distribution lie in three main areas: how to target subsidies so that their associated benefits reach those who need them most; how to leverage them so that their impact can be multiplied; and how to ensure that the poor themselves have access to capital subsidies. 'Where capital subsidies can only be accessed by formal financial institutions and developers the options for poor people to use such subsidies effectively are severely curtailed. Facilitating the development of capacity within community organizations so that they can manage capital subsidies themselves can provide an important means of creating more affordable and acceptable housing' (McLeod 2001a: 10).

Subsidies are delivered in a wide range of forms and at differing levels of administration that include:

- national government subsidies;
- state and regional subsidies;
- municipal and local authority subsidies;
- subsidies from bulk building material producers and suppliers;
- donor subsidies delivered through governments; and
- donor subsidies delivered through NGOs.

Subsidies of particular significance for slum upgrading include:

- free or 'cheap' land;
- technical assistance for land regularization and sub-division;
- incentives for negotiated land sharing;
- compensation for households involved in negotiated resettlements;

■ below-market interest rates on loans for land purchase, infrastructure provision, housing construction and home improvements;
■ allocation of land development rights[6];
■ reductions in costs of bulk utility provision;
■ wholesale pricing of building materials; and
■ technical assistance and equipment for land clearance and infrastructure installation.

Subsidies are by no means easy to access and, where they do exist, there are frequently bottlenecks in delivery. Also, the mechanisms used for delivery have often tended to favour formal sector developers rather than community-driven initiatives. Bottlenecks in subsidy delivery in India have been well documented by Burra *et al.* (2003). They cite the example of Pune, a city in Maharashtra that failed for 10 years to draw down sanitation subsidies available from the Government of India because of inadequacies in the local delivery system. The intervention of a visionary city administrator, Mr Gaikwad, enabled the development of a new delivery system that built on the capacity of communities to design and construct their own sanitation facilities. The result was an impressive increase in the number of facilities that became available, a reduction in development costs per facility and a reduction in long-term municipal expenditure on maintenance as communities took over responsibility for maintenance on a 30-year basis.[7] This new system in turn enabled the city to draw down national subsidies and to provide land and capital costs for the construction of the sanitation blocks. Replication of the approach in Mumbai demonstrated that innovation can be replicated rapidly when initiatives are seen to work at city level and to provide financial incentives both to communities and to city administrations.

Subsidies to developers rather than communities

One of the key issues in subsidy delivery is to whom and through whom they are delivered. Often subsidies are channelled through developers. The tendency for subsidy systems to favour private developers over communities is exemplified by the design of the South African housing subsidy programme. The programme aimed to facilitate private developer delivery of low-income housing; direct funding to communities was initially excluded as an option within the legislation that governed the system. It was only as a result of the lobbying of the South African Homeless People's Federation and their support organization People's Dialogue, that the legislation was amended. Their argument was strengthened because they were able to demonstrate that communities could produce significantly greater value for money than developers. In Maharashtra, the Slum Rehabilitation Act also assumed that private sector developers would play the lead role in organizing and implementing developments. However, when market conditions changed, reducing the financial incentive to participate, it was the Indian Alliance that took the initiative to demonstrate that local housing societies, with the provision of technical assistance and access to capital loans, could design and build high-rise developments of undisputed quality and acceptability to the slum dwellers who now live in them.[8]

Subsidies to communities

There are increasing examples of subsidies being made directly accessible to organizations of the urban poor. Local governments have provided land, or subsidized land purchase by federations, in a number of cities, including: Kampala, Nairobi, Mavoko, Nakuru and Phnom Penh. The Maharashtran Slum Rehabilitation Act granted land development rights to slum and pavement dwellers, which opened up completely new options for implementing slum upgrading in high-density areas. In Namibia, the government provided for special access by the Shack Dwellers Federation of Namibia to its Build Together Programme, building on the savings base that the federation had created and its demonstrable success in building good-quality, affordable housing. In Zimbabwe, despite a prolonged national economic crisis, local authorities have entered into partnership agreements with federations releasing land and collaborating on infrastructure and housing development. In Kenya the government has offered to match community savings with capital expenditure on the development of access roads in informal settlements.

Use of internal subsidies

One of the interesting developments in recent years has been the increasing use of internal subsidies. These have been necessitated where governmental subsidy options are unavailable but have also proved extremely useful where government provides land in excess of the immediate requirements of communities either being resettled or having their settlements upgraded. Systems of internal subsidy can be used within projects and also within project portfolios administered within an urban poor fund. CODI in Thailand provides an interesting example (Boonyabancha 2003). Within its national programme it provides differential interest rates on a range of financial products made available to communities. Loans for wholesale housing development by communities for example are made available at an annual interest rate of 3 per cent, whereas enterprise development loans are charged at a higher level. This allows the agency to support prioritized development areas whilst remaining financially solvent overall. In Mumbai, the Slum Rehabilitation Act makes provision for developments that incorporate commercial, residential and business units that can be sold to generate revenue to cover the costs of rehabilitation housing. The Act also allows for the sale of Transferable Development Rights (TDR).[9]

CONCLUSION

There are various options regarding the institutional means through which financial services and products needed by the urban poor can now be delivered, and may be delivered in the future. A diversity of facilities currently exists ranging from informal savings and loan systems right through to international donor-led facilities specifically designed to catalyse deepening of local financial markets. One of the major challenges, however, is how to approach the use of these facilities in a manner that optimizes the opportunities for the urban poor to improve their living conditions. It is not yet clear how far the formal financial sector will go in incorporating lending for housing and infrastructure provision into their core business strategies. Neither is it clear how far microfinance institutions will be able and willing to go in diversifying their lending portfolios to provide the medium- and long-term project lending required. It may be that totally new forms of institutional delivery will be required, as happened in the UK when poor people came together to form savings and loan groups that ultimately became building societies. However, financing for infrastructure provision and housing at scale is a critical requirement for sustainable development and its institutional delivery has a major part to play in the broadening and deepening of local financial markets.

CHAPTER SIX

Guarantees of success?

Malcolm Jack

INTRODUCTION

This chapter explores Homeless International's work in developing a guarantee fund. The fund was designed to provide guarantees that underwrite loans from formal finance institutions to Homeless International's partner organizations for increasingly large-scale community-led developments – particularly housing. Although the primary focus of Homeless International's work, and this book, is upon urban development finance, it is also necessary to examine some of Homeless International's work with partners in rural areas to understand how the guarantee fund was conceived, implemented and further developed.

The chapter begins with a reminder of the scale and complexity of the housing and infrastructure challenges facing poor communities, and then looks at the limitations of existing forms of finance in meeting these challenges. It was in recognition of these factors that Homeless International developed the guarantee fund concept. The chapter goes on to describe how the guarantee fund was structured and set up, before describing the first phase of projects supported by the guarantee fund and some of the refinements that emerged from the experience of negotiating and establishing guarantees in practice. A description of the second phase of projects then illustrates some of the challenges associated with establishing guarantee arrangements for housing projects in India's commercial capital, Mumbai, demonstrating the increasing scale of projects being undertaken by Homeless International's partner organizations. In the light of these experiences, the chapter concludes with some analysis of the achievements, limitations and realities associated with the guarantee approach, and hence some options and ideas to better support the work of our partner organizations in future.

A REMINDER OF THE CHALLENGES

In the face of an urbanizing world, the growth of slums, inadequate attention to housing provision for the poor and the need to ensure maximum impact from funds raised (as described in the earlier chapters of this book), Homeless International began exploring the concept of a guarantee fund in the early 1990s. A number of factors contributed to the decision to examine the guarantee concept. Firstly, as described in Chapter 1, the scale and complexity of the housing and slum upgrading challenge demanded responses at a similar level of scale and ingenuity. If Homeless International's development investment was to have any worthwhile or lasting impact in this environment, then it had to deal with solutions that benefited clusters of households, entire settlements and even to start influencing city-level development.

As described in Chapter 2, most national governments in developing countries had withdrawn from direct public provision of housing, instead seeking to play an enabling role that encouraged the private sector, in all its forms, to finance and develop housing. In this context, Homeless International was particularly concerned with supporting low-income groups to participate in the process of housing development, and hence the guarantee fund had to be equipped to deal with the specific requirements of this sector, and this target group. For example, housing is highly capital intensive, requiring large up-front investments. However, houses can also be improved or extended over time, requiring further capital investment. Large-scale housing developments can take years rather than months to design, negotiate and build, requiring the availability of capital finance throughout. The guarantee fund therefore had to help secure capital on a medium- and long-term basis, which would be flexible enough to deal with both initial construction and extension or improvements, to meet the varying needs of low-income groups in different locations.

Of course housing relies on the availability of land on which actually to construct. As described in Chapter 1, access to land with secure tenure is a particular challenge in commercially vibrant urban areas. Land can be expensive, politically sensitive, competitive, and therefore takes time to negotiate, indeed the urban poor face all of these pressures more acutely than most. Acquiring urban land is not something easily achieved by individual households, and often requires collective solutions at a community-wide level. In fact, it was initially planned to make guarantees available for loans to actually buy portions of land, but to date the guarantee fund has not been used for that purpose. It has however been used to underwrite loans for collective housing developments, which have been required in dense urban settlements where land is difficult to secure. The guarantee fund was also designed to underwrite loans to groups that are then on-lent to individual families who have the option to build or improve their own housing units.

Poor communities face an awkward and vicious circle in situations where access to land is difficult, in that they may need to demonstrate the availability of capital to build housing in order to secure land for development, but it is often very difficult to secure capital for housing prior to securing rights to develop land. As shown in Figure 9.1, the poor often invest in and develop housing in an 'informal' sequence which differs from the sequence anticipated by 'formal' institutions. Any attempt to support the poor in leveraging capital has to be able to deal with this informal sequence of events, and indeed to be available as a tool with which to negotiate for land in this context. The guarantee fund concept was developed precisely to address these complexities at the interface between the informal and formal development processes.

Homeless International's partners had already embraced the challenges of scaling-up, implying a corresponding need for Homeless International to complement their efforts with new scaled-up forms of support if it was to play a useful role. As Chapter 3 shows, an increasing number of Homeless International's partners were focused upon supporting a *process* of mobilizing and supporting large numbers of people in multiple locations, rather than supporting discrete *projects* with finite outputs. This resulted in a faster cycle of learning, capacity building, and identification of housing development initiatives, thus greatly increasing the number of viable demands for support, and for development finance.

In addition, savings and credit had become a central feature of most of Homeless International's partners' work, albeit in different forms. For example, in rural Tamil Nadu (India), the Integrated Village Development Project (IVDP) was developing a microfinance programme supporting a growing network of women's self-help groups. As described in Chapter 3, federations of the urban poor, such as the National Slum Dwellers Federation (NSDF) and Mahila Milan in India and the South African Homeless People's Federation in South Africa, focused upon daily savings as a means to encourage neighbours to meet regularly and gradually to prioritize how to utilize their scarce (collective) resources as a savings group. These varying approaches to savings and credit were bearing fruit. There was an increasing demand within communities to take on housing and infrastructure developments, and a growing capacity to carry out this work, not least in terms of a social infrastructure through which communities learned to manage increasingly large amounts of money. Unsurprisingly, these approaches also yielded a demand for housing credit. Furthermore, the Indian Alliance (SPARC, NSDF and Mahila Milan) had pragmatically decided that high-rise residential development would be required in high-density cities such as Mumbai, if large numbers of slum dwellers were to have any chance of acquiring decent housing with tenure security. If Homeless International was to play a meaningful long-

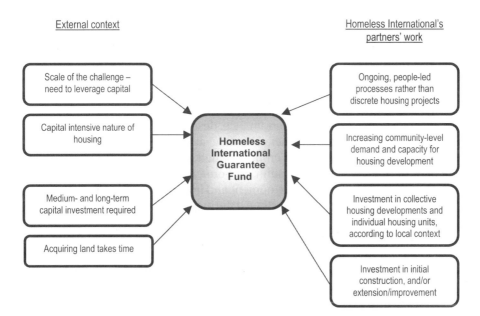

Figure 6.1 Factors influencing the guarantee fund concept

term role in supporting such processes, then it had to develop forms of financial support that matched this scale and diversity of demand.

BUILDING ON FOUNDATIONS – ADDRESSING THE LIMITATIONS OF EXISTING FINANCE

The factors described in the previous section compelled Homeless International to consider how to create access to finance, initially for housing and later for slum upgrading, at a scale that matched the demands and needs of the poor. Homeless International's grant-giving work in the early 1990s had proved successful. As described in Chapter 3, grant funds had, and have continued to, support organizations of the poor and their NGO allies in:

- building the capacity to manage scarce resources effectively, for community-determined priorities;
- successfully planning and developing small-scale, pilot housing and infrastructure initiatives;
- expanding their knowledge and experience of the institutions and regulations that affected the development of housing and infrastructure schemes;
- sharing learning through exchanges, creating demand for replication and scaling-up within communities and frequently amongst local government personnel.

However, grant funding clearly had limitations. Not only was it inconceivable that sufficient grant funds could be raised to match the scale of the housing and infrastructure challenges across the world, or even to meet the level of demand from Homeless International's partners, but there was a potential danger in relying on grant funds at the expense of finding and embedding local arrangements to sustain housing and infrastructure investments. Homeless International felt that grant funding was an essential, but not sufficient, component of financing for housing development, infrastructure improvement and slum upgrading. This begged the question as to what other sources of finance might be tapped to scale-up and sustain the finance available to poor communities.

One option appeared to be microfinance, described in more depth in Chapter 5. Characterized by short-term retail lending, at relatively high interest rates, to individuals and small groups, microfinance had grown into an important source of credit in many developing countries. Some microfinance loans were being 'diverted' for use in housing development and improvement, an area prioritized for investment by women who constituted the majority of MFI borrowers. However these diverted funds seemed largely to be used for home improvements and extensions rather than for larger-scale collective housing developments and slum upgrading. Short-term lending has severe limitations in high-density areas where options for incremental housing development may be extremely limited. Whilst microfinance can play an important role in enabling poor people to improve livelihoods and/or raise income levels, which can in turn help them to contribute resources to housing investments or better cope during relocation to new housing, it is insufficient to meet the medium- and long-term financing needs for housing and infrastructure. Nor is microfinance particularly well geared towards collective lending or project financing.

Various forms of capital funds (including revolving loan funds, urban poor funds and community development funds, as described in Chapters 3 and 5) were developed to offer loans and small grants to community groups, rather than individuals. Loans and grants of this nature enabled communities to take on collective development problems, including housing and infrastructure developments, on a small 'pilot' scale. Again these funds enhanced communities' capacities to manage money and manage projects, generating further demands for support. The funds generally relied on donor grants from European NGOs[1], community contributions through savings, and occasional capital injections by government for their capital base. As a result, although considered successful, few bi-lateral/multi-lateral donors or governments have felt able to channel substantial resources through such mechanisms, and hence these funds have mostly been unable to offer the scale of capital required to meet the scale of the challenges in many countries (the exception is CODI in Thailand – see Boonyabancha 2004).

Another option appeared to be housing finance institutions or banks with housing finance schemes within their portfolios of lending, which can offer longer-term loans. In countries such as India, housing finance institutions have been growing and developing, building up a substantial capital base in the process – certainly more than that available through aid programmes. In some cases these institutions had received soft loans from bi-lateral and multi-lateral agencies to on-lend and increase their (low-income) housing finance portfolios. However, even where housing finance markets and finance institutions have been relatively well developed, they have rarely proved able to lend to the majority of the poor, due to a range of factors detailed in Chapters 4 and 5, but summarized as:

- Low credit ratings amongst the poor (especially where poor people are unable to prove 'certifiable income' because they work in the informal sector).
- The poor having insufficient conventional collateral (particularly the lack of clear land title).
- Low or uncertain profitability in lending to the poor.
- Asymmetric information regarding ability to repay.
- Suspicious attitudes towards those living or working in the informal sector.
- Inability to lend to NGOs or community co-operatives, since institutions acting on behalf of the poor rarely have adequate collateral.
- Lack of loan products for collective development schemes, and lack of effective demand for such products because few NGOs or co-operative groups have had the capacity to work with banks to develop them.

Despite these obstacles, Homeless International and partners considered banks the most likely source from which to obtain finance for housing, infrastructure and slum upgrading. But the question remained how to get them to lend to the poor, for the sorts of housing, land and infrastructure developments described earlier in this chapter.

THE GUARANTEE FUND IN THEORY

Homeless International first started to develop the guarantee fund in 1991, to 'enable families unable to access conventional housing finance to obtain credit from local finance institutions for the creation of self-managed housing solutions' (McLeod 1994: 1). The guarantee fund was initially set up to underwrite loans from formal finance institutions to on-lend to poor families. As described in Chapters 4 and 5, Homeless International already recognized that poor communities had a variety of assets that were not recognized by banks as constituting appropriate collateral for loans. Homeless International believed that these assets gave good grounds to assume that poor communities had both the asset base and the capacity to successfully carry out self-managed housing schemes, and so sought to offer financial guarantees to banks to release loans for that purpose. In effect, Homeless International assumed that a financial guarantee would act as a 'formal' equivalent to the 'informal' collateral built up by poor communities, and hence alleviate the nervousness that banks and other financial institutions displayed (McLeod 2002a). This would in turn help to bridge the gap between informal and formal groups. Homeless International's guarantee would replace any requirements for personal collateral to be lodged with the banks by loan recipients (Homeless International 1992). Homeless International later modified this assumption, in recognition of the fact that guarantees could play a complementary function, with collateral being provided at several different levels (for example, loan recipients could make affordable down payments for loans, whilst guarantees would underwrite the release of group loans).

The guarantee fund was also developed to perform a 'leverage' function – in other words to provide guarantees for less than 100 per cent of the value of the loans secured. The assumption here was that some degree of 'gearing' would be possible – for example a 25 per cent guarantee would secure a loan of four times the guarantee amount. This multiplier effect was considered vital if Homeless International and partners were to scale up the impact of their development investments to assist larger numbers of poor people.

A further objective of the guarantee fund was to establish better links between the formal financial sector (the banks) and the poor. With Homeless International and local NGO partners acting as brokers, the intention was to enable poor families and community groups to further develop credit track records with local financial institutions. At the same time, the process of agreeing and managing loans would help all parties to better understand each other's ways of working, aspirations, terminologies and assumptions, hopefully leading to sustained working relationships. This would benefit poor communities firstly by increasing access to credit, and secondly by reducing their isolation from the range of institutions with which better-off citizens routinely engage.

Although not explicitly stated in the initial stages, but undoubtedly implicit in the thinking of those who established the guarantee fund,[2] was the need to mainstream workable local partnerships and processes involving not only communities and banks, but also government and other key agencies. This was particularly true in urban areas, where a greater number of agencies affect the possibilities for housing and infrastructure development by and for poor communities. Only through sustained engagement with these agencies would many poor communities be able to escape the cycle of poverty, insecurity and vulnerability associated with living in informal settlements.

Above all, it is important to reiterate that the guarantee fund was designed as a financial mechanism to support people-led approaches to tackling poverty. Inherent in the objectives was the concept of helping poor communities mitigate, manage and share the risks in investing in housing and infrastructure development. As described in Chapter 4, helping to minimize the financial risks incurred by those least well endowed with resources to invest, the poor, was only part of the story. In this sense, the guarantee fund concept differed from guarantee mechanisms planned or implemented by bi-lateral and multi-lateral development agencies, because it offered a 'portable' guarantee service to poor people, as a tool that they could use to negotiate with banks, rather than being offered as a guarantee service directly to banks. A 'portable' guarantee is an arrangement that enables a group to offer the guarantee to a range of institutions in order to obtain the best deal possible. As Homeless International and partners ventured further into housing developments and slum upgrading, which involved deeper engagements with government and with banks, we increasingly recognized that political risk was as important, if not more so, than basic financial risks. As the guarantee fund was further developed, and increasingly focused upon supporting developments in urban areas, it had to be able to support organizations of the poor in taking political and institutional risks associated with building the working partnerships described earlier. This is discussed more fully in the next section.

SETTING UP THE GUARANTEE FUND

Prior to a description in the next section of the development schemes supported by guarantees, and how the guarantees were negotiated and put in place, it might be helpful to explain how the guarantee fund itself was set up and structured. The diagram below illustrates this.

The Homeless International guarantee fund was capitalized in three ways. Firstly, Homeless International negotiated deposits from Housing Associations and other organizations linked to the social housing sector in the UK. These housing organizations initially agreed to deposit sums ranging from £5,000 to £100,000 for five- to ten-year periods with Homeless International in a UK bank account. They also agreed to forego interest accumulated by their deposits. In recent years, many depositors have extended the duration of their deposit or turned their deposit into a gift or grant.

Secondly, Homeless International successfully obtained grant funds from the European Commission, the UK Government's Overseas Development Administration (ODA, now the Department for International Development, DFID) and the Barings Foundation. Some grant funds were lodged in the fund as capital, but a proportion was also used to provide technical assistance and small-scale

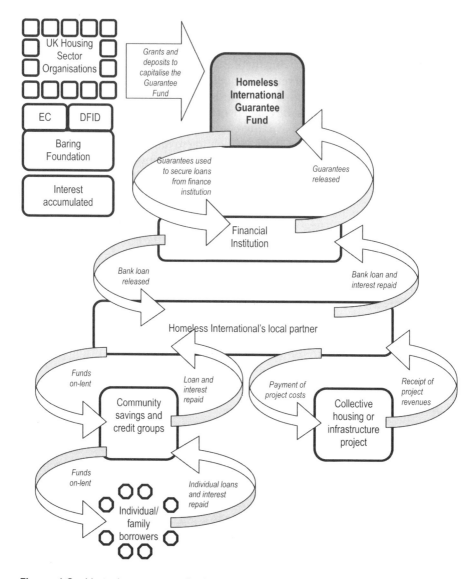

Figure 6.2 How the guarantee fund works

bridge financing to partners involved in the initial guarantee-supported schemes (particularly YCO, as described in the next part of this chapter).

Finally, interest accumulated on all deposits was used to increase the capital funds available. In the event of loan default and a call on a guarantee by a bank, a combination of interest and grant funds would be used to pay-off the default in the first instance, but depositors also understood that proportions of their capital deposits would be used to fulfil guarantee obligations if grants and interest proved insufficient to meet such calls. By structuring the guarantee fund in this way, Homeless International minimized the likelihood of calls on deposits, and ensured that risks would be shared amongst several depositors should their funds be called upon. Some of the interest generated within the fund was also used to cover the costs of developing new guarantees.

Once loan and guarantee arrangements were negotiated, Homeless International envisaged that it would issue 'letters of guarantee' to banks to release loans to its partner organizations. These 'letters of guarantee' would basically state that in the event of a default by partners, Homeless International would repay the per centage of the loan agreed with the bank. In practice Homeless International has been required to lodge funds in a designated account within the lending institution or a bank designated by them. These banks were usually in the UK, especially for loans in India where local regulations would make it difficult to repatriate funds lodged as a guarantee locally, but sometimes in the country where the loan is released as has happened in Bolivia (see later discussion). A variety of Memoranda of Understanding (MOUs) and multipartite agreements have also been required in practice, stating the obligations of Homeless International, Homeless International's partners, the lending institution, and any intermediate banks required where the lending institution did not have a UK branch in which to deposit guarantee funds. One of the reasons that the guarantee fund approach has proved so labour intensive is that Homeless International has usually had to draft these agreements from scratch.

As the diagram above shows, the institutional arrangements for releasing the loans vary according to the different types of loans. In general, the lending institution releases a bulk loan to Homeless International's local partner, which can be a local NGO, sometimes registered as a co-operative, or which can be some form of alternative financing vehicle (for example, a not-for-profit company) where this is required. The bulk loan may be released in one chunk, or in a series of smaller chunks, depending upon whether it is to be on-lent or to finance a particular development scheme. The bulk loan can then be broken down and on-lent to individual households or groups of families through whatever lending systems have been established locally, and repaid to the bank either directly by individuals, by community groups, by the NGO, or by any other vehicle set up to manage the loans. Alternatively, the loan can be managed on a project basis to pay for the costs of a specific housing, land or infrastructure development scheme. In this case the borrowing institution manages the loan directly, and repays the bank once project 'revenues' are received (as described in relation to the Rajiv Indira-Suryodaya and Bharat Janata housing development schemes described later in this chapter).

The interest rate arrangements can also vary according to local specifics and the purpose of the loan. In the case of a bulk loan to be on-lent to individual families or small groups, the bank will lend at a certain interest rate dependent upon a combination of several potential factors including local market conditions at the time of the loan; the influence of any concessionary interest rates the bank may wish to offer as a result of obtaining subsidized capital from government or a bi-lateral/multi-lateral development institution; and, the influence of any concessionary rates arranged by the lending institution itself, perhaps to explore the new (low-income) consumer market, or for philanthropic reasons.

The recipient of the bulk loan, such as Homeless International's partner NGO, a co-operative or other community-based institution, can often on-lend at a slightly higher rate of interest. The interest spread, as this is known, can be used to cover costs of administering the loan or to develop some form of hedge fund to buffer against defaults by families receiving the on-lent loan. Likewise, where communities' savings and credit networks have several layers (for example, where lending is decentralized through administration at cluster, village and savings group levels), each layer may include a small interest spread by agreement between the end recipients of the loans, the lender and the midstream institution. However, in some cases banks will not allow on-lending at a higher rate of interest, perhaps because government regulations have been designed to keep interest rates low for end recipients, or because banks themselves fear that loans will become too expensive for end recipients thus increasing the perceived likelihood of default. Where a loan is agreed for a specific (collective) housing, land or infrastructure project which will be repaid from revenues other than repayments by beneficiaries of the scheme in question, there is less scope for an interest rate spread. In this circumstance, the loan is simply repaid with the agreed interest rate over the agreed period of the loan.

Finally, it is worth noting that other aspects of the loan agreement may affect how the loan is repaid. It may be repaid periodically throughout the duration of the loan, for example on a monthly, six-monthly or annual basis. Alternatively the loan may be arranged in the form of a line of credit, which can be borrowed and repaid according to demand for on-lending and the pace of repayment by end recipients (in the case of a bulk loan for on-lending), or drawn upon and repaid according to the schedule of payments required and revenues received (in the case of a collectively managed development scheme). As another alternative, a loan may require a bullet repayment whereby the capital borrowed is returned to the bank in one bulk payment at the end of the loan period. In all these arrangements, variables such as a negotiated grace period (where no interest is charged, or no repayment required), the structure of interest charged (for example calculated on a compound or 'simple' basis), the magnitude of any guarantee arrangement fees levied by the lender, or the use of an agreed overdraft facility affect how and when the loan is actually repaid, and at what cost to the borrower.

The form of guarantee can also vary. The guarantee may underwrite a percentage of the overall loan, usually the 'top-slice', meaning the highest level of risk. For example, if a loan is issued for £100, a guarantor who provides a 20 per cent guarantee on a top-slice basis will pay for the first £20 of loss or default. The full guarantee would be called in for a default of only 20 per cent of the loan. This contrasts with a 20 per cent guarantee which is not top-sliced (effectively a 1:5 guarantee), where the guarantor would only cover 20 per cent of the first £20 of loss or default (i.e. £4), and then 20 per cent of all subsequent loss or default. Only if the entire loan of £100 is in default would a guarantor have to pay the full £20 in a '1:5' guarantee arrangement.

The guarantee may be devised according to the value of the 'peak' or 'maximum exposure' perceived by the bank. 'Maximum exposure' is calculated as the biggest financial gap between the amount lent by the bank for a project, and the value of the recoverable assets created within the project, at any time throughout the life of the project. For example, the 'maximum exposure' could emerge at the beginning of a housing project, when the bank has lent a large amount of money for the initial construction but few physical assets (for example houses) have actually been constructed and few revenues can be generated. Finally, it is worth noting that guarantees can be extended, by agreement amongst the guarantor, the lender and the borrower, where the duration of the project exceeds the initial agreement.

The following section describes the guarantees negotiated by Homeless International with partner organizations and local banks to support housing and infrastructure developments in India and Bolivia, illustrating the variety of different arrangements used in practice and the particular issues faced in different scenarios.

ARRANGING GUARANTEES IN PRACTICE – THE FIRST PHASE OF PROJECTS

YCO, India

The first programme to receive support from the guarantee fund was initiated by one of Homeless International's former partners in rural India, the Youth Charitable Organization (YCO). YCO was established in 1981 as a community development agency and registered Indian NGO supporting local economic development, particularly through agro-forestry, education and housing. Most of its work was located in over 90 villages along the coastal belt of Andhra Pradesh, which, though fertile, was also subject to droughts, floods and cyclones. YCO had focused much of its energy on assisting poor women in villages and small towns to establish and manage their own saving and loan systems. This microfinance activity was consolidated through the establishment of a network of women's savings groups (known as *mahila mandals*), which was increasingly interested in obtaining credit for housing but prevented from doing so because banks did not consider secure customary land tenure as sufficient collateral against which to lend for housing. For this reason, Homeless International sought to provide a guarantee in recognition of the 'informal collateral' represented by the *mandals'* track record in savings and loan repayment. YCO had also successfully managed several external credit lines for income-generating activities, enhancing its capacity and credentials to obtain external funding for a housing finance programme. More specifically, YCO had made loans available to women for milch animals, which had proved successful in increasing household incomes to a level that was judged sufficient to repay housing loans successfully.

Homeless International and YCO negotiated guarantees and loans with two Indian finance institutions, the Housing Development Finance Corporation (HDFC) and the Housing and Urban Development Corporation (HUDCO).

Between 1995 and 1996, Homeless International agreed two guarantees, each with HUDCO and HDFC for four phases of YCO's housing credit programme. Two further phases were also agreed in principle with each institution, but were not subsequently implemented. Negotiations with HDFC began in November 1993. Homeless International agreed to a guarantee equivalent to 109 per cent of the loan amount, which covered both the loan principal and interest at nine per cent. This may have seemed an illogical thing to do, but the organizations believed that it was vital to walk through the bank lending process in order to explore the terms and conditions that were expected in practice, and hence how these might be modified to achieve gearing in the future. Guarantee funds were deposited at Canara Bank in London, as part of a tripartite agreement between Homeless International, HDFC and Canara Bank itself. Homeless International successfully negotiated with Canara Bank to waive the guarantee arrangement fees. Separate arrangements between Homeless International and YCO were also put in place. It was not until March 1995 that the first tranche of funds was eventually released to YCO, despite agreement 'in principle' to an MOU in February 1994 and official sanctioning of the loan in December 1994. Delays within HDFC were caused by a combination of several factors, including:

- Requests for additional information on construction costs and socio-economic data about beneficiaries.
- HDFC's initial refusal to allow YCO an 'interest spread' for administration and hedging at both *mandal* level and NGO level by YCO.
- HDFC's subsequent insistence that YCO could apply a maximum of only 1 per cent 'interest spread', whereas YCO calculated that two to three per cent was necessary for sustainable administration of the programme.
- Poor communication and confusion between HDFC's central and local offices.
- HDFC's decision to refer the agreement to the Reserve Bank of India (RBI) for additional approval.
- HDFC's additional amendment that loan release would be conditional upon beneficiary families financing construction of each housing unit up to plinth level – equivalent to 43 per cent of the housing unit's total cost.

The delays and changes had numerous negative consequences, including cost escalation; difficulties mobilizing resources to meet the criterion of plinth construction prior to release of loans; frustration within participating communities; credibility of YCO undermined in the eyes of communities; and, deterioration of stored materials that people had been unable to use before the monsoon (Homeless International 1995). Homeless International and YCO were forced to use bridge financing totalling almost as much as the amounts sanctioned by HDFC for the first and second phase loans, in order to mitigate the negative impacts of the delays upon the families involved.

With HUDCO the process was considerably smoother, although not without its own delays and changes. Negotiations resulted in agreement for a guarantee of 25 per cent of the loan amount. Again Homeless International and YCO had to provide considerable bridge financing to mitigate the effects of delays. In 1999, Homeless International provided a fifth guarantee for YCO's housing work, this time for 16 per cent of a loan negotiated from the Small Industries Development

Bank of India (SIDBI). YCO provided its own guarantee for 20 per cent of the loan, marking a step forward in its own institutional development. In all guarantee arrangements with YCO, Homeless International successfully negotiated with the UK banks into which the guarantees were deposited, to waive any guarantee arrangement fees.

In total, the three guarantees enabled YCO to draw down loans totalling almost £400,000.[3] After nearly seven years of successful repayment and the construction of 850 new homes, however, YCO defaulted on its loan repayments to HDFC and HUDCO in 2001. The SIDBI loan was repaid in full. Calls were made on the guarantees provided to these financial institutions in early 2002 amounting to just over £150,000. The buffer of accumulated interest and grant funds within Homeless International's Guarantee Fund was used to cover this call. There were several contributory factors to the default, not least the introduction of State government housing programmes (ironically designed in collaboration with HUDCO) that seemed to promise 'free housing', which altered beneficiary families' perceptions of YCO's programme and hence undermined YCO's attempt to create a sustainable housing finance mechanism for low-income groups. A fire and crop failures also affected repayments. Nevertheless, Homeless International's work with YCO played an important role in the development of the guarantee fund and, experiences of dealing with banks fed into further guarantee-supported schemes in India.

IVDP, India

The second of Homeless International's partners to request a guarantee was IVDP. Homeless International had worked with IVDP since 1987, and had supported its development through grant funding (as described in Chapter 2). IVDP had been involved in the design and development of the guarantee fund from the beginning. IVDP is a registered NGO that had supported an innovative, experienced and growing network of women's self-help groups (SHGs) in Dharmapuri district, Tamil Nadu, in India. Although much of its work was in rural areas, IVDP later initiated the creation of SHGs in peri-urban areas and the town of Krishnagiri. Between 1977 and 2005, IVDP built up the network of SHGs to incorporate more than 75,000 women and their families across almost 4,000 SHGs. Many families lived in mud and wattle houses with thatched roofs, which were prone to leaks and flooding, required regular and time-consuming maintenance and provided cramped living spaces for families.

IVDP and the SHG network had developed an impressive array of loan products, management systems, decentralized administration arrangements and support networks, providing a strong institutional base with which to draw down bank finance. IVDP, and in many cases the SHGs themselves, also had a strong track record in negotiating and successfully repaying loans from local banks as part of the country's SHG-Bank linkage scheme, in which the National Bank for Agriculture and Rural Development (NABARD) refinanced local banks' lending for income generation and agricultural activity. However, larger and longer-term loans were required for house construction and improvement, and as a result banks were reluctant to lend without collateral. At the same time, however, the National Housing Bank (NHB) was willing to refinance local banks' lending for housing purposes, hence encouraging banks to explore such programmes. This presented an important opportunity to support IVDP in scaling up its affordable housing programme.

Homeless International and IVDP began to negotiate with the Bank of India, the major point of contention being the timing of repayments. IVDP were keen to re-pay quarterly, to match borrower's cycles of income in the agricultural sector, whilst the Bank preferred regular monthly repayments on the assumption that this reduced their risk. Homeless International and IVDP argued that the three-monthly repayment option actually reduced the risk of default, and the promise of a Homeless International guarantee proved enough to convince the bank to lend on that basis. In December 2001, the Bank of India approved a bulk loan of approximately £146,000 dependent upon a Homeless International guarantee of 25 per cent, a tripartite agreement was arranged, and the bulk loan was quickly released. Repayments of the principal and 10.5 per cent interest, were arranged on a quarterly basis, and IVDP was given permission to on-lend at 12 per cent to generate funds for administration. The loan was repaid in three years,

Photo 6.1 Peruma and her husband Munusamy borrowed Rs20,000 (approximately £260) through IVDP's housing loan programme, in order to build this two-roomed brick house with a tiled roof. Previously they had lived for many years in a thatched house (seen on the left of the photo) which leaked when it rained.

Source: Homeless International

one year ahead of schedule, enabling more than 500 households to develop permanent, safe and affordable housing.

In April 2004, Homeless International and IVDP arranged a second four-year bulk loan, this time for twice the amount, again with a 25 per cent guarantee. Arrangements and conditions were broadly similar, although a lower interest rate was agreed, partly as a result of lower base interest rates in India, and partly because IVDP accounted for an increasing proportion of the business conducted by the local Bank of India branch and was therefore in a position to negotiate a better rate. Homeless International has continued to provide small-scale grant funding to IVDP to support the demand-led expansion of the SHG network, in order both to enhance and scale-up the capacities of communities to draw down further credit, and to cover some of IVDP's costs in administering that expansion process. In early 2005, IVDP negotiated a third bulk loan from the Bank of India to on-lend for construction of toilets and bathrooms. IVDP provided their own guarantee of 25 per cent to secure a two-year loan of approximately £120,000, benefiting more than 1,000 families.

Fundación Pro Habitat, Bolivia

The first, and to date only, guarantee arranged with partners outside India was set up in Bolivia in 2002. Homeless International's partner in this initiative was Fundación Pro Habitat, a local NGO set up in the early 1990s to prevent the spread of Chagas disease in some of Bolivia's rural areas. Chagas disease is a fatal parasitic disease with no vaccines or effective treatment, spread by the bite of the vinchuca beetle, which thrives in cracks and holes found in mud, adobe and thatch commonly used to build Bolivian houses.[4] In 1994/95, Fundación Pro Habitat began Chagas prevention work in the peri-urban areas of two cities, Cochabamba and Tarija, through an education programme and by initiating a housing credit programme.[5] Few households had formal security of tenure, effectively preventing access to conventional bank loans.

Homeless International provided grant funds between 1989 and 2005 with the aim of supporting Fundación Pro Habitat's move into urban areas, with a particular focus upon the development of a sustainable housing loan fund available to poor households in the peri-urban *barrios* of Cochabamba and Tarija. Some of these grant funds were used to establish a revolving loan fund, which demonstrated people's capacity to repay and Fundación Pro Habitat's ability to manage such a facility. Sourcing and revolving loan finance from local financial institutions was an important component in the longer-term strategy for scaling-up the quantum of capital available and generating funds to assist in the costs of running the facility.

Homeless International and Fundación Pro Habitat held in-depth discussions with a number of Bolivia's financial institutions. A consultant, Rafael Rojas, also conducted further research into the institutional and regulatory frameworks which would affect credit activities, construction and NGO operations in these areas, as part of Homeless International's 'Bridging the finance gap' research project (see Rojas 2000). Eventually it was decided to proceed with an agreement with El

Fondo de la Comunidad, a Bolivian-based financial institution originally set up from the profits of a cement company for the purposes of supporting housing construction. As it transpired, El Fondo was reasonably confident in the capacity of Fundación Pro Habitat to manage and repay the loan, but sought a guarantee mainly to demonstrate to the Bolivian Central Bank that it had sufficient net worth to make the loan available.

The terms and conditions were agreed in principle in April 2000, although it took until July 2000 for the tripartite guarantee agreement to be signed by Homeless International, Fundación Pro Habitat and El Fondo. Homeless International agreed to a 100 per cent guarantee because it recognized the need to demonstrate the approach in a new country, and anticipated negotiating reduced guarantee rates in planned future guarantees. Fundación Pro Habitat and El Fondo arranged a separate agreement governing the loan itself. Together these two agreements had some notable features. Firstly, because El Fondo de la Comunidad did not have a UK branch or appropriate UK partner institution, Homeless International agreed to transfer the US$50,000 guarantee (approximately £35,000 at the time) to a deposit account in Bolivia. Secondly, the tripartite agreement stipulated that Homeless International would receive 7 per cent interest on its guarantee deposit, that El Fondo would lend to Fundación Pro Habitat at 11.5 per cent, and that Fundación Pro Habitat would be allowed to on-lend at between 14 and 18 per cent to maintain a balance between affordability and the need to generate an interest spread that would increase the capital base and/or contribute to costs of administering the Revolving Loan fund.[6] In comparison to standard housing loans available within the extensive network of Microfinance Institutions in the country at the time, demanding as much as 36 per cent interest per annum, these rates were considered acceptable by all parties. To further support Fundación Pro Habitat in expanding its capital base and sustainable operation, the agreements also confirmed that Fundación Pro Habitat would repay interest on the loan periodically, but that the principal amount ($48,000[7] equivalent to £33,500 at the time) would be repaid as a bullet repayment five years after the release of the loan. The idea was to enable Fundación Pro Habitat to revolve the capital within the five-year period, thus generating additional funds for capital and operational costs.

The loan and guarantee were extended for a further year in 2005, and the bullet payment arrangement changed to facilitate gradual repayment of the principal during the course of the additional year. This was partly due to a slower than anticipated release of loans to low-income families in the first three years of the arrangement. The slower than anticipated release was caused by a combination of Bolivia's political and economic crisis during that period, lower than anticipated demand within communities and by limitations in Fundación Pro Habitat's capacity to process and administer the loans. The extension was also caused by increased demand in the latter years of the agreement, which encouraged Fundación Pro Habitat to make loans available without fully considering whether it could make the bullet repayment on the date stipulated. This was partly down to limitations in the loan monitoring systems, and partly down to Fundación Pro Habitat's perception that Homeless International would turn the guarantee into a form of grant. As described in relation to 'limitations and realities' later in this chapter, the experiences in Bolivia generated some important lessons that have fed into the guarantees fund's ongoing evolution.

SPARC, India

Throughout the development of the guarantee fund, Homeless International and SPARC had been considering the use of guarantees for large-scale housing developments initiated by the Indian Alliance in Mumbai, indeed Ruth McLeod and Sheela Patel (the respective directors of Homeless International and SPARC) had discussed the idea as far back as 1989. Homeless International and SPARC examined the financing patterns associated with one of the first and most challenging community-led developments to go ahead in Mumbai, the Markandeya scheme, in which SPARC had negotiated with HUDCO to provide a loan and raised grant funds to guarantee it. The Markandeya experience gave some insights into the complex institutional and policy-related environment that could affect the finances of such a project and hence affect suitable guarantee arrangements (Sanyal and Mukhija, 2000). In 1995, the Government of Maharashtra introduced the Slum Rehabilitation Act and created the Slum Rehabilitation Authority (SRA) to implement the policy (see Box 6.1). This provided a missing piece in the slum development jigsaw, and 'provided possibilities for co-operative societies of slum

---

Box 6.1   The Slum Rehabilitation Act and Transferable Development Rights (TDR)

The Slum Rehabilitation Act recognizes the right of slum and pavement dwellers, who can prove residence in the city on 1st January 1995, to 'avail of a permanent house'. Under the Act a slum landowner, a co-operative society of slum dwellers, a NGO, or any real estate developer having individual agreements with at least 70 per cent of eligible slum dwellers, is entitled to become a developer. Until the Rajiv Indira-Suryodaya development, however, all the schemes developed under the policy had been developed and implemented by conventional developers rather than communities themselves. Under the Act, each eligible family is entitled to develop 225 square feet of floor space, and developers who implement projects under the Act are expected to provide self-contained rehabilitation tenements of this size free of cost to slum dwellers. A land development incentive is made available to developers based on a Floor-Space Index ratio (FSI), which determines the permissible ratio of built floor-space to building plot space and varies in different parts of Mumbai, depending on real estate prices and the state's interest in minimizing development density. The FSI used on a particular site cannot exceed 2.5 times the available land area, but if the FSI entitlement is greater than the amount that can be used on the site, the balance can be awarded in Transferable Development Rights (TDR). TDR is awarded in square feet and allows developers to access an equivalent area of land in specified areas of the city which can then be used for development. TDR awards can either be used for construction or sold on the open market.

Extract from *Homeless International* 2003: 10.

dwellers to participate in their own redevelopment and... provided a financial mechanism to do so' (Burra 2005: 87-88). Slum dwellers in Dharavi, reputedly Asia's largest slum, formed a co-operative and asked their colleagues in the National Slum Dwellers Federation to help develop a multi-storey housing scheme in which to house 54 families. The Indian Alliance agreed to help, and the Rajiv Indira scheme began in 1997. Two neighbouring co-operatives later joined the scheme, enlarging the scheme to include five buildings between five and seven storeys high, which would benefit 209 families. It then became known as the Rajiv Indira-Suryodaya scheme.

SPARC had already been in discussions with Citibank about financing slum developments, in part because Citibank was seeking to establish its ethical credentials within India whilst its business expanded in the country. Homeless International and SPARC were able to use the offer of a guarantee to 'open the door' to in-depth discussions with them, and Citibank subsequently expressed interest in supporting the Rajiv Indira-Suryodaya scheme. Following lengthy negotiations, particularly in relation to cash-flow assumptions, the lending terms were set. Citibank agreed to lend SPARC and the Rajiv-Indira co-operative US$750,000 (approximately £464,000 at 1999 rates); Homeless International agreed that, in the case of the project's default, it would reimburse the bank for the first 20 per cent of the loan – an amount seen as the difference between the most optimistic and pessimistic financial scenarios. The loan would be repaid using sales of apartments, commercial units and TDR permissible under the SRA legislation, which would cross subsidize the costs of the rehabilitation units.

In early 1999, construction got underway, although no formal loan or guarantee arrangements had been signed. There were also delays awaiting construction permissions and formal registrations. The Indian Alliance and the co-operatives decided to take a risk by using scarce bridge funds held by SPARC to start the development and maintain the project's momentum, whilst the process of seeking registration and permissions continued. Slum dwelling families took massive personal risks in demolishing the slum housing in which they previously lived (and had invested money to develop), vacating the land and moving to transit housing to enable the scheme to begin.

Formally agreeing the loan arrangement with Citibank was not easy, and it took until an official project launch in 1999 for Citibank to issue an advance of Rs3 million (approximately £43,000) (see Spicer and Husock, 2003 for a fuller story of the pressures this placed upon the stakeholders involved in the Rajiv India – Suryodaya scheme). Citibank later released another Rs3.5 million (£50,000), but the introduction of Coastal Regulation Zone (CRZ) legislation in 2001 reduced the financial viability of the scheme by apparently limiting the height of buildings permissible on sites close to creeks, and as a result Citibank decided to withdraw from the loan arrangement (Burra 2004; Homeless International 2004). The limited bridge funds that SPARC held, including a rapidly arranged grant injection from Homeless International (£60,000), were soon used up and construction progress slowed. This continued until in March 2003, capital funds from the Community-Led Infrastructure Finance Facility (CLIFF – see Chapter 7) were eventually approved and disbursed for the scheme. Negotiations with Citibank

Photo 6.2 The Rajiv Indira-Suryodaya scheme, Mumbai, India, at an early stage of construction

Source: Homeless International

reopened soon after, and, towards the end of 2003, Homeless International and Citibank eventually finalized the guarantee arrangement that had initially been agreed years before. Ironically, the amount of financing that was required at this late stage in the scheme's development was much less than originally required, and the bank actually lost out in terms of the revenue it could have gained from the project.

REPLICATION IN MUMBAI – THE SECOND PHASE OF PROJECTS

Whilst the protracted negotiations with Citibank were frustrating, they did produce results beyond the scope of the Rajiv Indira-Suryodaya scheme. In particular, as a result of significant media attention, they opened up space for SPARC, and to some extent Homeless International, to showcase their work to a range of institutions, and to engage other banks in considering similar schemes. Although the guarantee fund was not of course solely responsible for these opportunities, it undoubtedly played a part in maintaining these conversations, and resulted in two further guarantees for housing developments initiated by the Indian Alliance within the SRA framework.

Bharat Janata is in a slum settlement in the middle of Dharavi, Mumbai, whose residents learnt from the experiences of the Rajiv Indira-Suryodaya scheme, and decided to design, construct and manage an *in situ* housing project for themselves.[8] The project, which consists of five buildings containing 197 residential units (of which 50 are for sale) and eight commercial units, began in 2003 following four years of planning and site clearance. The Bharat Janata scheme aimed to set an important precedent, namely that a slum housing development could be financed through revenues from TDR and the sale of housing and commercial units in a less commercially attractive area of Dharavi than was the case with the Rajiv Indira-Suryodaya scheme. It would prove that there was a market for housing within Dharavi, and hence that similar schemes could help redevelop most parts of Asia's largest slum. However, it initially lacked an access road to the property, which hampered construction and reduced the price expected for units to be sold. In early 2003, India's National Housing Bank (NHB) approached the Indian Alliance with a view to learning from their experiences in slum housing developments. NHB does not ordinarily lend directly, as it is a housing refinancing subsidiary of the Reserve Bank of India, but saw the Bharat Janata scheme as an opportunity to develop experience and credibility in lending for slum upgrading with which to catalyse, support and refinance similar lending by commercial banks.

The NHB guarantee arrangement differed from all previous guarantees, in that it was calculated on the basis of NHB's 'peak exposure' during the project. Peak exposure occurred near the beginning of the project, when NHB was required to lend large amounts of money to initiate construction of the first three blocks, but, according to SRA rules, had no rights to the housing units actually built. The SRA rules basically stipulated that all houses for slum dwellers must be built before any

Photo 6.3 NHB calculated its 'peak exposure' as the point when it had lent large amounts of money to construct the first three of the five blocks in the Bharat Janata scheme, which constituted the free housing for slum dwellers under SRA rules. Because NHB had no call on the houses in these three blocks in the event of a loan default, it required a guarantee from Homeless International.
Source: Homeless International

'for sale' units could be built, in order to prevent developers benefiting from development rights without actually building houses for slum dwellers. As a result, slum dwellers rather than the developer (in this case Nirman[9]) owned the first units completed in the Bharat Janata scheme. In this situation, NHB had no call upon the housing owned by slum dwellers, and could only treat the 'for sale' units as loan collateral.

Discussions with NHB began in early 2003, and arrangements between NHB, Nirman and Homeless International were concluded in November 2004. Although this was the first guarantee where an arrangement fee was charged, Homeless International negotiated successfully to reduce it. Not only was this the quickest guarantee negotiated in the guarantee fund's history, it also resulted in the lowest rate of guarantee – just 16 per cent of the loan amount. There are several reasons for this success. Firstly, the Indian Alliance had sufficient finance from CLIFF to complete the Bharat Janata project, which not only meant that NHB effectively had a competitor, but also enabled the Indian Alliance to start construction and show NHB that the project was going ahead on the ground. The Indian Alliance began the discussion with NHB before loan finance was needed, giving the kind of head start needed for the bankers to go through the due diligence process and understand the workings of the Indian Alliance, and hence to complete their internal risk assessments. Each time representatives from NHB visited the scheme, construction had progressed at a significant pace. The Indian Alliance invested a great deal of time and energy exploring options with NHB staff.

Secondly, the Indian Alliance had a number of projects in its portfolio to show NHB (including the Rajiv Indira-Suryodaya scheme which had attracted and secured bank financing). This enabled the Indian Alliance to demonstrate both its capacity and its future potential, in contrast to negotiations with Citibank where it was the first bank to come into the process and the Rajiv Indira-Suryodaya scheme was one of only two or three large housing schemes in the portfolio. Thirdly, the Indian Alliance had gained more experience in dealing with banks since the Rajiv Indira-Suryodaya scheme, and so was in a stronger position to negotiate with them. Fourthly, the Bharat Janata project, having incorporated many of the lessons from the Rajiv Indira-Suryodaya project and not falling under CRZ legislation, was a much more attractive project in terms of its projected financial viability by the time NHB was actively considering the loan (the access road had by this time been put in place). Finally, NHB was at a stage where there was some drive internally to finance such a scheme, as a basis for developing a framework for NHB to refinance commercial banks lending to such projects. The NHB front negotiator was also familiar with the SRA framework within which the scheme was developed.

The Bharat Janata scheme has influenced bank policy and practice by:

- Convincing NHB to lend for housing on un-mortgaged land (because the SRA only hands over ownership rights after construction is completed).
- Proving that SRA housing schemes are indeed bankable – in particular proving that such schemes are viable in less commercially attractive slum areas away from main roads.
- Demonstrating a tripartite agreement whereby the SRA and the Indian Alliance agree that the bank has lien on all cost recoveries including TDR.
- Initiating an ongoing dialogue between the SRA and NHB to set up a partnership for other SRA slum development schemes.

Homeless International and the Indian Alliance are involved in discussions with another Indian bank, ICICI, with a view to securing loan finance for the Indian Alliance's largest housing development to date. The Oshiwara II scheme will involve 18 high-rise buildings and provide housing and secure tenure benefiting 2,500 slum and pavement-dwelling families (more than 10,000 people). The project is allied with a community-led relocation process, in which the Indian Alliance is supporting tens of thousands of families currently living in pavement dwellings in dangerous locations alongside roads to plan and manage their relocation to decent housing and settlements, as part of the Mumbai Urban Infrastructure Project (MUIP) to improve Mumbai's transport network (Burra 2005).

At the time of writing, ICICI had sanctioned a Rs190 million loan to Nirman (approximately £2.4 million at January 2006 rates), calculated as the 'peak borrowing requirement' during the Oshiwara II development, which would cover 100 per cent of the financing requirement. ICICI initially requested a guarantee of 50 per cent from Homeless International, but subsequent negotiations and analysis encouraged ICICI to sanction the loan in principle with only a 25 per cent guarantee. In particular, ICICI took the initiative to suggest a loan with two components that would reduce the interest burden borne by Nirman, and hence increase the likelihood that the project will break even, in turn reducing the level of guarantee that ICICI felt would be necessary.

The loan comprises a standard loan component, on which monthly interest is charged on the amount sanctioned (rather than the amount actually drawn down), and an Overdraft Facility in which interest is only charged on the amount of money actually utilized (i.e. any repayments of the overdraft will reduce the amount on which interest is charged). ICICI proposed this loan structure in recognition that the Indian Alliance, unlike conventional developers, expects minimal if any profits on developments and hence the viability of projects is more sensitive to increases in costs such as interest. However, a guarantee is still required when loans are for projects with low or minimal profits like this, as described by Anil Kumar (Assistant General Manager of the Rural Microbanking and Agribusiness Group at ICICI Bank):

> The guarantee facility takes care of two things. One is the lack of a profit component, which is, to all effects, not built into the projects, which are even more difficult to build because of all the social components involved. Secondly because both sides of the cash flow – the revenue streams and the input streams – are open to fluctuation on both sides. There are certain risk swings from 15 to 20 per cent that the project may not be able to absorb. If the project moves the way it has been scheduled and all the assumptions prove correct (for example if the market remains stable) then there will not be a need for a guarantee. But if the market moves the other way and there is a delay, or a cost escalation, then there is a possibility of deficit. Both your streams are not fully covered – unlike a [conventional] builder where inflow stream is almost fully covered, reducing risk. A guarantee helps to cover that additional risk exposure – to provide additional comfort that makes the bank feel more confident about lending. (Homeless International 2005c).

Finally, the proposed ICICI arrangement is also significant because ICICI is approaching and analysing the loan from a purely business perspective, not for philanthropic reasons. ICICI views slum upgrading schemes of the sort pioneered by the Indian Alliance as an important new market in which to expand its business. Before assessing the challenges that this potential expansion poses, particularly in terms of the size of guarantees that this might imply in future, it is worth stepping back to consider the limitations and realities of the guarantee fund revealed in the process to date.

GUARANTEES OF SUCCESS? ACHIEVEMENTS, LIMITATIONS AND REALITIES

When the Homeless International Guarantee Fund was first established in the early 1990s, the use of guarantees by NGOs was relatively new. Guarantees had also only had limited application in the realm of housing finance (Platt 1997). The guarantee fund therefore marked a significant development not only in

Homeless International's organizational development, but in the broader context of testing new mechanisms for housing finance.

This chapter is deliberately entitled as a question, not a statement. The original assumption was that the guarantee fund could fill the gap between, on the one hand, banks unwilling to lend to poor people due to lack of formally recognized collateral and, on the other, poor people with the capacity to repay and having a range of informal assets on the other. As the stories related earlier reveal, Homeless International began to recognize that the nature of this 'gap' was more nuanced. In particular, the nature of the 'informal' collateral was difficult for banks to identify, and hence they found it difficult to analyse the risks associated with lending to the poor. Banks' assumptions were consistently risk averse, and Homeless International and partners found themselves disagreeing with them on every assumption. The role of the guarantee fund therefore changed, in that it contributed an opportunity to debate these different perceptions of risk. Although these discussions have taken a long time, they have contributed to an increasingly promising range of relationships between banks and organizations of the poor and their allies, with signs of increasing collaboration in future.

Before looking in more depth at the broader lessons emerging from Homeless International and partners' experiences with the guarantee fund, it is worth considering how the guarantee fund fared in relation to its four broad objectives, namely:

- securing bank finance;
- leveraging resources;
- linking the formal and informal sectors; and
- encouraging the development of local partnerships between the poor, banks, local government and other key development agencies; and thus supporting people-led approaches to development.

Firstly, the guarantee fund has achieved positive results in relation to its objectives to secure bank financing for self-help housing and to support the varying housing and infrastructure priorities of poor communities in different local environments. By 2005, the guarantee fund had supported three organizations in India, and one in Bolivia, to secure bank financing for housing development schemes. It had provided a total of ten guarantees, drawing down loans from seven different financial institutions.[10] At the time of writing, a further guarantee was under negotiation with ICICI in India, to support the Indian Alliance's Oshiwara II housing scheme. A total of 3,800 families will have benefited from new or improved housing as a direct result of these loans, with an additional 2,500 projected to benefit from the Oshiwara II development. As the case studies also demonstrate, the guarantee fund has successfully secured bank financing for a diverse range of projects – in rural, peri-urban and urban areas; for on-lending to individual families and for project lending for large-scale collective housing developments; for individual housing units and for high-rise developments; and for projects varying between three and ten years in duration.

Excluding the planned Oshiwara II scheme, the guarantee fund has provided guarantees to the value of just over £480,000, to secure bank loans totalling £1.8 million – an overall guarantee-to-loan ratio of 26 per cent. There is a mixed picture with regard to the multiplier effect of guarantees. The negotiations for the first guarantees in both India and Bolivia resulted in guarantees of more than 100 per cent of the loan secured, which Homeless International and partners accepted primarily to make steps towards the objective of better linking formal financial institutions with the organizations of poor people. This worked to the extent that 25 per cent guarantees were later secured for loans for housing programmes carried out by both YCO and IVDP. The lowest guarantee rates have been secured for housing developments undertaken by the Indian Alliance in Mumbai. However, it is perhaps unhelpful to compare the YCO/IVDP/Fundación Pro Habitat guarantee arrangements with the SPARC arrangements, because they were very different types of loan. The former loans were bulk loans for on-lending to individual families (effectively microfinance products), the latter were project finance arrangements. These lower rates achieved for the Mumbai housing developments with SPARC are probably more indicative of the different ways guarantees can be calculated for project financing as compared to microfinancing, rather than necessarily indicative of greater confidence among banks to lend with minimal guarantees. Nevertheless, there are good grounds to assume that similarly low rates of guarantee can be negotiated for similar projects in Mumbai (with the Indian Alliance) and Tamil Nadu (with IVDP) in future, particularly if NHB promotes the concept amongst commercial banks, and new agreements are secured with current lenders who have more familiarity with the development processes and borrowers in question.

The guarantee fund has also made progress in terms of facilitating linkages and working relationships between the poor, who generally live and work in the informal sector, and banks. In the case of YCO, in spite of the default, women's co-operatives were able to secure additional loans for both income generation and housing, without any involvement or guarantees from Homeless International. IVDP has scaled up its engagement with local banks to a remarkable extent; its network of women-led SHGs have secured and repaid upwards of £12 million in loans through India's bank–SHG linkage programmes benefiting tens of thousands of families. Several different banks are involved in this programme. Since 2004, as a direct result of its relationship and track record with the Bank of India, IVDP has worked with them to develop a brand new credit package to extend loans to SHG members for the installation of toilets and washrooms in houses. The first phase began in 2005, benefiting 100 families, again without the need for external guarantees. The continuing value of the working relationship between banks, IVDP and its network of SHGs is illustrated by IVDP's receipt of an excellence award from the Bank of India in 2004, First Prize in NABARD's SHG–Bank Linkage Awards 2004 and numerous local and district level awards. The situation in Bolivia is less clear, as the first loan has not yet been repaid nor the guarantee released.

As illustrated by the second phase of loans for increasingly large-scale housing developments initiated by the Indian Alliance in Mumbai, there is a growing relationship with banks concerning these sorts of development schemes. In addition, the Bank of Baroda approved loan financing for a very large housing scheme called Poonam Nagar (for which the Indian Alliance submitted a tender in 2003), although the Indian Alliance later decided not to go ahead with the scheme primarily because communities felt the location was inappropriate. The Indian Alliance also negotiated a new form of financing arrangement with the Unit Trust of India Bank (UTI Bank) for its sanitation work.[11] Significantly, it is a locally negotiated, locally financed guarantee arrangement between the Indian Alliance and UTI Bank, requiring only a 'letter of comfort' from Homeless International. The Indian Alliance's guarantee deposit secured UTI's agreement to lodge performance and advance bonds with the Brihanmumbai Municipal Corporation (BMC), thereby securing an advanced income payment of 10 per cent of the contract for the Indian Alliance's toilet construction work in the city and providing the BMC with the performance bond required.[12] The UTI Bank arrangement stemmed largely from the Indian Alliance's investments in developing a working relationship with UTI Bank, but was also due in part to the influence of the Citibank story described earlier. It is also important to note that the Indian Alliance is in discussions with an increasing number of banks (with regard to project lending, income generation and other initiatives), and is working with the Reserve Bank of India to channel learning from current schemes into broader policy work within the financial sector (see SPARC 2005b: 24).

It is also fair to say that the guarantee fund-supported initiatives have played a role in strengthening the capacity of communities and their allies to build up working relationships with government agencies. As McLeod puts it, 'guarantees and security deposits buy space within which negotiations with formal financial institutions can take place.' (2002b: 19). The *mahila mandals* supported by YCO began negotiating infrastructure and service provision with local authorities, and worked in partnership with them to build schools, roads, community centres and irrigation systems in several villages. Fundación Pro Habitat also facilitated links between community groups and municipalities, leading to, for example, joint initiatives to install street lighting and improve roads. Long before the guarantee fund came to fruition, the Indian Alliance had centred its attention upon establishing working partnerships with city, state and national authorities. The relationships developed by the Indian Alliance with a range of banks, particularly where guarantees helped secure loans for actual implementation of development projects, undoubtedly enhanced the credibility of the Indian Alliance in the eyes of those in government with whom they sought to build working relationships. The agreement with UTI Bank, for example, certainly enhanced the Indian Alliance's credibility in the tendering process for community construction of toilet blocks in slums, whilst its ability to finance housing schemes has further enhanced its relationship with the SRA. In all the cases described above, however, a wide range of activities have contributed to the creation of such working partnerships, with the guarantee fund considered only as one tool amongst many to enhance such relationships in favour of the poor themselves.

The projects described earlier in the chapter highlight a number of realities, and it is worth pausing to consider these. The first thing to highlight is that almost all guarantee negotiations have taken a long-time to achieve signed agreements and the release of funds, and several have been subject to numerous delays and frustrations throughout the negotiation periods. The brief descriptions of these stories possible within this chapter probably do not do justice to the myriad of twists, turns, hoops and pitfalls that Homeless International, partners and indeed communities have had to navigate. This is even true where there is genuine enthusiasm and in principle agreements within banks to pursue such arrangements. As described in more detail in Chapter 4, there are several general reasons for this state of affairs, as well as some specific reasons in the case of lending for slum developments in India. They are:

- *Rapid staff turn-over and limited institutional learning within banks.* 'Where no mechanisms exists to "capture" the insights and learning that individuals develop at an institutional level, staff relocation means that the negotiation process has to start all over again from the beginning.' (McLeod 2002b: 19). This was particularly noticeable during negotiations for the Rajiv Indira-Suryodaya scheme (see Spicer and Husock 2003).
- *Bureaucratic bottlenecks and problems with internal communication* within banks, such as between central headquarters and local branches during the YCO guarantee negotiations with HDFC.
- *Lack of 'datasets'.* Banks have no significant experience in the slum upgrading sector, particularly those with substantial community involvement; as a result, there are little if any available datasets or comparable experiences with which to analyse schemes proposed by organizations of the poor and their allies.
- *Standard lending criteria inapplicable.* Standard models for lending encourage banks to lend to construction firms on the basis of their balance sheet, rather than on the basis of the perceived viability of a particular project – in other words the criteria for lending is based upon the financial well-being of the organization in general rather than the project in question. These criteria preclude relatively young or small organizations working on behalf of the urban poor (like Nirman in India), and demand that banks develop new models with which to assess the credibility of the organization and its ability to implement the project under scrutiny.
- *Fears about control over revenues.* Banks may consider some form of project lending whereby they have first call on project revenues, and hence analyse the sensitivity of key variables, particularly revenue sources, to assess viability and risk. However, because there are several stages in the process of raising revenues from sources like the SRA's TDR mechanism over which banks have little control, they are reluctant to make a decision to lend on that basis. In the case of TDR, for example, the bank is reliant upon the Indian Alliance's ability to navigate the institutional arrangements within government to obtain TDR certificates, and upon the Alliance's ability to operate successfully in the TDR market to turn the certificates into revenues. Only at that stage can the bank have legal agreements with SPARC/Nirman to have first call on the revenues raised.

The overarching feature of Homeless International's protracted engagement with banks has been the search for the elusive 'comfort factor' as described in Chapter 4, the intuitive feeling amongst banks' decision-makers that a loan 'feels right'. Bankers have been forced to develop more qualitative criteria in order to assess loan applications of the sort put forward by the Indian Alliance. The criteria tend to be based partly on an assessment of the borrowing organization and their past record in similar schemes, and partly based upon demonstrated progress, including construction visible on site. In the case of SRA schemes for example, the bank has no legal avenue through which to lay claim to TDR certificates and instead has to develop a confidence that the Indian Alliance has the capacity to (1) complete projects, (2) navigate the government systems to draw down TDR certificates and (3) operate effectively in the TDR market to sell the certificates. This reveals the limitation of the guarantee fund on its own: it does not have the facility to provide funds to kick-start projects in advance of bank agreements and hence cannot easily contribute to demonstrating in practice that a project is going ahead. The guarantee fund is therefore most effective when allied with a venture capital facility such as CLIFF (see Chapter 7), which makes bridging loans available to kick-start projects and to enable projects to proceed whilst negotiations for bank finance go ahead, or if bank financing is delayed.

Where the guarantee fund has proved useful, particularly in its early stages, has been in helping to open the doors to initial negotiations with banks. At the very least, the guarantee fund (because it was in a form readily recognizable by banks) probably helped to wedge the door open longer whilst banks were shown other aspects of the community development process that helped to build their confidence. In this sense it helped demonstrate the credibility of Homeless International and partner organizations. Discussions about the possibility of loans underwritten by Homeless International guarantees also helped Homeless International and partners to learn the language of the banking fraternity, and to refine our own articulation of community-led housing and slum developments in financial terms. The guarantee fund undoubtedly made a contribution to Homeless International and partners' increased familiarity with banks and to the relationships developed with key personnel over the years. McLeod (2002b: 19) describes the importance of such a process:

> The risks undertaken by the poor when engaging with the state and with the formal financial sector need to be acknowledged. At the same time a far greater degree of understanding needs to be developed by both banking institutions and organizations of the urban poor as to what lies behind the differences in perception and judgement that are so apparent between them. Without better understanding, the chances for improved mediation between the formal and informal financial sectors seem remote. One of the entry points to building understanding in this area is that of providing support for risk analysis, management and mitigation by organizations of the urban poor so that space for dialogue and negotiations with banks can be created.

The guarantee fund has proved most effective in India, where a combination of factors has contributed to its success. Firstly, Homeless International has worked with several Indian partner organizations that have considerable capacity and experience in housing development or slum upgrading, grounded in strong links with organized networks of communities. By contrast, the guarantee arrangement with Fundación Pro Habitat was set up quite soon after Fundación Pro Habitat had begun work in peri-urban and urban areas, and before it had in-depth experiences of, and partnership with, communities in those areas. Nor did Homeless International and Fundación Pro Habitat have the same depth of relationship or experience of collaborative working that Homeless International had with partners such as SPARC and IVDP. These factors contributed to slower than anticipated growth of Fundación Pro Habitat's housing credit programme, and to the need to negotiate an additional 12-month period of the guarantee to ensure that Fundación Pro Habitat could fully repay the loan. The lesson here is that guarantee arrangements are best set up with experienced organizations with whom a wide range of collaborative activities have already taken place. Where this is not the case, preparatory work through, for example, grant-funded initiatives, research or other forms of collaborative work can help create the basis for future guarantee-supported work. Grant funds can also help with aspects of institutional development that are particularly pertinent to guarantee-related work, such as:

- administrative capacity to manage a portfolio of development schemes;
- technical capacity and/or access to appropriate technical assistance to construct at the quality and scale required; and
- networks of relationships with government agencies required to negotiate hurdles in permissions or to draw down revenues from government.

By extension, because the guarantee fund is a demand-based mechanism, it also relies on capacity at community level to manage money and make repayments where funds have been on-lent to individual families. The guarantee fund is therefore most effective when allied with grant funding initiatives to expand and deepen communities' capacities, and when part of an integrated programme of poverty reduction activities. For example, the Indian Alliance, IVDP and YCO all supported communities in developing social security mechanisms, income-generating activities as well as planning physical improvements to slum settlements.

Thirdly, the guarantee fund has been effective where there is a relatively well-developed, competitive and well-resourced banking sector in place. The obvious counter-argument is that guarantees cannot be set up where formal finance institutions are few and far between.

WHAT NEXT? FUTURE PROSPECTS AND NEW IDEAS

The Oshiwara II scheme described above marks a major milestone in terms of scale: it is the biggest development scheme undertaken by any of Homeless International's partners, it is the largest financially, and it will stretch Homeless International's guarantee fund to its limits. This poses new challenges, not least because developments of this scale are required to make significant progress in supporting slum and pavement dwellers to escape the poverty associated with insecure housing and poor living conditions. Replication, of course with alterations suitable to the projects and contexts in question, is vital, and as described above guarantees will continue to be essential, if not necessarily sufficient, to support this scaling-up. Homeless International has two main options, at least over the next few years. Firstly, Homeless International can seek to build up its own guarantee fund, encouraging investors to make interest-free deposits or grants to the fund. Secondly, Homeless International may have a role in facilitating linkages between partners such as the Indian Alliance and other organizations with larger guarantee facilities, such as bi-lateral and multi-lateral development agencies. This would hopefully enable agencies to build upon Homeless International and partners' experiences to date, but would pose questions in relation to how Homeless International and partners would cover the costs of their 'technical support' work in this process.

This second option will also pose questions to bi-lateral and multi-lateral agencies about whether they have the inclination or capacity to effectively support innovations like the guarantee fund that operate explicitly to meet the needs and realities experienced by the urban poor. This in itself is couched within the broader question facing these agencies as to whether they are willing to embrace the issue of urban poverty more effectively, and whether they are willing to engage with local, community-led processes.

CHAPTER SEVEN

The Community-Led Infrastructure Finance Facility

Ian Morris

WHAT IS CLIFF?

The Community-Led Infrastructure Finance Facility (CLIFF) provides project loans and other support to organized communities, so that they can access subsidies, and borrow from formal finance institutions, in order to scale up community-driven housing and infrastructure initiatives that benefit the urban poor. The CLIFF project is co-ordinated internationally by Homeless International and is being piloted in India and in Kenya. It is funded, via the World Bank Cities Alliance programme, by DFID and Sida, which have committed £6.84 million and 20 million Swedish Krona (£1.5 million equivalent) respectively. Homeless International is providing guarantee funds worth £600,000. Pre-existing local capital has been provided by SPARC/Nirman in India (£1.2m equivalent) and the Pamoja Trust in Kenya (£250,000 equivalent).

This chapter outlines the background to CLIFF's development (drawing on McLeod 2002b) before detailing the CLIFF implementation process (drawing on Homeless International 2002a and 2005), including its aims, the organizations involved, the products that the facility offers. The chapter then goes on to examine CLIFF implementation in Kenya and India in more detail. Finally, the learning emerging from CLIFF is considered, together with options for replicating or building on the CLIFF experience in the future.

THE NEED FOR CLIFF

Work during the 'Bridging the finance gap' research project (see Chapters 4 and 5) showed clearly that organizations of the urban poor, and the NGOs with whom they work, were making significant investments in urban development and in doing so managing substantial levels of risk. The solutions they developed were extremely valuable in the longer term because they provided precedents that had the potential for scaling-up. However, there were major constraints to actual scaling up because the urban poor did not have access to the financial resources needed to finance large projects. Government agencies were unable to deliver subsidies because there were no funds to pre-finance projects and their delivery mechanisms assumed reimbursement rather than payment in advance, and banks and other financial institutions were unwilling to provide project loans because they had no experience of assessing such initiatives from a risk perspective.

In theory the provision of guarantees, particularly hard currency guarantees such as those provided by Homeless International, should have helped to alleviate the nervousness of formal financial institutions and governmental agencies. However, in practice, guarantees have proved difficult and expensive to negotiate and by themselves have rarely resulted in loans being extended in time for the projects to be implemented as planned. The complexities of guarantees have already been discussed in the previous chapter. It is important to note that while guarantees can create valuable space for dialogue, banks and governmental bodies require evidence of successful construction on the ground before they are willing to provide finance or agree to contractual arrangements. Initial projects therefore require financing from other sources so that construction can begin and potential achievements be demonstrated. CLIFF has been designed to provide project loans to fill this gap because this level and kind of financing cannot be covered by conventional NGO funding.

Once financing is available to provide initial working capital for projects that demonstrate real scaling up, important breakthroughs can be achieved. Large projects on the ground, being implemented in practice, demonstrate the capabilities of organizations of the urban poor in project design, negotiation and delivery. Construction standards can be assessed, costings can be tested, and cash flows can be monitored so that financial planning can be improved over time. Not only can the possible be demonstrated, but also people from a range of institutions then have the opportunity to visit and learn from a project as it is implemented. This makes negotiations with formal financial institutions easier because they have real evidence and data to consider when analysing project risks. If, in addition, those risks can be shared by the provision of a guarantee, then a loan for project working capital from a formal financial institution becomes a viable proposition. In addition, it becomes easier for organizations of the urban poor to bid for state contracts and to access state subsidies because they can provide a track record of performance not only in terms of successful construction, but also successful financial management of complex projects.

THE CLIFF IMPLEMENTATION PROCESS

A CLIFF approach can only ever work in situations where communities have already developed the organizational capacity needed to take a lead role in the implementation of slum development projects. CLIFF has been designed to enhance this capacity by providing financing that will help organizations of the urban poor to scale up the solutions they have already tested as precedents. It cannot replace the grant funding that is necessary to support the basic mobilization of communities through the processes described in Chapter 3.

The CLIFF Project

The CLIFF Project was designed as a 10-year project and its implementation envisaged in three main phases. Following an initial mobilization period beginning in June 2002 and lasting six months, Phase 1 began in April 2003. It was predicted that by the end of the first phase, in March 2006, all the capital funds would have been drawn down and lent to projects in the first pilot area, India. It was also anticipated that preparations would have been made to initiate a second CLIFF in sub-Saharan Africa. The second phase, extending from April 2006 to March 2008 was expected to result in the consolidation of CLIFF in India and a second CLIFF being implemented in sub-Saharan Africa, providing the necessary funding could be mobilized. At the global level there would be an exploration of the potential to establish a permanent global CLIFF facility, and a discussion regarding the details of such a facility should it be seen as desirable. Finally, provision was made for a third phase running to 2011, during which a global facility, if agreed, would be established.

The overall aim of the CLIFF project is to 'achieve reductions in urban poverty by increasing poor urban communities' access to commercial and public sector finance for medium to large-scale infrastructure and housing initiatives' (Homeless International 2002a). The aim is to achieve this by developing a sustainable finance facility that can assist organizations of the urban poor to carry out successful community-driven infrastructure, housing and urban services initiatives at city level, in conjunction with municipalities and the private sector, and to do this in at least two countries. Each country-level facility is meant to be used to increase the availability of local market financing for community-driven infrastructure and housing initiatives and, where applicable, to facilitate improvement in the use of government subsidies by municipalities supporting community-driven initiatives. The project design emphasized the importance of shared learning, with an assumption that lessons emerging from the project will be disseminated widely to enable a wide spectrum of local authorities, communities, donors and other interested parties to learn from the project as it is implemented. By the end of the project, it is envisaged that there will be demonstrable improvements in infrastructure and housing for the urban poor living in the cities where CLIFF has been operational, with commensurate improvements in the local policy, regulatory and legislative environments.

Who is involved in CLIFF, and how?

Local level. It had already been agreed during the design of the CLIFF project that the first pilot would be implemented in India, with the Indian Alliance composed of SPARC, the National Slum Dwellers Federation and Mahila Milan, via their construction and financial management company SPARC Samudaya Nirman Sahayak – Nirman (SSNS). The formation and structuring of the Indian Alliance has already been described elsewhere (see Chapter 2 Box 2.1). Then, in 2004, at a much earlier stage than had been envisaged, it was agreed that a second pilot CLIFF should be initiated in Kenya, using £100,000 of the capital funds initially allocated for India. In Kenya the initiative is being implemented by a national alliance that is structured similarly to the Indian Alliance but is considerably younger, having been in operation for around five years at the time of writing. It is made up of a national federation of saving and credit groups known as

Muungano wa Wanavijiji, which is supported by the Pamoja Trust, a Kenyan NGO that aims to facilitate community-led solutions to homelessness and related problems in Kenya. Muungano wa Wanavijiji and the Pamoja Trust have together established a separate institution to finance projects implemented by members of the Federation called the Akiba Mashinani Trust (AMT), which is playing a key role in implementing CLIFF.

International level. As already indicated, the UK Department for International Development (DFID) and Sida (the Swedish International Development Cooperation Agency) have provided the major funding for the first phase of CLIFF. Their grants have been channelled through the Cities Alliance programme, which is located within the World Bank. Cities Alliance was launched in 1999 by the World Bank and UN-Habitat as a multi-donor collaboration with cities and their development partners to facilitate developments in the living conditions of the urban poor. The advantage of locating CLIFF in this way is that Cities Alliance takes fiduciary responsibility for the DFID and Sida funds but also provides a platform that enables a wide spectrum of agencies to have direct access to the lessons emerging from CLIFF. Funds are channelled from Cities Alliance to Homeless International in the UK. Homeless International co-ordinates planning, monitoring and reporting of the CLIFF project, as it is implemented, and also takes a hands-on role in collaborative development and testing of the systems and procedures necessary to manage a complex portfolio of projects supported by CLIFF.

In addition to the agencies that have legal and contractual responsibility for implementing CLIFF, there are a range of advisory groups that review progress and plans on a regular basis. The CLIFF Advisory Group (CAG) is made up of the donors to CLIFF, organizations co-ordinating and implementing CLIFF, and potential stakeholders. It is essentially a steering group and meets twice a year to learn about and review progress as well as make decisions that affect the future implementation of CLIFF. In the UK and in India there are also technical advisory groups. The Nirman and Homeless International technical advisory groups are made up of relevant local individuals who advise the respective staff and Boards of each organization on the implementation of projects and related matters. They have expertise in areas such as construction management, law, banking and financial services, international development and organizational management and development.

CLIFF financial products

CLIFF provides a variety of financial support to a portfolio of community-led projects:

- Technical assistance grants,[1] to cover costs such as professional fees that are required to support communities implement such projects.
- Capital funds for project loans, to enable projects to begin and continue at a pace unhindered by the timings of project cost recoveries. As projects are completed, loans are repaid and this capital is recycled at the local level to support additional projects.

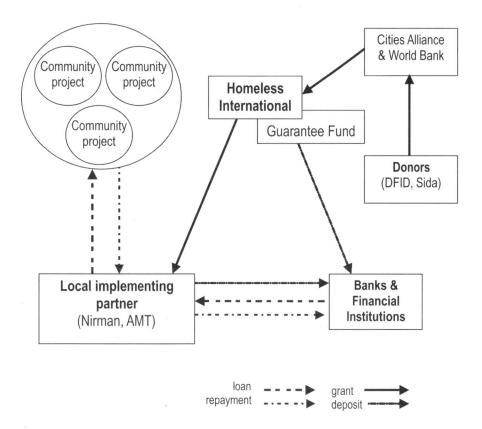

Figure 7.1 CLIFF, bank financing and associated financial flows

■ Knowledge grants, to allow the learning from projects to be shared with as many people as possible to help achieve change beyond the project.
■ Management grants, to cover the related management costs of the organizations implementing CLIFF.
■ Financial guarantees, Homeless International's Guarantee Fund can be used to complement CLIFF by helping to secure loan finance from financial institutions.

The diagram above shows how CLIFF funding flows from donors through the co-ordinating organizations to implementing partners at the local level, and how loans are then disbursed to and repaid from projects. The diagram also shows financial flows associated with securing loan finance from banks, including guarantees from Homeless International or implementing partners at the local level where required.

More about the loan finance component

Capital for loans to projects is the most important form of financial support that CLIFF provides, and so represents the majority (around 75 per cent) of the total

CLIFF budget. Loans are allocated to projects on the basis of agreed criteria. The projects must demonstrate that they:

- have the potential to be implemented as a flagship that will provide a precedent for future scaling-up, replicability and pro-poor policy change;
- have emerged from strategies developed by organizations of the urban poor and their existing relationships with local authority and municipal officials, and have the potential to strengthen such city–community relationships;
- actively include and benefit the poorest and most marginalized members of the community in the area where the project is to be implemented;
- are properly costed, financially viable and offer options for negotiating loan finance from commercial banking institutions and municipal/state subsidies where necessary;
- include an analysis of the major project risks, identifying what form these risks will take, who will bear the burden of these risks, and how CLIFF will assist in the management and mitigation of these risks;
- incorporate a management strategy that identifies how project responsibilities will be allocated and undertaken;
- include long-term planning for sustainability and maintenance of the assets developed as a result of the investment;
- incorporate a learning and knowledge-sharing agenda to ensure that other communities and actors in urban development can benefit from the experience.

These criteria were largely developed based on findings from the 'Bridging the finance gap' research, which had identified approaches that helped organizations of the urban poor to manage risk more effectively. However, very early on in the implementation of CLIFF it became clear that a reasonable amount of flexibility would need to be applied in applying the criteria to individual projects put forward by implementing partners. This was necessary to ensure that projects that rated very highly on strategic criteria such as their potential for scaling-up but which had, say, a strong likelihood that they would incur some level of financial loss (and so did not meet the criteria for being financially viable), could still receive a CLIFF loan. At the same time it was agreed that the loan criteria should be applied to the portfolio of projects as a whole so that while individual projects might be expected to suffer losses the portfolio as a whole would not be put at risk. This flexibility is a vital component of CLIFF because one its most important functions is to provide a means to share risk taking with the urban poor, and to understand this risk taking better so that it can be more effectively managed and mitigated.

Learning

CLIFF is innovative in a number of respects, and it was recognized from the beginning that it was likely to produce important lessons for scaling-up the provision of suitable housing and related infrastructure for the urban poor. It was therefore important to set up structures and systems to capture and share this learning. One of the most important steps in this direction was the design of a framework for the monitoring and evaluation of CLIFF. The framework is

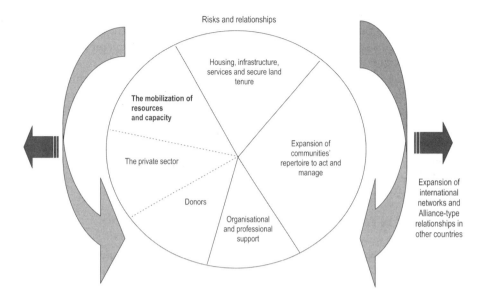

Figure 7.2 The CLIFF monitoring 'pizza'

summarized as a '360 degree process', which in practice means that all those involved in the development and implementation of CLIFF are monitored and evaluated, rather than just 'the project', as would happen in more conventional approaches. A monitoring 'pizza' (see Figure 7.2) was also developed as a part of the framework. This guides the monitoring process by identifying the broad spectrum of areas about which information needs to be collected in order to determine the impact that CLIFF is having.

Learning and information exchange takes place at many different levels. At a community-level, learning takes place on a day-to-day basis. Exchanges and visits within cities, between cities and between countries are ongoing, and may be supported by CLIFF Knowledge Grants. These visits often bring teams of slum dwellers and government officials to the projects to discuss the rationale that lies behind them and to explore the nitty-gritty of implementation on the ground. Information at community level is compiled by the federations through their own processes and recorded by SPARC, Nirman, Pamoja Trust and Akiba Mashinani personnel for monitoring purposes. Homeless International staff visit India and Kenya regularly to track progress and discuss issues that have arisen as a result of the projects. In addition, there is almost daily contact between Homeless International staff in the UK and the implementing agencies in India and Kenya. Homeless International produces an official CLIFF Annual Review that brings together progress reports and reflections from the experiences in India and Kenya, and which also provides a space for donors, bankers and government officials to give feedback and comments on what has happened.

At the international level, the CLIFF Advisory Group meets twice a year to discuss progress, with at least one of these meetings being held in a city where

CLIFF-supported projects are being implemented. Meeting with communities implementing projects and having an opportunity to discuss the approaches used in detail with local actors helps to keep CAG discussions centred on the realities that are being tackled on the ground. There is also an expectation that all those involved in CLIFF will utilize and share the learning that is emerging within their own organizations and networks and will subsequently feed back how that learning has been used through the CAG meetings. Furthermore, lessons from CLIFF are being shared internationally through the SDI and ACHR networks. Homeless International and the Indian and Kenyan Alliances have participated in numerous meetings, given lectures and presentations, and made visual and written documentation available in printed form and through web sites.

IMPLEMENTATION TO DATE: INDIA

CLIFF is now into its fourth year of operation in India. The achievements made by the Indian Alliance, using the facility, have been significant, despite considerable constraints and obstacles encountered on the way. The portfolio of projects supported by CLIFF is outlined below, together with an analysis of additional resources mobilized. Finally, key elements of the monitoring framework (see Figure 7.2) are examined: impact on policy and practice, the community's repertoire to act and manage, organizational and professional support, and risks and challenges. This information and analysis on implementation in India is largely based on the most recent CLIFF monitoring reports, which provide more detailed information (Jack *et al.* 2005; McLeod 2005a).

Portfolio overview

A review of the portfolio's performance, summarized in Table 7.1 below, demonstrates the scale of the achievement by June 2005, with 5332 families set to benefit from the housing projects and more than 279,000 families from the sanitation projects supported by CLIFF.

Resource mobilization

Resource mobilization in this context refers to a range of additional resources for slum upgrading and infrastructure provision that have been mobilized by using CLIFF. Resources include land; local infrastructure such as water, sewerage, electricity and roads; loan finance from banks for projects; and project cost recoveries such as government subsidies and contract payments, commercial and residential unit sales and community contributions. The sources of these resources span both the public and private sectors. Table 7.2 provides an overview of the range of resource mobilization resulting from the portfolio of CLIFF-supported projects, as of June 2005.

Table 7.1 Overview of the current portfolio of CLIFF projects

Name	Location	Type	Number and type of buildings	Number of families benefiting	For-sale component
Rajiv Indira-Suryodaya	Mumbai, Maharashtra	SRA – upgrading	5 multi-storey buildings	209	27 residential units + commercial space
Bharat Janata	Mumbai, Maharashtra	SRA – upgrading	5 multi-storey buildings	147	50 residential units + 8 commercial units
Milan Nagar	Mumbai, Maharashtra	SRA – resettlement	5 multi-storey buildings	327	30 commercial units tbc
Oshiwara I	Mumbai, Maharashtra	SRA – upgrading and resettlement	6 multi-storey buildings	780	38 residential units
Oshiwara II	Mumbai, Maharashtra	SRA – upgrading and resettlement	19 multi-storey buildings	2,480	120 residential units + commercial space
Jollyboard	Mumbai, Maharashtra	SRA – resettlement	2 multi-storey buildings	101	5 residential units
SRA HOUSING PROJECT TOTAL				**4,044**	
Solapur bidi	Solapur, Maharashtra	Subsidy drawdown test	Ground-level housing units	501	Commercial space
Sunnuduguddu (Ph 1)	Bangalore, Karnataka	New slum development exploration	4 multi-storey buildings	74	11 commercial units
Hadapsar 1 + 2	Pune, Maharashtra	Subsidy drawdown test	713 housing units in low-rise buildings	713	–
OTHER HOUSING PROJECT TOTAL				**1,288**	
BSDP	Mumbai, Maharashtra	Sanitation	208 toilet blocks	Over 200,000	
Pune sanitation (Ph 4)	Pune, Maharashtra	Sanitation	23 toilet blocks	Over 13,000	
Tiruppur sanitation	Tiruppur, Tamil Nadu	Sanitation	88 toilet blocks in four phases	Over 66,000	
SANITATION PROJECT TOTAL				**Over 279,000**	
GRAND TOTAL				**Over 284,000**	

Table 7.2 Overview of the projected costs and resource mobilization of the portfolio of projects supported by CLIFF loan finance, as of June 2005

Name	Total cost (£)	Resources mobilized Land (m²)		Main cost recoveries (£)			Bank finance/ guarantee sanctioned (£)	CLIFF financing required (£)	SPARC/ Nirman non-CLIFF financing required (£)
		From government	From private sector	Government subsidies and contract payments	Sales	Community contributions			
Rajiv Indira-Suryodaya	1,319,736	3,972		0	1,442,902	0	250,000	393,914	381,920
Bharat Janata	1,002,743	2,507		0	1,059,298	0	775,853	213,855	17,569
Milan Nagar	1,380,756	4,710		0	1,375,624	21,800		513,833	660,391
Oshiwara I	3,197,877		8,351	0	3,331,266	0		1,151,622	86,133
Oshiwara II	10,670,224		29,249	0	10,999,174	0	2,666,667	74,397	4,174
Jollyboard	388,010		2,071	0	431,781	0		87,115	0
Solapur bidi	849,108		54,001	267,200	490,031	100,200		365,809	338,524
Sunnuduguddu (Ph 1)	139,985	3,390		0	97,636	19,733		120,032	28,818
Hadapsar 1 + 2	686,668	28,105		475,333	0	206,000		418,934	120,000
HOUSING PROJECTS TOTAL	**19,635,107**	**42,684**	**93,672**	**742,533**	**19,227,710**	**347,733**	**3,692,520**	**3,339,510**	**1,637,528**
BSDP	4,043,710	208 toilet blocks		3,560,069	0	0	859,768	893,257	897,192
Pune sanitation (Ph 4)	168,334	23 toilet blocks		154,618	0	0		94,600	21,667
Tiruppur sanitation (Ph1)	833,731	88 toilet blocks in 4 phases		967,847	0	0		to be confirmed	0
SANITATION PROJECT TOTAL	**5,045,775**	**319 toilet blocks**		**4,682,534**	**0**	**0**	**859,768**	**987,857**	**918,859**
OVERALL TOTAL	**24,680,882**	**42,684 m² and 319 toilet blocks**	**93,672**	**5,425,068**	**19,227,710**	**347,733**	**4,552,288**	**4,327,368**	**2,556,387**

Project cost recoveries

The variety of sources of project cost recovery reflects both the different locations that the Indian Alliance operates in across the country and the utilization of different policy and legal frameworks associated with those locations. Perhaps the most complicated policy environment has been that of Mumbai, particularly in testing how the Slum Rehabilitation Act (see Box 7.1 below) can be implemented in practice using a community-led process.

Box 7.1 Slum rehabilitation policy

The Slum Rehabilitation Authority (SRA) was created in 1995, when a new act was introduced which recognized the rights of any slum and pavement dwellers who could prove residence in the city of Mumbai on 1 January 1995 to 'avail of an alternate permanent accommodation'. A slum landowner, a co-operative society of slum dwellers, an NGO or any real estate developer having individual agreements with at least 70 per cent of eligible slum dwellers is entitled to become a developer.

Under the act, each family is entitled to a unit with a floor space of 225 square feet (21 square metres), and developers implementing slum rehabilitation projects must provide this unit free of cost to the slum dwellers occupying their land. The act gives incentives to developers to construct rehabilitation housing in slum areas of Mumbai. The amount of development rights generated by a project is dependent on the location of the plot and the building design. Developers may use development rights in excess of those needed to build rehabilitation units to construct additional units for sale if space allows, or to sell the rights as Transferable Development Rights (TDR).

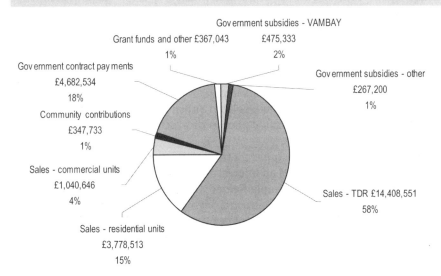

Figure 7.3 Projected cost recoveries from the June 2005 portfolio of CLIFF-supported projects

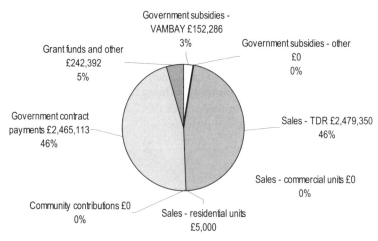

Figure 7.4 Actual cost recoveries from the current portfolio of CLIFF-supported projects

The hub of the Indian Alliance's activity is in Mumbai. Mumbai is also where the scale of projects is the largest, as reflected in Table 7.1. However, it is worth noting that the number of projects supported by CLIFF in Mumbai makes up only around half of those in the India portfolio as a whole.

A deeper examination of each project highlights the diversity of environments in which projects are being implemented, ranging from the Mumbai SRA projects already mentioned to special housing initiatives for *bidi*[2] makers and projects to test new approaches to slum upgrading in specific cities such as Bangalore. The different policy and legal frameworks within which projects are being implemented have an important influence on how efficiently project cost recoveries are achieved. In virtually all cases, project cost recoveries are scheduled to be received both during construction – i.e. upon pre-set stages of construction being completed – and after construction has been completed. However, the timing of payments and the percentages of costs reimbursed at any given stage differ from policy to policy and even project to project. In many instances projects are selected for support precisely so that they can test state delivery processes for specific subsidies that have historically failed to reach the poor as no practicable delivery mechanisms have been put in place.

In the BSDP project, for example, there were no takers for the delivery contract until the federation expressed an interest and took steps to submit a tender. Yet, as the BSDP project has been implemented, the Indian Alliance has experienced substantial delays in receiving contracted payments from government. Figure 7.5 shows that there have been delays of between 18 and 24 months in receiving payments following actual expenditure. At the time of writing, this amounts to around Rs50 to 100 million (approximately £0.65–1.35 million) owed by the state to the Indian Alliance. Drawing down subsidies from government authorities has also been difficult. Despite initial success in drawing down Valmiki Ambedkar Yojna (VAMBAY) housing subsidies for the Hadapsar projects in Pune, the Indian Alliance was unable to draw down virtually any subsidies during 2004, as Figure

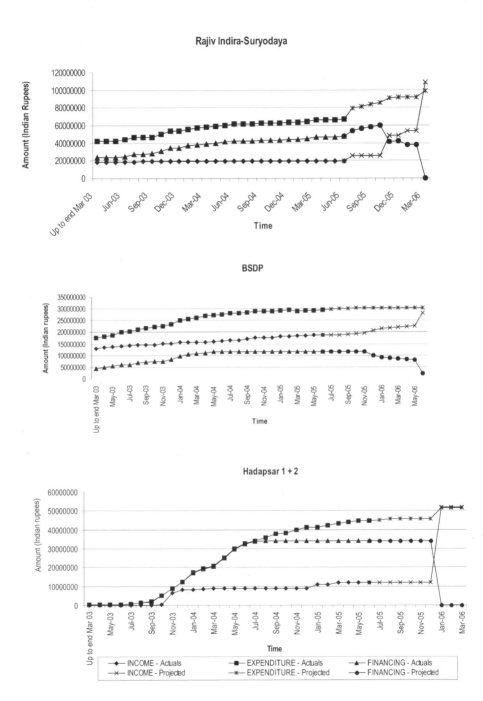

Figure 7.5 Financial profiles of the Rajiv Indira-Suryodaya, BSDP and Hadapsar projects

7.5 shows. Most of these delays have resulted from bureaucratic obstacles. There has also been reluctance, in some cases, to authorize or make payments without a bribe. The Indian Alliance refuses to pay bribes, because it believes that corrupt practices undermine the long-term goal of achieving accountable and transparent investments in development that benefit the poor. When delays associated with corruption do occur, the Indian Alliance sits them out, and works together with government officials who share the same principles to pressurize for payments to be made as they ought to be. The problem is that, in the short term, the cost of not paying bribes can be significant because the resulting project delays extend the time for which loans are required and therefore the overall cost of project finance.

Finance

The graphs in Figure 7.5 demonstrate more clearly than any written explanation both the need for project loans and, in the absence of bank loans for such projects, the need for CLIFF. Without CLIFF and the project loans that SPARC/Nirman have themselves provided, these projects simply could not have taken place. However, in the space of only three years, the situation has changed quite significantly. When CLIFF started, in June 2002, nearly all the project financing required for the selected portfolio was provided from pre-existing SPARC/Nirman funds or from CLIFF. However, by July 2005, one-third of the financing required by the portfolio of projects supported by CLIFF was projected to come from banks, and virtually all of the projected bank loans had been officially sanctioned. These loans are from Citibank, NHB and ICICI for the Rajiv Indira-Suryodaya, Bharat Janata and Oshiwara II projects respectively as detailed in Table 7.2. It is important to note that all of them have required guarantees ranging from around 10 to 25 per cent.

As the Indian Alliance has gained more experience it has not only obtained more bank loans, it has also found ways to reduce the amount of financing that projects require, and the amount of time that financing is required for. The Indian Alliance has done this in two main ways. The first has been to include the ability to pre-finance construction to pre-set stages of construction in the selection criteria for building contractors, where possible and practical. What this means in practice is that building contractors have to invest their own funds (typically representing 20–30 per cent of total construction costs) in the construction of the project, and these funds are then reimbursed when the stages of construction have been completed as contractually agreed. The pre-financing arrangement allows the Indian Alliance to start projects without needing to have full project financing in place from day one, leaving more time during which arrangements can be negotiated with other sources such as banks or CLIFF to cover the complete financing needs of the project.

The second method that the Indian Alliance has used to reduce financing costs is to accelerate revenue payments into projects. They have used their influence within state bureaucracies to put pressure on bureaucrats sitting on approvals and payments, but more specifically they have also discovered that, for SRA projects,

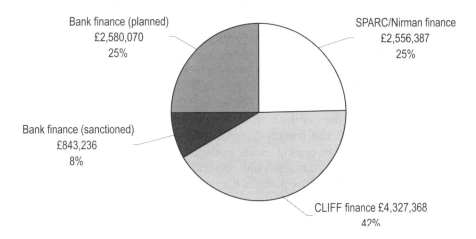

Bank finance (planned)
£2,580,070
25%

SPARC/Nirman finance
£2,556,387
25%

Bank finance (sanctioned)
£843,236
8%

CLIFF finance £4,327,368
42%

Figure 7.6 Projected financing from the current portfolio of projects supported by CLIFF loan finance during project construction.

they can apply for smaller quantities of TDR on a more frequent basis during project construction. With SRA projects representing such a large proportion of the portfolio of projects supported by CLIFF, this is already beginning to have a significant impact on the financial performance of projects and the portfolio as a whole.

Land and infrastructure

Land is one of the most valuable, and therefore hotly contested, assets in cities, particularly in commercially vibrant cities like Mumbai and Bangalore. For example, in Mumbai 60 per cent of the population lives in slums on about 13 per cent of the land (SPARC 2005a:4). At the same time government authorities appear to be pursuing an inequitable and misguided strategy to free further land for speculative development, as exemplified by a series of major slum demolitions in January 2005. In general, it is extremely difficult for the urban poor to secure land and tenure, and almost all attempts to do so are contested at every stage by political interest groups across the city. The success of the Indian Alliance, supported by CLIFF, in securing land and tenure for slum and pavement dwellers is all the more impressive and important in this light.

The mechanisms and arrangements to access both land and infrastructure differ from project to project within the CLIFF portfolio. Land and infrastructure is sometimes obtained directly from the respective municipalities. In other cases community savings and grant funds from other sources are used to buy land. As demonstrated by the Oshiwara project, land is also now being obtained from private landowners in joint ventures because the landowner does not have the capacity to realize its value through SRA-linked development. With respect to infrastructure, in some cases obligatory fees are paid by the project for extension of bulk infrastructure. Sometimes temporary measures are also necessary. For example, temporary provision of water from a nearby well has been arranged until connection with the piped water supply of a neighbouring housing development scheme has been negotiated.

Impact on policy and practice

CLIFF impacts upon policy and practice most directly by providing loan finance to projects that 'have the potential to be implemented as a flagship that will provide a precedent for future scaling-up, replicability and pro-poor policy change', as listed in the CLIFF loan criteria earlier in the chapter. The aim is to catalyse change not only within government but also within other institutions such as banks and donor agencies. The projects that receive CLIFF loans and support have been designed to either:

- create and implement new policies;
- catalyse implementation of dormant policies; or
- improve policy implementation, particularly focusing on re-orienting recognized practice such that communities control, steer and manage slum upgrading initiatives and the resources involved.

Measuring the impact that CLIFF has had on policy and practice can be complex and difficult to assess, since there are numerous other factors that may result in any particular outcome. However, it is possible to identify some of the ways in which CLIFF either has played or is playing a significant role in influencing policy and practice. These include:

- Testing and improving the SRA policy and underlying systems, to see how they can successfully enable community-led housing developments to go ahead. For example, developing projects in different locations around the city; carrying out relocation and rehabilitation as well as *in situ* upgrading developments; implementing developments on private as well as public land; and improving design and quality standards.
- Influencing policy and practice within banks towards lending for community-led slum development projects, using the growing portfolio of projects to demonstrate both organizational capacity and future business opportunities.
- Testing and improving VAMBAY housing subsidy policy and practice, for example, by changing policy on the use of housing subsidies in the city of Pune to emphasize cluster developments; by supporting the blending of subsidies with savings and loans so that housing can be built to a higher specification; and by encouraging communities from other cities and states to explore such an arrangement with their respective municipalities.
- Providing a means for previously unutilized *bidi*-worker housing subsidies to be drawn down, and testing and improving policy and practice in the process.
- Demonstrating the first large-scale community-led slum development project in the state of Karnataka.
- Contributing to the Indian Alliance's ability to engage in significant national-level debates, committees and task forces on improving India's housing and

sanitation strategies, and improve norms and standards in resettlement, through supporting relocation and rehabilitation projects.

How CLIFF has influenced the policy and practice of international development agencies is less clear, and more needs to be done to understand this better. However, within Homeless International, CLIFF has proved to be an experience that requires an engagement and relationship with partners that is far deeper than that required for standard grant giving. Interfacing between international development agency protocols such as the World Bank Trust funds and local community processes has required capacity building within Homeless International. It is challenging to make both local and international requirements align in a manner that ensures that issues of governance, transparency and procurement procedures are not ignored or side stepped, but adapted within the local context in a manner that strengthens and assists the scaling-up process. This has been a learning experience for Homeless International, as well as for Nirman and the wider Indian Alliance, and at times the relationship between Homeless International and the Indian Alliance has involved a high degree of tension. This has been because, within a new context, disagreements and contention over ways of understanding what has happened have arisen and taken time to be resolved. Without the long-standing relationship that preceded CLIFF and the high levels of trust that had developed historically between the two agencies, it would have been far more difficult to negotiate solutions and emerge from the tensions with a greater degree of collaborative understanding. That said, CLIFF has had an enormous influence on Homeless International and helped to focus its commitment on continuing to broaden and deepen the range of financial services that are made accessible to the poor.

Impact on the community repertoire to act and manage

The community repertoire refers to the strength and scale of community organizations, which through their federations are able to access the support provided by the Indian Alliance and CLIFF. Measuring impact in this area is as complex as that of measuring impact on policy and practice, but again it is possible to identify some of the ways in which CLIFF has had an influence. These include:

- An increase in the number of people and communities that have been exposed to the processes associated with community-led slum development projects, including negotiations with government authorities, project design and development, and construction management.
- Deepening the skill base of individuals within Mahila Milan and NSDF who have taken major responsibility for implementing and managing larger-scale projects.
- A larger number of locations in which there is capacity at the community level to undertake community-led slum development.
- Stronger construction skills and more people benefiting from construction-based livelihoods. For example, construction contractors are now required to

give a minimum of 30 per cent of the unskilled work and skilled work to slum dwellers, and the Indian Alliance has helped many slum dwellers to set-up their own construction businesses.

Organizational and professional support

The relationship between communities and professionals has been subject to considerable discussion within the Indian Alliance and Homeless International. The monitoring framework for CLIFF specifically addresses this issue:

> *The [Indian] Alliance's approach to resettlement and rehabilitation which forms part of the portfolio of projects that CLIFF is supporting, challenges the traditional notion of the professional as 'expert' in the planning and implementation process. However, while many of the activities that professionals undertake in a traditional process are challenged, there are still nevertheless important areas where professional support to the community is necessary. It has been widely shown that professionals hold a number of class, gender and ethnic-based stereotypes about the poor, which hinders their understanding and ability to address poverty. The [Indian] Alliance has challenged these assumptions and has created a new way for professionals to work with community organizations that are based on building respect, equality and trust, and these are crucial to the success of CLIFF-supported initiatives. (Satterthwaite* et al. *2004).*

The development of capacity by professionals to engage with communities as equals and offer appropriate support is therefore very important.

The Indian Alliance has developed working relationships with a number of professionals, some of whom have continued to work with the Indian Alliance

---

Box 7.2   Developing the Oshiwara I housing scheme

'The neighbours were watching. When it was clear that the Nirman-constructed Oshiwara I project of 780 households was going ahead smoothly, the landowners of the adjoining site approached the Indian Alliance with an even more ambitious project. Their proposal was for the Indian Alliance to build tenements for over 2,000 households – the Indian Alliance's largest construction project in Mumbai. Discussions led to a Memorandum of Understanding being signed in August 2004 and foundation work began shortly after.

In what is named Oshiwara II, *tabelas* or buffalo sheds figure prominently among the encroachers. In all, 372 slum dwellers on site will be given tenements in four buildings, many *tabelas* need to be shifted, and negotiations are underway with three printing presses on site to exchange their land for free space in new multi-storeyed buildings. Since large parts of private land have been encroached upon, the landowners are keen to partner with the federation, which can negotiate with residents who have encroached on the space. This is one of the federation's key strengths: the ability to negotiate with slum dwellers on site, and protect their interests, while simultaneously taking into account the other's point of view...'

Extract from SPARC (2005a: 39)

Photo 7.1 The first phase of the Oshiwara housing scheme with the buffalo sheds in the foreground
Source: Homeless International

for many years. The number of professionals that are required to support the Indian Alliance's operations has increased with the implementation of CLIFF because of the size of the project portfolio that is now being managed. Professionals who work with the Indian Alliance have in some cases found the federation process frustrating, and have on occasions attempted to take control of projects, particularly during the initial stages. Some have become more accustomed to community-led approaches and continue to work with the Indian Alliance, but some have not. Experience to date reveals that professionals require both the necessary technical skills and the right attitude to allow them to support communities. In particular, the Indian Alliance is clear that professionals must treat communities as the clients who control the process. Perhaps one of the biggest achievements in the area of professional support is that the Indian Alliance has signed a Memorandum of Understanding with two civil service training institutions and is involved in programmes designed for senior civil servants who will be responsible for implementation of city-wide sanitation and water provision.

Main risks and challenges

Delays. Delays in obtaining permissions and payments from government authorities can prolong construction and lead to an increase in financing requirements and associated costs. CLIFF has helped mitigate some of this risk by providing the financing required to continue construction when payments from government have been delayed. In addition, the Indian Alliance has become far more efficient in putting together the necessary paperwork to obtain permissions and repayments quickly. However, delays continue and still represent a significant obstacle to the smooth implementation of projects.

Resistance from vested interests. CLIFF has sought to support community-led projects that challenge and change existing policy and practice, in other words projects which seek to change 'business as usual'. As a result, those who have long benefited from the status quo have begun to feel threatened, and in some cases have sought to undermine the more transparent processes promoted by the Indian Alliance's community-driven models. Those who have found the developments particularly challenging include commercial contractors and their

Box 7.3   Political interference in the BSDP project

In August 2004, the Indian Alliance received a legal notice regarding one of the toilets it was constructing as part of the BSDP. This toilet was being built in a slum at Juhu Tara Road, Santa Cruz (W) in the K-West Ward of Mumbai. The president of the community-based organization in this slum at Santa Cruz accused SPARC, among others, of delaying and obstructing construction. This baffled Indian Alliance members, considering that SPARC, despite local political opposition and threats, had been pushing forward to complete construction work. There had been a temporary pause in construction work because, on two different occasions, local police officials had detained labourers on site and in one case, even the contractor who was building the toilet.

The politics behind this slum toilet is that a local MLA (an elected representative) does not want the Indian Alliance to build a community-style toilet block: he wanted to build toilet blocks in 'his' slum with the help of Minister of Parliament funds. The fundamental issue here was that the municipality-commissioned federation-built toilets opposes the patronage-style delivery of toilet blocks. The federation approach also involves community contribution, participation and control, which is deeply threatening to local politicians.

SPARC filed a reply in the Mumbai High Court that the Indian Alliance was ready to construct toilet blocks. However, once again construction work was stopped by police authorities, who arrested the labourers, but this time the Indian Alliance contacted the Police Commissioner who instructed the Santa Cruz police officials to let the labourers go as they were being held on baseless charges. Subsequently, the city authorities withdrew permission to build a toilet in this slum. The Indian Alliance must constantly manage and attempt to mitigate such political risks, but delays and, as in this case, stoppages are often problematic. Juggling between two opposing perspectives is a tough process for the municipality as well.

(extract from SPARC 2004: 26)

allies within government authorities, local politicians and individuals with vested interests within particular communities. As the Indian Alliance grows in capacity and expands its operations, it will become more of a threat to more parties, and so this risk is likely to grow.

Loss of knowledge and relationships. Another major risk faced is that of loss of learning within key institutions resulting from staff turnover. Maintaining constructive relationships with government agencies, banks and international development agencies means an ongoing investment in developing relationships with key staff to ensure that they understand the work of the Indian Alliance and develop trust in the processes involved in community-led developments. It is a common policy in Indian government institutions for officials to be in post for a maximum of three years, and the reality is that officials often get transferred before this time period is up. In Chapter 4 it has already been mentioned that in the corporate sector staff turnover can also be high. This is understandable given the nature of the sector, where people leave positions more frequently for promotions and higher salaries. For example, between 2000 and 2001, all of the 15 bankers from Citibank who had helped put the loan agreement together for the Rajiv Indira-Suryodaya scheme were transferred out of Mumbai (Spicer and Husock 2003). The Indian Alliance has sought to mitigate the risks associated with staff turnover by broadening relationships within institutions. However, the Indian Alliance is often proposing a departure from 'business as usual,' by requiring decisions from senior personnel whose longevity in a particular position may be insufficient to get the job done.

Securing bank financing. Convincing banks to lend for community-led slum upgrading has proved extremely difficult and time consuming. Banks are beginning to see lending for slum development as a future growth area, and are using the Indian Alliance's demonstrated capacity as a way to explore this. However, nobody knows whether lending for slum development will become a norm in banks and, even if it does, whether NGOs and communities will be the parties to whom they will lend. In most cases banks still require guarantees to secure loans because of requirements laid down by the Reserve Bank of India, which regulates banking practice within India. The requirement for guarantees can be a constraint requiring additional resources as well as time and effort. One thing is, however, clear. The attempt to engage banks must go on because it is only by mobilizing significant levels of domestic capital that the financing requirements of large-scale upgrading in a city such as Mumbai will be met.

Policy change. A significant risk encountered has been that of unanticipated changes in governmental approaches and policies, at different levels of government. For example, no one could have foreseen the manner in which the Coastal Regulation Zone legislation was to be implemented in Mumbai and how it would affect the Rajiv Indira-Suryodaya scheme. A more worrying trend has been the increasing threat of forced eviction by the state. CLIFF and the long-standing experience of the Indian Alliance have provided a basis for projects to be implemented in times of policy uncertainty, whilst simultaneously negotiating with the state for a partnership approach that can create alternatives to forced evictions. Riding out political uncertainty becomes a feasible option when communities are well organized and have financial resources and external support available. However, policy change still presents a significant risk and is discussed at greater length in Chapter 4.

IMPLEMENTATION OF CLIFF IN KENYA

Implementation of CLIFF in Kenya began in 2005. This section is largely based on the 2005 CLIFF Annual Review (Homeless International 2005d) and begins with a consideration of the contrasts with the Indian experience, before outlining the portfolio of projects and assessing the lessons to date. More information on implementation in Kenya can be found in the first monitoring report (Hughes 2005).

Contrasts with India

There are many parallels between the challenges facing the urban poor in India and Kenya, yet there are also significant differences. Whereas India has relatively well-developed policies for slum development at various levels of government, local and national government in Kenya is still going through the process of policy formulation regarding land, housing and basic services for the urban poor. Government spending on housing declined from KSh136.6 million (approx. £1,000,000) in 1998 to nil in 2002/2003. Despite new initiatives like the Kenya Slum Upgrading Programme, the national housing budget for 2004 remained a mere KSh23 million (approx. £165,000, Government of Kenya 2003). Investment in infrastructure has also been minimal, particularly with respect to provision of services to poor urban communities. By ratifying the Millennium Development Goals, however, the Kenyan Government has made political commitments to dealing with urban poverty. Local government has had an increased focus on poverty alleviation in the last five years, but poor urban governance makes the creation of effective financing partnerships with bi-lateral and multi-lateral agencies, NGOs, the private sector and communities difficult. It is however worth appreciating that some local authorities like Nairobi City Council have illustrated a willingness and capacity to partner with slum communities and to introduce flexibility in applying planning and development regulations.

Whereas India has a relatively well-developed financial sector that has become aware of the bankability of community-led development projects and has at least begun to invest in these initiatives, the financial sector in Kenya is generally much further removed from the urban poor. While conventional housing finance for the middle- and high-income segments of society is available, there exists a vacuum for low-income housing finance, as the poor cannot provide security for credit. Microfinance institutions have proliferated, but have yet to offer the kind of medium- and long-term financing required for major housing development. Kenya's policy environment currently lacks instruments that would mitigate against risk or encourage private sector investment in the lower end of the market. Poor settlement planning, lack of secure tenure and high poverty levels also hinder investment by the formal financial sector in what is potentially a huge low-income market.

It is also important to note that the Kenyan Alliance is at a much earlier stage in its development than the Indian Alliance. Whereas the Indian Alliance has been working together for around 20 years, the Kenyan Alliance has only been working together for about 5 years. Furthermore there are key differences in the implementation of CLIFF in Kenya and India: in Kenya implementation only began in 2005, with a budget of just £100,000, whereas in India CLIFF officially began in 2003 with a much larger budget.

The portfolio of projects supported by CLIFF

The £100,000 allocated to Kenya from the original budget for India has been used to provide £15,000 for operational costs and £85,000 of capital. The £85,000 capital will support five community projects. The strategic intention in financing these projects is to build precedents in community-led development and to further strengthen the financing systems within the Kenyan Alliance. The projects are described briefly below.

Huruma and Soweto Kahawa housing. In 2003 and 2004 communities in Huruma and Soweto Kahawa negotiated for permissions from Nairobi City Council to carry out *in situ* development of the lands they occupy and for agreement that they would be given secure land tenure by the City Council thereafter. By early

Photo 7.2   Housing in Kambi Moto, Nairobi, Kenya
Source: Homeless International

2004, 34 houses had been completed in Kambi Moto, one of the Huruma settlements, funded by AMT bridge funds and repayable by the community over a period of five to seven years. CLIFF has provided loan finance for a further 10 houses at Kambi Moto plus an initial 11 houses at Soweto Kahawa. In both cases, the houses being built are intended to be the initial phase of whole settlement developments, of 270 houses in the case of Kambi Moto and 673 houses at Soweto Kahawa. Through the two projects the processes used by the federation, such as enumeration and community planning, are becoming recognized as legitimate slum development tools by the city.

Toi Market sanitation block. Toi Market is an informal market within Kibera, the largest slum in Nairobi, which has approximately 3,000 trading stalls. The market's saving scheme has a membership of 1,000 members who consistently save a total of £1,000 a week. The scheme has a well-developed loaning system, with up to 65 per cent of the savings continually in circulation as small business and welfare loans. Sanitation facilities in the market consisted of a few pit latrines around the market and construction of a City Council toilet block within the market had stalled years ago. The saving scheme negotiated with the City Council for transfer of ownership and management of the part-built toilet facility. The saving scheme then applied for a loan of around £2,000 from AMT to complete the construction. The toilet block was completed in 2005 and is being managed by the savings scheme on a pay-per-use basis.

Toi Market and Ghetto land purchase. Members of the Toi Market savings scheme have also used CLIFF loan finance to purchase 80 acres of land on the outskirts of Nairobi for settlement. The land cost £65,000, the community has raised £12,250 upfront and CLIFF has provided £52,750 in loan finance, to be

Photo 7.3 The new toilet block at Toi market, Nairobi, Kenya

Source: Homeless International

repaid by the community over a period of 1 to 2 years. The savings scheme at Ghetto, part of the slum area of Huruma, has gone on to buy land on a similar basis, in their case costing £14,000, of which 80 per cent has been financed via CLIFF.

Lessons to date from Kenya

In Kenya, where there are no existing land or housing subsidies for the poor, providing financing to poor communities has proved an effective way to obtain resources from the state. In three of the projects that CLIFF is supporting the communities have been able to obtain planning assistance and free transfer of land ownership. In the other two projects, for land purchase, the community will negotiate with local government for water, sewage and road access as they undertake development of the land. Demand for financing community projects has been higher than the supply of funding; AMT has considered four applications for land purchase alone. Capital funds in addition to the £85,000 are therefore urgently needed. Community-led development of housing and services requires considerable investment in community mobilization, technical support and negotiation with local authorities. Whilst there are several communities moving towards such projects, there will be a need for significant grant funds for technical support in addition to loan funds for construction costs if the process is to succeed.

LEARNING EMERGING FROM CLIFF

A detailed analysis of the learning emerging from CLIFF can be found in McLeod (2005a); key lessons are summarized below.

Risk. 'Bridging the finance gap' identified a spectrum of risks that were being shouldered by the urban poor when they proactively engaged with local authorities and started to negotiate with banks to finance slum upgrading, resettlement and the construction of basic infrastructure. Experience in implementing CLIFF has helped to clarify which of these risks poses the greatest challenges, and has provided an opportunity to develop and test a range of risk management and mitigation strategies. In the case of India, these risks and challenges have been discussed earlier in this chapter.

The interface between informal and formal systems. One of the biggest challenges in establishing CLIFF has been to find the right balance between formal systems recognized by professional agencies, and informal systems upon which community organization and networking is based. This conundrum applies in areas such as financial management, procurement, communication and governance. Experience to date has shown, for example, that formal CLIFF prescriptions and the associated logic of professionals involved can be alienating for the communities who established the social infrastructure on which CLIFF is based. At the same time, it is difficult for professionals to absorb or understand the complex nature of informal community systems that have enabled CLIFF to function successfully. As a result, in India, SPARC, Nirman and to a lesser extent Homeless International have had to act in a mediating role, negotiating and navigating a bridge between formal and informal processes. Inevitably this has placed significant pressure on the agencies, their staff and their relationships with other stakeholders

Efficiency and efficacy. Precisely because all of the projects supported by CLIFF either challenge or test assumptions that exist regarding how slum development can most effectively be addressed it is vital to maintain an open mind about what might constitute 'efficiency' in the long run. CLIFF-supported projects are primarily chosen to establish whether the approaches that are being used are effective in delivering solutions that work for the poor, the state and banks. This involves a considerable degree of experimentation and learning on the part of all those involved. The costs involved arguably amount to the 'research and development' input of new approaches. Over time, as the lessons become clear, it should become far easier to focus on efficiency.

Scale. As CLIFF projects prove successful, new opportunities arise for scaling up. For example, the success of the Oshiwara I housing scheme has made bank financing of a much larger scheme, Oshiwara II, far easier. As banks become familiar with the community-led processes involved there is some evidence that they also begin to think about longer-term financing, and discussions are now underway for accessing credit lines for the Nirman portfolio as a whole. This rapid expansion in effective demand and in potential financing requires increasingly detailed planning and co-ordination to ensure that the portfolio as a whole is not placed at risk.

Both the Indian and Kenyan Alliances have been able to use CLIFF loan finance to challenge planning regulations and practice. This is going to be more and more important if planners' thinking is going to move beyond the existing urban population and to look at housing that will be affordable for the next generation. The capacity to challenge existing planning and building policies and standards will be important for both *in situ* and new site developments because both will be needed if delivery at scale is to be achieved. Variation in project size is also likely to be necessary, combining some much larger projects with many smaller-scale initiatives.

Continuity and replication. When a project has demonstrated real success, there is frequently a drive to replicate at the earliest opportunity. CLIFF cannot operate without a significant level of community capacity within organizations of the urban poor. The success to date of CLIFF in India is to a large extent due to the organizational base built within the Indian Alliance over the last 20 years, and it is critical that this is understood and recognized.

The CLIFF Advisory Group asked Homeless International to work with SDI to determine a list of criteria that they felt reflected the items that are required for successful replication of CLIFF. In response SDI has developed criteria for the development of facilities that focus upon the use of financial resources from external non-grant sources. These criteria are divided up into 'internal' criteria (i.e. within poor communities and their support networks) and 'external' criteria (i.e. broader contextual factors). External criteria:

■ Land policies that allow the poor to take on housing development.

■ A stable economy, and with single digit interest rates.

■ A banking sector with whom the urban poor can talk and with money to lend over and above routine operations.

■ A willingness within municipal authorities to consider working partnerships with the urban poor.

Internal criteria:

■ A federation that saves and has the capacity to manage and supervise a savings and credit process.

■ The capacity to examine and support community federation networks in exploring options and visions for housing and related ingredients.

■ The capacity and demonstrated ability to dialogue with state and municipal institutions around the issues of land, policy and other resources which are needed to supplement what people cannot obtain themselves.

■ The capability to design and manage pilot projects, technically and organizationally.

■ A strong relationship of trust between the community federations and their support organizations (NGOs).

Moreover, it is important to consider what criteria might determine an institution's ability to implement CLIFF-like facilities. CLIFF is, amongst other things, about innovation, taking risks and challenging 'business as usual.' This risk-taking ethos separates CLIFF from many other development interventions. In order to be able to implement a facility such as CLIFF, experience to date suggests that the institutions most directly involved in implementation need to possess quite specific characteristics as part of their beliefs and working style. They need to be innovators, risk takers and challengers of 'business as usual approaches', even where this may raise initial obstacles to a given project or process.

Different national and city contexts mean that lending priorities may vary between and within countries. For example, collective land purchase has emerged as a priority lending area in Kenya, whereas in Mumbai land prices are so high that land purchase would be out of the question. More needs to be understood about the conditions under which collective land purchase by the poor is worthwhile. It is important to identify how variation in the development of local financial markets and in the availability of subsidies determine the most effective means of ensuring access to development capital by the urban poor.

During the start-up phase of CLIFF there were some confusions about priorities. On the one hand, communities were pushed to negotiate and begin projects to prove that there was a demand for a capital financing facility. On the other hand, new institutions such as advisory groups and existing institutions, for example management boards, needed to take time to deepen their understanding of community processes; their natural tendency has been to recommend slower disbursement of capital until they feel confident about projects and processes. There is a tension between the need for action on the ground to demonstrate what is possible, and caution and clarification from advisers who have to ensure systems are devised and procedures created to ensure accountability to those who give funds. On the funding-side, therefore, it might be useful when planning new CLIFF-like programmes to allocate a portion of the capital budget as a grant given immediately to the local implementing partner, the use of which is not reliant on formal approvals from newly emerging advisory groups. This would enable current projects to maintain at least some continuity of funding, whilst enabling participating institutions to build the systems, relationships, understanding and channels of communication required to establish formal approval systems and advisory roles that add genuine value. The first CLIFF monitoring report emphasized that future CLIFF-like facilities may need to incorporate such a grant-funding component, particularly in countries where organizations of the poor do not have the same length and depth of experience as the Indian Alliance.

Contributing to the agendas and priorities of donors and government authorities. It is not clear as yet how donors and government authorities will be able to use the learning that is emerging from CLIFF. There are some interesting possibilities. For example, the potential for using debt forgiveness funds, debt-equity swaps and donor grants for slum upgrading and infrastructure provision through CLIFF-like facilities is considerable. If slum upgrading, resettlement and infrastructure pro-vision in urban areas becomes more effectively integrated into Poverty Reduction Strategy Papers (PRSPs) and the other national strategy documents this potential would be greatly enhanced. It is clear that interventions of the kind that CLIFF supports have a major role to play in addressing the broader challenges of the Millennium Development Goals. The challenge now is to mainstream the approach.

FUTURE OPTIONS

At the moment CLIFF remains a pilot project. It is reaching the end of its first phase and has already demonstrated that providing direct access to project loans for community-led initiatives can have an important multiplier effect. In India just over £5 million in capital has so far been utilized and, as a result, a portfolio of projects valued in excess of £25 million is being implemented with the active engagement of four banks and a range of government agencies. The second local CLIFF has been initiated in Kenya, but it is far too early to judge how effective it will be. A mid-term evaluation of CLIFF is scheduled to take place early in 2006 and will hopefully provide some conclusions regarding the efficacy of the approach and some guidance on how the process should be developed in the future.

From the perspective of the teams implementing CLIFF there is concern regarding how other national alliances might be able to benefit from the approach. There are national alliances that have already established a track record in implementing projects that have set new precedents and which appear to be scalable. However they do not have access to the level of capital financing that CLIFF has provided in India and donors have not, as yet, been willing to look at wider replication of the CLIFF approach. The evaluation should provide some guidance on how this obvious demand can be met. The other question is clearly how the principles and processes emerging from CLIFF can be used by other agencies – particularly governmental agencies that are managing large infrastructure and settlement upgrading projects. Donors negotiating large-scale grants and loans for such purposes might also benefit from an exposure to the lessons that are emerging.

CHAPTER EIGHT

'This house believes that the private finance market will never fund major slum upgrading'

Ruth McLeod with Dave Hughes

INTRODUCTION

We as urban development professionals sometimes try to protect ourselves from the scale of the challenge, from the awfulness of what is happening, by the terminology we use, but really we're talking about places where people live in wretched, squalid, overcrowded conditions, where they are vulnerable to being turned out at any moment. The scale of the challenge takes my breath away, and the scale of the investment needs are staggering. If you take the one billion slum dwellers who will live in cities by 2020, the investment expected to be needed is something like US$1 trillion (over £500 billion). (Gavin McGillivray, DFID, chairing a debate on the motion that 'This house believes that the private finance market will never fund major slum upgrading' at the World Urban Forum in September 2004.)

In this statement Gavin McGillivray provides a graphic backdrop to the need to engage the formal private sector in financing investment in urban infrastructure and housing. Without their engagement it is difficult to envisage the scale of intervention that is clearly needed. Although the debate organized by Homeless International at the World Urban Forum focused upon the financial sector, our work with partner organizations across Asia and Africa emphasizes that the private sector is not just made up of financiers. It is composed of a diverse array of organizations and individuals located in both formal and informal markets. This chapter explores how that diversity of interest is currently engaged in the activities that Homeless International supports, and suggests how future work with the private sector might be strengthened. Throughout the chapter we have interspersed comments from some of the speakers who participated in the World Urban Forum debate chaired by Gavin McGillivray in Barcelona.

CONSENSUS OR DIVERGENCE?

The introduction to this book summarizes the historical context within which Homeless International's work has developed, and identifies the prominence given to market-based solutions during the 1980s and 1990s. As the World Bank, UN-Habitat and donors began to talk in terms of the 'enabling' role of government, discussion also focused on the crucial contribution that could and should be made by the private sector. It was assumed that their involvement, particularly as financiers and developers, would provide the basis for developing solutions at scale and, within the international development sector, a broad consensus has emerged on the importance of private sector involvement in poverty reduction. However this surface consensus masks a considerable divergence in opinion over the nature and remit of the private sector role. Different stakeholders, even where they are attempting to co-operate, can comprehend the private sector in entirely different ways. There are differing opinions of what constitutes the private sector, differing views on what its role can be in slum upgrading, resettlement and infrastructure provision, and contention over the promotion of privatization of utilities and other services.

Perhaps most significantly from Homeless International's perspective, discussions have centred upon 'public–private' partnerships with relatively little attention to 'people–public–private partnerships' that recognize that the involvement of poor communities is also essential in urban development. We feel that discussion of 'people–public–private partnerships' brings an additional question to the fore, namely 'what are the terms of engagement by which the private sector is drawn into the process of urban development, and who defines them?' Homeless International's experiences of private sector involvement, described in the following paragraphs, illustrate both the diversity of the private sector and the way in which organizations of the poor and their NGO partners have sought to harness private sector involvement to further benefit the urban poor themselves.

Over the last decade, Homeless International has worked extensively to develop partnerships with banks and other formal financial institutions, and to facilitate links between these financial institutions, Homeless International's partner organizations and the organizations of the poor with whom they work. Some of these institutions are clearly identified as private sector – Citibank, for example – whereas others may increasingly operate along private sector lines but technically belong to the realm of the public. The National Housing Bank (NHB), a subsidiary of the Reserve Bank of India, is a case in point. The NHB is a secondary lender. It refinances banks that have provided housing loans to low-income households via rural self-help groups. If it can develop an understanding of lending for upgrading and infrastructure provision in urban areas, and support other banks in extending these kinds of loans, the potential for scaling-up financing through commercial (i.e. private sector) banks is significant (this was discussed in greater depth in Chapter 6).

As the example of NHB demonstrates, the line separating private from public sector can be quite blurred. This is even more so where parastatal organizations and public–private partnerships have been established, for example, in the provision of utility services. A further complication arises because the private sector is not necessarily located entirely in the formal sector. There are many enterprises operating in the informal sector that may not be formally registered in the sense that they report to a regulatory body and pay taxes. However their day-to-day operations are essentially those of commercial enterprises within a competitive market. They operate for profit, they make investments that entail risk, and they compete in a large and dynamic market where supply and demand determine price. In practice they are dynamic parts of the private sector and their dynamism has been increasingly evident, as our partners' work has scaled up. In recent years, as projects have increased in size and complexity (particularly with the support of CLIFF, as described in Chapter 7), a growing number of community-based enterprises have become established in different areas of construction and have collectively submitted competitive tenders for the delivery of municipal infrastructure in the form of community toilets. The individuals involved have taken on responsibility for managing specific projects such as the construction of a toilet block, and some have also become subcontractors on larger sites (with responsibility for internal brickwork or tiling, for example). In both cases, over time, the nascent businesses become registered for tax purposes. So, as community capacity has grown, slum and pavement dwellers have become active members of the private sector themselves, frequently moving from informal to formal status as they become recognized community subcontractors, developing skills and experience particularly in construction and maintenance-related areas. Indeed the Indian Alliance have encouraged this, providing start-up capital and technical support to slum dwellers setting up such businesses, reasoning that the poor can and should be able to benefit from the work generated by investment in improving slums.

As the scale of the work that Homeless International supports has increased, our understanding of the diversity of the private sector has also increased. Private land owners, commercial contractors, construction professionals, bankers, building material suppliers, and businesses ranging in size from tiny to huge have played their part in the development of initiatives on the ground. Sometimes relationships with these agencies have been competitive. For example, the success of community tendering for contracts to construct toilets in Pune and Mumbai created considerable resentment among contractors and a backlash of resistance with contractors trying to prevent members of Mahila Milan submitting tenders (see for example SPARC 2004: 14). There have also sometimes been conflicts in relationships with private landowners and commercial enterprises competing for land.

Fortunately, in a growing number of cases, new partnerships have developed which have been able to draw on the strengths of a range of organizations to the benefit of all. For example, the Oshiwara housing scheme in Mumbai, which was described in more detail in Chapter 7 and in Box 8.2, exemplifies the potential for community–private sector partnerships involving organizations of the urban poor, private landowners and large contractors. In Malawi, the local federation is entering into a joint-venture partnership with a private entrepreneur to produce lime, which is needed for masonry and paint in the housing schemes being implemented by its members. In Kenya there are plans for the Pamoja Trust and Muungano wa Wanavijiji, the local federation, to collaborate with a commercial newspaper and distribution agency to print and circulate community newspapers. The growing recognition that community-driven projects can be more viably financed when they incorporate internal cross subsidies from commercial sales is also beginning to lead to an exploration of how such commercial development can be enhanced by effective marketing and sales promotion, a feature normally associated with private sector real estate developers.

As described in Chapter 6, the origins of Homeless International's engagement with the private sector emerged from a concern with scaling up our access, and that of our partners, to capital financing for housing and infrastructure development. When it became clear that Homeless International's grant funding would be insufficient to support scaling up of community-driven approaches, we established a guarantee fund in order to encourage banks to fill the glaring financial gap that existed. The story of the guarantee fund has been related in more detail in Chapter 6 and will not be repeated here. However it is important to note that much of our understanding of the private sector has emerged through using the fund in practice. With the guarantee fund, Homeless International took its first steps in seeking to obtain resources from the commercial banking sector. The first phase of loans to YCO, described in Chapter 6, relied for their original source funds on KfW (the German Development Bank), channelled through a private sector institution (the Housing Development Finance Corporation, HDFC), and a government agency (the Housing and Urban Development Corporation, HUDCO). The lending that both organizations extended to low-income groups was, in effect, subsidized by KfW, although their lending practices, at least in the case of HDFC, proved highly risk averse.

Our next foray into guarantees was with Citibank, exploring options for financing the Rajiv Indira-Suryodaya scheme that has been described in more detail in Chapter 6. With Citibank the situation was rather different. Citibank was not being asked to lend funds that had been sourced from a donor. It was lending its own funds but it was not entirely clear whether this initiative was being driven by notions of philanthropy, or constituted a serious exploration of potential market extension. Indeed initial negotiations with Citibank tended to involve more personnel from their marketing and PR department than their credit assessors. Certainly one of the key questions, when considering the role of the private sector in banking, is whether collaboration with NGOs and communities amounts only to an attempt to demonstrate corporate social responsibility, or whether it can form part of a genuine business model. The two are not necessarily incompatible, but it is important to be clear where the emphasis lies.

For the private sector role to be fulfilled in the manner envisaged in the Habitat Agenda adopted at the Second United Nations Conference on Human Settlements (Habitat II) held in Istanbul in 1996, their input has to coincide with their business interest. Investment in housing, infrastructure and related services has to be a strategic and substantial element within their business model, if the kind of scaled interventions needed to address current and future urban growth are to occur. At the moment there does not appear to be convincing evidence that this level of involvement is occurring, although it could be argued that it is still relatively early days and financing from banks for CLIFF-related projects now seems to be accelerating (Jack *et al.* 2005). It is also true that, in the early stages of a bank's involvement, banks, NGOs and community groups face an extremely steep learning curve. The role of individuals (leading bank staff, NGO staff and community leaders) in developing and maintaining a working relationship is very important. Over time, however, it is vital that these relationships be institutionalized, such that the learning that emerges from their experiences is captured and codified into systems that provide the basis for replication and scaling up. Often this is problematic because of the extremely high turnover of staff in banking institutions, particularly in a context of rapidly expanding financial markets.

WORKING WITH THE PRIVATE SECTOR: KEY LESSONS

Working with a range of actors

As has already been noted, it is important to recognize that the private sector is made up from a far wider and more diverse constituency than just financial institutions. In slum upgrading, for example, building links with banks is crucial to leveraging the local resources that are the prerequisite for genuine scale, but the actual process of large-scale upgrading can only be realized if it also includes involvement of a wider range of private sector groups. These can vary from community contractors to private landowners; from architects to commercial contractors; or from skilled tradesmen and women to building material suppliers. The following case boxes describe projects being implemented by Homeless International's partner in India (the Alliance of SPARC, the National Slum Dwellers'

Photo 8.1 Community toilet block in Dharavi, Mumbai, built by the Indian Alliance through the BSDP project

Source: Homeless International

Box 8.1   How the Bombay Sewerage Disposal Project created a new level of private sector involvement

Numerous small-scale community contractors have been involved in the Bombay Sewerage Disposal Project (BSDP), which is a World Bank-funded programme for universal sanitation in slum areas of Mumbai (formerly Bombay). As part of the overall programme, community contractors, organized through the Indian Alliance of SPARC, National Slum Dwellers Federation and Mahila Milan, succeeded in bidding for a contract to build 211 toilet blocks, such as the one shown in the photo. After the Indian Alliance had bid for the blocks en masse, the construction of individual blocks was then subcontracted to numerous small-scale community contractors. The vast majority of them would not have been able to set up in business in the first place were it not for the programme. In essence, the programme has therefore created a whole new level of the private sector, made up of slum residents themselves.

Given that comprehensive slum upgrading needs to be not just about housing but also about sustainable sources of income for residents, this must be seen as a significant progression, as it ensures that benefits are retained within communities rather than going to outside speculators. It should also be noted, however, that such a shift requires significant support from NGOs during the transition, enabling community contractors to get to grips with tax regulations and to withstand pressure from vested interests.

Federation and Mahila Milan), and demonstrate what this diversity within the private sector can mean in practice. Both projects have received bridge financing via the Community-Led Infrastructure Finance Facility (CLIFF, see Chapter 7), but the level of financing required from CLIFF has declined as private sector involvement has increased.

Maintaining a poverty reduction focus through communities' involvement

Private sector institutions are primarily motivated by minimizing their costs and maximizing their profits in the shortest possible time. The challenge for those seeking private sector involvement in poverty reduction is to harness their involvement without losing the focus on effective poverty reduction. The two projects described in Boxes 8.1 and 8.2 show the importance of a civil society counterpart to the public and private sector institutions, such that they contribute to development solutions determined by organizations of the poor and the NGOs with whom they work. In other words, organized community groups and NGOs have developed the capacity to set the terms of engagement in a way which does not disenfranchise the poor, which maintains the poverty reduction focus but which also appeals to the private sector. Perhaps most importantly, organized communities directly monitor the performance of private sector institutions in such projects, helping to ensure that profit motives do not overshadow the poverty reduction objectives upon which the projects are based. The 'people' dimension of 'people–public–private partnerships' is vital in this regard.

Box 8.2   Diverse private sector involvement in the Oshiwara housing scheme, Mumbai

The Oshiwara scheme is a large and complex project developed to house families being resettled as a result of city-wide infrastructure upgrading in Mumbai. The project, one of the most recent CLIFF projects, demonstrates a number of levels of engagement with the private sector. In all cases, Homeless International and the Indian Alliance provided the links bringing the organizations together to implement the project. The development is at a significant scale, with 760 families to be housed in the first phase and 2,500 families in the second phase. Private sector involvement occurs in four main areas.

Private landowners. Private land owners approached our local partners, the Indian Alliance, for assistance in developing their land for a number of reasons. Firstly, they recognized their own lack of competence in dealing with the complex social issues associated with resettlement; secondly, they lacked the capacity to navigate the government systems and procedures associated with designing and implementing a project of this type; and they also knew that financing such a large development would be difficult. Their motivation to enter into a development partnership was, nonetheless, high, because the scheme would take place as part of the World Bank-funded Mumbai Urban Infrastructure Project, which had as one of its terms that there are subsidies – in the form of development rights that can be sold on the open market – both for the landowner who gives their land for resettlement and for the developer who builds on it. Creating a development partnership therefore made sense to both the private landowner and to the Indian Alliance.

Private contractors. The Indian Alliance also negotiated with commercial contractors, and employed them to take on parts of the housing scheme. Between them, 10 private contractors agreed to provide pre-financing of 30 per cent of total project cost. This meant that less CLIFF bridge financing was needed, and that the risk was being shared between the Indian Alliance and the contractors. The Indian Alliance negotiated contracts with them that stated that a certain proportion of labour or subcontracting had to be sourced from slum communities, ensuring the transfer of skills for even larger-scale community contracting in future and providing income-generating opportunities for the urban poor. The contracts also stipulated high quality and design standards developed and approved by communities over time during previous construction projects.

Commercial bank involvement. Impressed by the speed and quality of construction on the first phase, ICICI, one of the largest banks in India, has provisionally agreed to provide around £2.4 million in financing for the second phase, in turn encouraging more banks to see community-led slum upgrading as a viable lending area. Homeless International will underwrite the loan using its guarantee fund, as described in Chapter 6.

Selling in the real estate market. In both the first and second phases, a small percentage of units will be sold on the open market so as to provide an element of cross-subsidy for slum dwellers. This adds a further aspect of private sector involvement, whilst also making it vital that slum dwellers understand the dynamics of the market in order to get the best possible prices.

The importance of intermediaries

All our experience supports the view that intermediary organizations are needed to bridge both informal and formal financial systems and to broker dialogue between organizations of the urban poor and government regulators. The intermediary role can be extremely difficult, as it has to carry and buffer the expectations and assumptions of all the parties involved. It is also a role, which, if successfully carried out, eliminates itself as the main actors take on full responsibility for carrying the working relationship forward. Chapter 10 looks in more detail at Homeless International's experiences in operating as an intermediary organization.

Getting to know each other

If you look at the figures all over the world for how many poor people have relationships with financial institutions, less than 5 per cent save their money in banks or take loans. Very few poor people living in urban areas have a relationship with the banks. But it's not a problem of money. Banks have lots of money – they want to lend and they make all kind of incentives to lend money to people who already have money. For the poor, their language, their way of dressing, everything is anathema to the banks. People have an irregular income, and the banks want something more recognizable, more predictable. Banks have a culture of their own, they aren't a local organization, they are not devoted to local development. (Somsook Boonyabancha, Managing Director of Community Organisations Development Institute, Thailand, speaking at the CLIFF World Urban Forum debate in June 2004.)

It is almost a truism to say that poor people are as afraid of banks as banks are of poor people. Financial exclusion has become a topic of hot debate in recent years but it is clear that one of its fundamental causes is a lack of mutual understanding and trust between the formal financial sector and the poor. Bridging the finance gap in the provision of decent shelter and infrastructure requires that this misunderstanding be addressed so that confidence in lending to the poor for housing and infrastructure can be strengthened. This process of building confidence is complex because it depends on a hard-to-define 'comfort factor', which is the intangible, intuitive sense on the part of the banker that lending in a particular context feels right (McLeod 2001a). Over the years we have found that negotiations around loans and guarantees, whilst ostensibly concerned with the details of project financing, are also in a broader sense about creating time and space for this 'comfort factor' to emerge.

This takes time, exposure to real success stories on the ground and a willingness on the part of individuals and organizations to take risk. It also takes a commitment to openness and a recognition that there may be new ways of doing things. A good example is that of the Managing Director of Citibank in Mumbai who, when asked what he had learnt from visiting the savings schemes of Mahila Milan, replied that he had been inspired by the women's recognition that 'loans work better when the borrower designs the product'. He was referring to the Mahila Milan practice of members deciding how large a loan they need and over what time they can feasibly repay it.

Establishing a mutual interest

The private sector's first, second and third priorities are profit, profit, profit. We also seek to minimize risk in order to maximize our profit, ensure management stay in their jobs and ensure stakeholders are paid enough in dividends to keep them committed to what we are doing. For slum upgrading, you are often talking about places where it is not appropriate for people to live. There is disease, you have displaced people who just stop wherever they can find somewhere to lie down – we don't even know who these people are. You [the urban poor] need to come to us, to make an approach to us, so we can assess your credentials and we can believe that you will pay us back. We need a clearly defined project where the numbers make sense. (Stephanie Baeta Ansah, Managing Director, Home Finance Corporation Bank, Ghana, speaking at the CLIFF World Urban Forum debate in June 2004.)

As projects financed by CLIFF have become larger and more complex, there has been a concomitant growth in the level and complexity of the engagement of the private sector in the schemes. This has been strongly related to the increased capacity of local slum dwellers organizations to deliver, making the potential advantage of entering into joint ventures with the private sector increasingly apparent. Interesting community–private sector partnerships are also developing in other areas of our partners' work. We have already referred to the joint venture being entered into by the Malawian Federation to ensure that they have ready access to affordable lime products. They are also exploring investing in one of the banks they use, which plans to go public in the coming year. In nearly every project, partnerships between local communities and skilled trades people are negotiated and mutually beneficial arrangements are also frequently worked out with building material and equipment suppliers.

The challenge with the banks, however, remains that of establishing the exact nature of mutual interest that might exist. That in turn requires the 'translation' of community-driven projects into a conceptual language and form that the banks can recognize and make sense of. The interview with Anil Kumar of ICICI Banks in India, which follows later in this chapter, gives some cause for optimism, tracing how the bank has developed an understanding of the work of the Indian Alliance. However Stephanie Baeta Ansah's challenge remains very real and much more structured support is needed to assist the dialogue between organizations of the urban poor, their support NGOs and banking institutions.

Developing mechanisms for practical partnerships

The question isn't really whether banks will fund slum upgrading but whether this will ever be on sufficient scale to make a difference. What we've heard is that there are lots of examples where it has been made to work, even in places where you would think it would be extremely difficult to make it work. But what we have seen is that you can't say, 'in that corner there's the banks, and in that corner the poor'. We've actually got to look at what makes these examples work; what combination of political will, regulatory frameworks and intermediaries make it as interesting for the banks to get involved in slum upgrading as it is for the poor communities. (Derek Joseph, HACAS Chapman Hendy, UK and Homeless International adviser, speaking at the CLIFF World Urban Forum debate in June 2004.)

Derek Joseph's point stresses the importance of having practical projects on the ground, which can be understood in detail from the perspectives of different interest groups. Nobody becomes properly engaged on the basis of a theory. They respond to practical demonstrations that allow people to test how effectively different approaches have worked and to decide where and how improvements can be made. Again this emphasizes the importance of capital funds with which to kick-start practical demonstrations.

Supportive state regulation

The practical aspect is that no bank will turn away a well-defined project that has the backing of the local government or municipality, but we don't have the expertise. We welcome those intermediaries who can prove that they are credible, because most banks will want to deal with people who are willing and able to pay back loans. We want government to have a clear policy and direction for the private sector. Where governments are not focused in this way, we will not take the risks. So we ask that you educate the government in the same way you are educating us. There is no stigma against poor people – the banks have a social responsibility to participate in having a cleaner and healthier environment. We are all speaking the same language, but you need to come to us. (Stephanie Baeta Ansah, HFC Bank, Ghana, speaking at the CLIFF World Urban Forum debate in June 2004.)

The role of government will be discussed in more detail in Chapter 9. Suffice to note here that a genuinely facilitative state regulatory system can make a huge difference to the capacity of the urban poor to form working partnerships with the private sector. We have been very fortunate in a number of countries to engage high-level personnel within central and reserve banks in discussions regarding scaling up financing of slum upgrading and infrastructure provision. If commercial bankers believe that central banks have a genuine interest in exploring new operational mechanisms for providing such finance their confidence to engage with organizations of the urban poor can be greatly enhanced.

Mutual learning: interview with Anil Kuma of ICICI Bank

An interview between Ruth McLeod of Homeless International and Anil Kumar of ICICI Bank in September 2005 gives an insight into how banks are learning to work with the urban poor and their support NGOs, but also into how much further development of that relationship is still required.

'*How and why has ICICI Bank entered into a loan arrangement with SPARC*[1]*?*'

'The first thing we look at is the implementer. The second is the project. Both have to be stand-alone viable. If you ask me why I deal with SPARC it is purely because of their track record of implementing projects of varying sizes, from Rs50 million to Rs430 million [£628,000 to £5,402,129]. The size of the projects they are implementing has scaled up by a factor of 10 over the last five years and this has been achieved in very adverse areas. That's the first point. The second point is that they have a strong presence and relationship with the slum dwellers and this is particularly important because they work well with the communities affected by resettlement. This community linkage has been built up over 20 years, whereas their implementation competence as a builder has come up over the last five or six years.'

'*How do you view the lending relationship that is being established, as philanthropic or as commercial?*'

'The scales are different. This Oshiwara II project is large-scale and we expect the money to come back. It's a commercial arrangement for us. Philanthropy would focus far more on social impacts. In a commercial arrangement there is also an impact on lives and on livelihoods but the most fundamental thing is risk: how effective you can be in lending money and getting your money back. This risk aspect is completely absent within a philanthropic approach.'

'*Is this an entry point into a new market for ICICI?*'

'Yes. We see a large potential – not just in slum rehabilitation but also other areas such as micro-lending to individuals for housing. Also the potential for cross-selling of other financial products. There is a large unexplored market.'

'*How does SPARC differ from a large conventional builder or developer?*'

'A large developer works with a clear commercial orientation and brings in substantial liquidity, which supports their balance sheet. There's the support of a large commercial enterprise. In contrast, SPARC is clearly not working with a profit motivation. A commercial project is clearly designed to have a profit margin which also takes care of any adverse moments with input prices and so on, whereas SPARC is looking at the project with virtually no profit orientation so the margins may be very narrow or non-existent.'

'*What transition have you gone through as a banker in dealing with SPARC?*'

'ICICI are now substantially more sensitized to working with NGOs as clients. Microfinance developments have meant that we might be working with 20 or 30 NGOs at any one time so it's clearly accepted to take NGOs as clients. Within ICICI we're working with around 65 NGOs, including SPARC. However, almost all of them are in microfinance. So banks *per se* understand that NGOs can work in the field, with communities, and can deliver, so the initial mind set within banks has improved. Now banks have proven experience so they are beginning to be prepared to look at larger exposures. With NGOs the presentation of data has progressed considerably. Now the incoming data is being professionally managed and we are getting the precise data that we are asking for.'

'*What do you think is the future of the relationship between ICICI and SPARC?*'

'Internally SPARC/SSNS will remain one of our key partners not just in Bombay but in other cities, and not just in housing and sanitation – we want to work with them on a whole range of financial services. We see this as a long-term partnership built on a commercial basis.'

'*So you are talking about jointly designing completely new financial products?*'

'Clearly. It will help us to reach a large clientele to whom we have no real access at the moment because of our own current infrastructure constraints.'

'*Are there other NGOs working in this area?*'

'We have not met many. Unlike microfinance, there are very few NGOs involved in infrastructure and housing. If you remove SPARC/SSNS from this handful, the others are in rural areas, and yet the requirements are much more acute in urban areas. Most of the NGO projects, apart from SPARC/SSNS, have only been on a demonstration project level, which is not scalable, so I don't have too many NGOs to work with. Also the microfinance institutions have difficulty in this area, apart from home improvements, because the end price that you can charge for housing loans that are medium- and long-term may not absorb your administrative cost. Your typical Grameen microfinance model and pricing can support a 52-week loan at 32 per cent. However to build a new house you need a minimum loan of Rs50,000 and, at a 30 per cent interest rate, this is not supportable. There has to be an input that takes away the delivery cost if housing finance for the poor is to be a viable proposition.'

This dialogue demonstrates that, in India, there is potential for collaboration between the formal private sector and the urban poor and their support organizations, but it is also clear that there is much still to be done in deepening and widening this dialogue, in going beyond new projects to new products, and in taking the whole process to the scale needed if it is to have an impact across cities and across the country. Similar challenges are faced in many African countries faced by rapid urbanization and a lack of the effective regulatory/ financing mechanisms needed to provide alternatives to slum formation. In these countries, though, financial markets are at a much earlier stage of development and so the task faced is even greater.

THE WAY FORWARD

Effective working partnerships between organizations of the urban poor and the private sector around slum upgrading are still in their early stages and are frequently contentious. In some countries, such as India, significant progress has already been made and the possibilities for future collaboration look strong, but there still remains much to be done on both sides as community organizations develop and demonstrate further their organizational capacity and skills, and as private sector groups refine their criteria to make large-scale collaboration a realistic option. In other countries, such as Ghana and Kenya, discussions with the private sector, particularly banks, around slum upgrading are only just beginning and progress will depend on demonstrable capacity of the community process, which will depend in turn on greater levels of donor and other resources for community capacity-building and precedent-setting. New initiatives such as UN-Habitat's Slum Upgrading Facility (SUF) offer the possibility or greater support in packaging community projects and in drawing in investment from the private sector, but, given that initiatives such as SUF lack funds for mobilization and demonstration of capacity at community level, other complementary approaches will clearly be needed. Homeless International is already exploring new options for mobilizing investment funds, particularly in the UK, but it remains to be seen how effective these will be in catalysing greater private sector interest in slum upgrading and infrastructure provision in developing countries.

CHAPTER NINE

Working with government

Kim Mullard

INTRODUCTION

Homeless International's aim of supporting processes that have the potential to scale up and achieve policy change cannot be achieved without some form of engagement with government. However, the nature of Homeless International's approach – working through local partner organizations – means that this engagement is often indirect. This chapter aims to reflect briefly on some of the experiences of Homeless International and its partners in engaging with government. The policy and practice of all forms of government – from local and city government, sub-national government, national government, donor governments to intergovernmental organizations – has an important influence on the context for urban development and its financing in a particular city. The discussion that follows is therefore, by necessity, wide ranging. Its central theme, however, is more focused, concentrating on the processes that have enabled collaborative partnerships between organizations of the urban poor and government at both national and sub national levels.

The approach to government that our partners have developed can perhaps be best described as 'critical engagement', a practice which recognizes that government has an important role and significant responsibilities in urban development, for which it should be held accountable, but at the same time proactively seeks to engage and work with government to help it to discharge those responsibilities. It is important to note that critical engagement is very different from partisan alliances; maintaining neutrality with respect to party politics has proved extremely important in safeguarding the long-term effectiveness and credibility of organizations of the urban poor.[1] Critical engagement assumes that government's most vital responsibility in urban development, at national and sub-national levels, is that of guardian of the public good. Land and infrastructure constitute critical elements of this public good and their development and management are crucial in determining how effectively a city ensures adequate shelter for its citizens. These are also the elements that have the greatest impact on the quality of life of the urban poor and it is therefore not surprising that our partners' critical engagement with government has been concentrated on land and infrastructure access and development. Inevitably this has also required an engagement with the whole issue of capital financing and the ways in which cities resource their growth and development. To understand how this engagement has evolved it is necessary to begin with a discussion of the manner in which governmental practice has changed in this area over the last 20 years.

When Homeless International began giving grants, our partner organizations had little involvement with their local or national governments, and those relationships that did exist were frequently adversarial and contentious. As our work expanded, our support increasingly focused on the federation process (see Chapter 2) and engagement with government at all levels, from local government to intergovernmental organizations, developed. Subsequently, as community-government interaction emerged within this continuum of relationships on the ground, engagement with city government has proved to be the strongest starting point for seeking to scale up. This city focus is consistent with recent global trends associated with decentralization, which have placed an emphasis on the city, and led to a recognition that the relationship between the nation state and cities is changing. Government has increasingly been expected to take on a facilitative rather than direct delivery role. In this context the creation of city development strategies is viewed as a critical ingredient in ensuring cities remain competitive in a globalized marketplace. Another trend has been that public utilities, previously owned and operated by local or national government, have been subject to differing degrees of private sector involvement or privatization in many countries, with consequent impacts on affordability for the poor and on the likelihood of services being extended to low-income settlements. In addition, local government is seen as having an increasingly important role in mobilizing domestic capital for infrastructure development, but to be able to do this effectively It needs both the technical capacity and access to reliable support from central government.

GOVERNMENT'S ROLES AND RESPONSIBILITIES IN URBAN DEVELOPMENT

Local, sub-national and national governments have a number of roles and responsibilities that influence the context for financing urban development, but the distribution of these roles between levels of government varies between countries, and is changing as processes of decentralization and devolution accelerate. Important government roles and responsibilities are:

- determining the policy and legal framework for urban development, including financial regulations;
- enforcing legislation and regulating urban development, including responsibility for planning and building;
- government ownership of land and other physical assets;
- provision of infrastructure and the delivery of services; and
- responsibility for the welfare of poorer sectors of society.

Often delivery of the final two roles – supplying infrastructure or services, and welfare provision – may be contracted out or provided in partnership with the private sector or civil society. Government's responsibility for welfare provision is linked to wider policy and attitudes towards poverty, often determined at a national level and outlined in documents such as Poverty Reduction Strategy Papers (PRSPs). In terms of the work Homeless International supports, there are three areas of government action that are particularly important: policy implementation and regulation (including urban planning and building regulation, regulation of financial institutions and banks, local authority regulation and fiscal management, regulation of NGOs and other civil society organizations); ensuring land availability and tenure security; and policies regarding poverty alleviation.

Accepting that there are general government responsibilities for facilitating urban development, it is also important to recognize that the extent to which local and sub-national governments can influence the national or city-level budgets for urban development differs across localities. Roles and responsibilities may have been decentralized without a concomitant flow of resources. There can be significant disparities between the policy on paper and the practice in reality. Policies may not be fully implemented for a variety of reasons, including not only a lack of technical or financial capacity but also a lack of political will, government not being held to account, or a poorly designed policy. The quality of governance has a huge influence on the environment for financing urban development; the incidence of patronage, corruption, and forced evictions are important in this respect. The story told in Box 7.3 is just one example of how political interference can hinder urban development projects. A final factor is the frequent changes of both elected representatives and officials within the administration; obviously such changes can have both positive and negative impacts on the environment for financing urban development. However, in general terms personnel changes result in a lack of continuity in relationships, policy and practice that can be disruptive given that urban development is a long-term process. As Hasan *et al.* point out, 'It is challenging for any newly elected government to meet ambitious commitments to low-income groups. Legal and institutional changes are difficult to implement and need to be negotiated; their impacts are cumulative but can take longer to establish than a three-to-five year election cycle' (2005: 13).

Policy implementation and regulation

Policy and legislation, and how they are enforced and regulated, impact upon financing urban development in three main areas: land, building and the financial sector. In addition, policy and regulation can limit or enhance the ability of community-led organizations and NGOs to become involved in large-scale urban development initiatives, such as slum upgrading. Planning legislation may make plots unaffordable, for example, through minimum plot sizes, 'set backs',[2] and infrastructure standards. Many cities lack adequate land registration or cadastral systems, making formal transfer of land title unaffordable or unfeasible. Building legislation may require standards that are unaffordable or inappropriate (for example, not allowing incremental development). Or the process of gaining building approvals may be expensive or entail long delays.

Government policy and practice influences the development of the financial sector. Financial regulations govern how both civil society and government institutions can borrow and lend to finance urban development. In relation to local government borrowing, Sierra argues that: 'Global experience clearly demonstrates that, with an appropriate policy and a legal and regulatory framework, cities successfully access private capital markets in order to finance urban infrastructure. Indeed, financing infrastructure in this manner also provides strong and tangible incentives for improved urban governance, efficiency and accountability' (2005: 1).

Ensuring land availability and tenure security

Government policy and practice has a massive impact on the land market not only in terms of planning and building regulations and systems for land registration, but also on price and availability if it owns large amounts of land within a city. In relation to slums, government policy can make more affordable land available and improve the security of tenure for those in slums. Inappropriate policy makes land unaffordable for large sections of the population; for example, land use policy in Ethiopia has resulted in a situation where only the top fifth of the income distribution can afford housing plots (Cities Alliance 2004: 7). City development policies that focus excessively upon providing land for commercial use can also raise land prices and effectively prevent the poor from accessing urban land. Increasing the supply of affordable land can entail: changing cumbersome administrative procedures; tackling corruption or changing regulations in the systems for land registration and permission to occupy or develop; surveying and planning new areas; or intervening in the land market, through for example subsidies or releasing vacant government land on to the market. In Mumbai, the slum rehabilitation legislation and the establishment of transferable development rights (see Box 6.1) have made slum upgrading feasible in a city with extremely high land values. However, as Mukhija (2001) describes, Mumbai's strategy of enabling private sector involvement in housing through market mechanisms has proved complex and not resulted in the level of slum redevelopment that was hoped for.

Tenure security is a multifaceted and locally specific concept, and can only be touched upon here. Indeed, Payne argues that tenure systems are 'the outcome of historical and cultural forces and reflect the relationships between people and society and between people and the land on which they live' (2002: 4–5). It is important to note that, as described in Chapter 4, our experience has been that *de facto* tenure security can have more influence on families' decisions to invest in permanent housing than *de jure* security. However, the lack of secure tenure has wide-ranging impacts, as the UN Millennium Project points out.

> Insecure tenure has multiple ramifications for poverty. Legal tenure at the settlement level is often a prerequisite for the provision of basic services. Without security of tenure, newly serviced settlements are vulnerable to market pressure. Lack of tenure hinders most attempts to improve shelter conditions for the urban poor, undermines long-term planning, and distorts prices for land and services. It has a direct impact on investment at the settlement level and reinforces poverty and social exclusion. Its effects are most destructive for women and children … From the point of view of governments, insecure tenure also has a negative impact on local taxation on property and economic activities. Cost recovery for services and infrastructures is also difficult or impossible without proper identification of beneficiaries. For all these

reasons, ensuring security of tenure is an effective tool for alleviating poverty in slums (UN Millennium Project 2005b: 49–50).

Governments have taken a variety of approaches to improving tenure security for the urban poor; for example, the Baan Mankong programme in Thailand improves tenure security for slum dwellers in four ways: land purchase, land lease, land sharing and relocation (Hasan *et al.* 2005: 10; Boonyabancha 2005). Depending on the local context, government may be able to fund or facilitate these options.

The final point to make about land is that, except in a very few cities, the issue facing slum dwellers is not an absolute lack of land within the city, but a relative lack of affordable, accessible, surveyed, well-located land with access to bulk infrastructure. Often governments do not know how much land is vacant within the city, or who owns the land, due to a lack of cadastral records. Searching for land by comparing city plans with the reality on the ground has become one of the tools used by the federations that Homeless International supports (see Box 9.1 below).

Poverty alleviation policies

Although we live in a world where nearly one in six people live in a 'slum' and, as Chapter 1 describes, there is a complex interplay between such living conditions and many aspects of poverty, governments' poverty alleviation policies and plans frequently make little reference to slum upgrading. In a review of 23 PRSPs, Mitlin concluded that 'nearly all PRSPs have a strong emphasis on the relative importance

---

Box 9.1 Land search as a federation tool

'When cities claim there is no land left for the poor, don't believe them – they're almost always fibbing. And when poor people get to know their own cities and educate themselves about development plans, they can challenge this bunkum. Land searches in cities all over Asia and Africa have helped poor communities to negotiate countless resettlement deals.

'An early land search in Bombay went like this. "We thought we could find places for the poor to stay: there must be some land allocated for poor people's housing, you can't have a government and a city corporation which doesn't plan for people's housing! So we got these silly development plans, and, along with a big group of Mahila Milan women, we went all over the city, locating every single place marked 'housing for the poor' on those plans. What an eye-opener! Whatever was 'green belt' on the plan was actually industrial belt. And whatever was meant for housing the poor was upper-income housing, or warehouses and factories – all kinds of things. With the same naiveté, we went to the Chief Secretary and asked him why this is happening? He told us, this is a notional plan, this is how we'd like it to be! And that's what it is – it's a dream plan".'

Sheela Patel of SPARC in ACHR (2000: 28)

of rural poverty. However, many appear concerned that their poverty estimates do not fully represent the situation with respect to urban poverty' (2004a: 1). Government policy may seek to intervene in the complex interplay between poverty and living conditions through changing policy and practice to make formal housing more affordable or through subsidizing slum upgrading.

The affordability of any planned housing or infrastructure improvements is determined by a multitude of factors: poor people may have to purchase water from informal vendors, paying more than they would for a formal supply, but moving from 'slum' housing to formalized or upgrading housing may entail additional costs such as taxes and maintenance. Ultimately, affordability can only be assessed with detailed local knowledge. Within the federation process community-led enumerations and subsequent community-level discussion of development options are crucial in ensuring that housing or infrastructure development plans are affordable for community members. In Kenya there are no subsidies for improving slum housing,[3] but Nairobi City Council has agreed to designate certain slums – for example Huruma and Soweto Kahawa – as special planning areas, relaxing strict building standards (Hughes 2005: 17), hence improving affordability.

Channelling subsidies

Subsidies are a complex issue, which cannot be dealt with in detail here. As Chapter 5 outlined, the experience of our partners suggests that it is unrealistic and unfair to expect poor households to bear all the costs of land, housing and infrastructure development through loans to individual families. Some form of subsidy, or an intervention in the land and housing market, is therefore necessary if poor urban communities are to be able to gain access to adequate, affordable housing and infrastructure. However, subsidies need to be carefully designed and targeted if they are to benefit the poor. Subsidies are not necessarily cash payments from government to individuals or projects; Chapter 5 lists the various forms that subsidies can take, from provision of free or 'cheap' land and infrastructure through to market-based subsidies, such as transferable development rights in Mumbai.

One of the challenges in the provision of government subsidies is the creation of delivery mechanisms that ensure the subsidies reach the intended beneficiaries and are used effectively. The existence of well-organized civil society organizations, such as federations of the urban poor, can help to ensure that delivery systems actually work in practice, both by creating effective demand for subsidy draw-down and by scrutinizing the process. Homeless International's grant funds have helped, for example, the Namibian Federation to negotiate with national government to better implement its 'Build Together' subsidized loan programme. In terms of larger-scale subsidy programmes, such as those for housing projects undertaken by groups of people rather than individuals, bridge financing has proved valuable in initiating developments; in buying time for subsidy systems to be unlocked; and in channelling subsidies to community-led, rather than developer-

Box 9.2 *Bidi* workers' subsidy in Solapur

Bidi workers roll traditional Indian cigarettes, for which they receive a small daily wage. *Bidi* factories pay a 'cess' to the funds of the state and central government for each packet of *bidis* sold, and as a result, *bidi* workers are entitled to a Rs20,000 housing subsidy each from both the state and central governments in India. However, these subsidies have not been drawn down effectively or very often, because the Maharashtra Housing and Area Development Authority (MHADA) could only build houses for *bidi* workers at a cost of over Rs75,000 per unit, which is generally considered unaffordable by most *bidi* workers. Prior to the Solapur *Bidi* Workers' project, described here, only about 3,000 housing units had been constructed using the subsidy.

The Indian Alliance's project with *bidi* workers in Solapur has catalysed implementation of the subsidy policy in three ways. Firstly, it has helped *bidi* workers to adapt the designs of housing to develop an affordable house that includes space for *bidi* rolling. Secondly, bridge financing provided by CLIFF has been crucial in creating the breathing space required to submit the paperwork and push for the release of subsidies. This has helped establish a system for *bidi* workers to apply for, and central and state government to release, the subsidy payments to which they are entitled, although there are still delays associated with corruption and bureaucratic bottlenecks in drawing down subsidies. Finally, other *bidi* workers have observed the project and begun to pressurize their own *bidi* unions to begin similar housing schemes. As a result, a second *bidi* workers' union is implementing a scheme for 10,000 houses independently of the Indian Alliance, drawing down further state and central subsidies. A third group of 2,000 *bidi* workers has organized, borrowed money to buy land (required to qualify for a subsidy), and then approached the Indian Alliance with a view to planning for 2,500 more houses and some collectively owned work sheds. The national Ministry of Labour is also interested in expanding the programme to other Indian states, and has raised the subsidy level to Rs40,000 each from central and state governments. This is a major achievement, and an example of how scaling-up can occur once successful solutions have been demonstrated.

(taken from Jack *et al.* 2005: 45)

led, housing developments (Jack *et al.* 2005). Box 9.2 describes a particularly interesting example from Solapur, a city in the Indian state of Maharashtra.

FACING THE CHALLENGES AND RISKS OF CRITICAL ENGAGEMENT

As discussed in Chapter 4, the formation of city–community partnerships entails significant political challenges and risks, particularly during changes of political control. These challenges and risks are complex, because they result from actions at various locations from local to global. Understanding the relationships that operate across this global continuum has become an increasingly important feature of developing effective city-level development strategies in which the urban poor can play a leading role.

It can be argued that with urban growth, many cities are becoming increasingly dysfunctional. The urban poor provide many of the basic services and much of the pool of labour that keep cities running, but struggle to find adequate, affordable places to live. The existence, and projected growth, of slums is the most significant manifestation of this contradiction. As Chapter 1 outlined, nearly 1 billion people already live in slums, and the urban areas of the less developed regions will absorb 95 per cent of the world's population growth between 2000 and 2030 (UN-Habitat 2003: 54). Hasan *et al.* provide a clear analysis of slum causation: 'Slums and squatter settlements are the result of people being priced out of legal land for housing, and housing markets. Increasing the supply and reducing the cost of land for housing and related infrastructure is central to meeting the MDG targets for extending provision for water and sanitation, and for significantly improving the lives of slum dwellers. Finance systems also have a critical role, increasing what low-income households can afford' (2005: 9). The lack of adequate, affordable housing raises issues of governance and whether the poor are accorded the citizenship rights enjoyed by better-off city dwellers. This lack also affects a city's competitiveness in globalized markets. It is within this context that governmental policies and practice become so crucial, because they can influence all these determining factors in a city's land and housing markets. As a result, effective critical engagement requires that the urban poor find a means to work constructively with the level of government that has most impact on land and housing markets. This increasingly means finding ways to work with government at sub-national levels, usually focused on the city or specific areas within cities.

The risks associated with critical engagement largely arise as a result of a core paradox that exists in approaches to city development. This paradox was identified and discussed during the 'Bridging the finance gap in housing and infrastructure' research, and is shown schematically in Figure 9.1. Both the poor and government

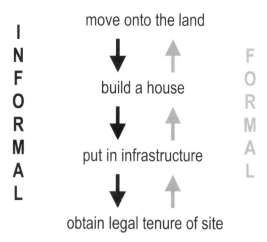

Figure 9.1   Informal and formal approaches to settlement development

recognize that there is a problem of inadequate shelter and a lack of services within cities, but the informal processes depended on by the poor, who in reality deliver the majority of housing construction within cities in developing countries, work according to a logic that is almost totally inverse to that of the formal planning system. So government and other formal institutions subject to government regulation may want to work with the poor, but the planning and building systems they regulate, and which regulate them, make this extremely difficult. The rules of the formal game exclude many of the options presented by informal solutions. In summary, the urban poor rely for their survival on their capacity to break the rules, whilst the state relies for its success on enforcement of the rules. Neither side succeeds in solving the problem and other players such as formal financial institutions remain on the outside not knowing how, why and where they can fit in. No one wins.

This paradox becomes amplified when communities, building on the creativity of their informal processes, begin to demonstrate that they can scale up successful solutions that could work for cities as a whole. Their success nearly, if not always, results from 'breaking the rules'. However, in order to gain financing from banks (regulated by the government) or to receive government subsidies, they have to demonstrate that they have followed the rules. The pragmatic response of the organizations of the poor with whom Homeless International works has been to complete at least 20 to 50 per cent of a housing project without formal permissions and use its visible success to create more flexibility in the rules, or to change them altogether. By proceeding with the project and reaching certain stages of construction the balance of power shifts, creating pressure for the release of subsidies or for bank loan applications to be seriously considered. CLIFF was designed to provide the bridge finance that would allow the federations to go through this process of engagement and to straddle the demands of the informal and formal approaches, in effect enabling a resolution of the informal–formal paradox (see Chapter 7).

Resolving the informal–formal paradox requires engagement, which in turn requires a clear view of the roles and responsibilities that government should assume, and the roles that organizations of the urban poor have the capacity to manage. It also requires that governmental agencies enter into partnerships with the urban poor on practical issues prioritized by the poor rather than limiting engagement to the superficiality of 'consultative workshops' that have no follow through in actions on the ground. However, within most cities there are few effective mechanisms that allow city authorities to engage with the poor in a manner that builds on the resources that the poor themselves have at their disposal[4] and there is generally little experience in building relationships in a way that gives credence to the poor as dynamic subjects within a change and development process that can benefit the city as a whole. This gap in connection requires a focus on the formation and nurturing of on-going relationships, of connection, of communication and of practical collaborative action. Short-term, spasmodic interventions simply do not work. This is as true in addressing questions of urban finance as it is in addressing challenges of social welfare in general. When resources are scarce, the lack of collaboration between government and citizens, particularly the poor, becomes more than inconvenient – it becomes actively dysfunctional. Frustration, anger and resentment dominate interactions between city authorities and vast numbers of urban residents, to the cost of everyone. So how can investment in the creation of long-term constructive relationships be developed? What are the basic ingredients? What are the processes that create dynamic and pro-active engagement?

WHAT HELPS IN CREATING ENGAGEMENT WITH LOCAL AND NATIONAL GOVERNMENT?

Homeless International's relationship with local and national government has been less direct than that with the donor governments and other international agencies; our focus has been on supporting partners to engage with their governments. Several of the forms of financing outlined in Chapter 5 have been utilized to support this engagement, including:

■ external grants for financing basic capacity, to build the economic and social base;
■ grants for financing learning, knowledge creation and capacity building; and
■ grants and revolving loan funds for financing development of small-scale pilot and demonstration (precedent-setting) projects.

Perhaps the most impressive engagement between communities and government has been through the data that emerge from community-led enumerations. As detailed in Chapter 3, grants for financing basic capacity have supported community-led enumerations, the data from which have enabled communities to negotiate with government over land, infrastructure and housing issues. Local government does not often have equivalent information to that collected by communities; by offering their information, communities are able to change the balance of power in their relationship with their government resulting in a more equal partnership (Mitlin 2004b: 7).

Grants for financing learning have been used not only to support exchanges of federation members between communities, cities and countries, but also to support exchanges where government officials are part of the team (see Chapter 3 for more information on exchanges). Exchanges where officials are able to meet their counterparts and see how a project, together with the associated community–government partnership, has worked in practice were vital in expanding the Indian Alliance's toilet-building work from Pune to Mumbai (see Box 9.3) and in convincing the Kenyan authorities that community-led resettlement of railway-side slum dwellers could really work. Box 9.3 tells the story of the Kenya–India railway exchange from the perspective of the Indian Alliance.

Finally, Homeless International has provided grants and loan fund capital, to support our partner organizations' development of precedent-setting projects, which have demonstrated new ideas to government. However, Homeless International's ability to provide the bridge financing that may be necessary for projects to access subsidies, and grant or loan capital more generally, has been constrained by our funding base. Donor rules have often viewed such capital

Box 9.3 The Kenya–India Railway Exchange

In February 2004, the Kenyan Railway authorities started to demolish houses in Kibera that were along the tracks. As the local communities watched in great distress and the eviction watchers of the world began to fill cyberspace with news of the doom facing the communities and protesting against what was happening, Muungano (Muungano wa Wanavijiji, the Kenyan Federation) and Pamoja Trust went to their railway authorities to talk to them about a new way of dealing with this process. They asked them to explore working together with the poor to solve the problem of land so that the poor got alternate housing and the city got back their land along the railway tracks. They were told the story of how 10,000 families in Bombay moved from the railway track, and that, within three years, 120 kilometres of track had been cleared – 30 feet on either side. The Kenyans invited their officials to go to Bombay and learn more about this. On 2 April, a team of seven Kenyans arrived in Mumbai to learn about this resettlement. They had many discussions both with NSDF and Mahila Milan communities as well as the Indian Railway officials. At the end of the trip, they agreed to explore how they would also undertake a similar partnership in Nairobi.' SPARC (2004: 30)

'The land on which those slum dwellers are facing demolitions in Kibera belongs to the Kenyan Railways. So the delegation that came with Jane Weru comprised of three senior members of the Kenyan Railways, one senior official from the government department of Land Affairs, a professor from the university and a member of the Mungano federation. In the week that they were in Mumbai, they first of all spent time understanding the processes that the federation uses to generate data about themselves, and how they get that data accepted by the state agencies and land owners. As the process in Bombay also demonstrates the importance of the relationship between the Indian railways, the State Government of Maharashtra and communities, the delegation spent a great deal of time meeting with officials in the Indian railways and the Government of Maharashtra. The process also allowed those in the delegation to see themselves as *Kenyans*; and to see those who are poor and living in slums as people who had come to cities to improve their lives and that of their children. Often you need to travel somewhere else to focus on your identity and reflect on your work and values. Most of the officials began to see their larger goals as improving the lives of their fellow Kenyans as they do their jobs and in fact one of the Kenyan officials actually admitted that he never thought about people when he ordered the demolition because he was thinking of them as structures.

'... As Kenyan and Indian railway officials began to reflect on their roles, it became clear that the railways all over the world have not guarded their lands, and poor people forced by economic conditions squat wherever they see land, and this comes to a head-on collision and a war between the land owners and communities when the land owner suddenly wakes up to wanting to use this land. The role of the national government in this kind of crisis is very important as its role requires a delicate balancing act of arbitrating the interests of the poor and the land owner. The Kenyan Government officials quickly picked that up, and suggested the possibility of federations and communities undertaking joint surveys with railways and state, and this process to feed into the national land policy that was being reviewed. One visit does not solve all problems, and the challenges to work together were identified and opened up in this visit and will emerge as events unfold in Kenya. But a federation of poor people in India helped its counterpart to open up this debate.'[5]

investments as consumption, rather than productive, and as service delivery rather than necessary to realize rights and achieve change. Only with the advent of CLIFF has Homeless International been able to provide bridge financing on a significant scale.

Homeless International has focused on supporting partners to engage with government to change practice, not just policy in the abstract. In engaging with government, our partners have generally adopted a similar approach to the Indian Alliance:

> The Alliance has an unusual way of advocating changes in state policy. Most NGO advocacy first targets policy changes, and then works for implementation of the results. In contrast, the Alliance seeks to create community-centred practices that can be enshrined in policy, or to set pro-poor precedents on the ground that can then inform policy frameworks. This has the distinct advantage that even before the policy becomes articulated, clear strategies for its implementation have already been honed. What is more, when resistance has been encountered from officials, thanks to anti-poor biases or red tape, large numbers of people have already asserted persistent demands, or higher-level officials have been brought in to reinterpret rules and practices to facilitate the necessary change. Through this complex and cyclical process, a web of relationships is created that ultimately enable both the articulation of new policy as well as its implementation in a manner that actually allows the poor to access resources and entitlements.' (Batliwala 2005: 10)

The story of the Indian Alliance's growing community toilet-block programme, told in Burra et al. (2003), illustrates many of the complexities of the relationship between urban development finance and government, some of which are drawn out in Box 9.4. Burra et al. analyse the politics of sanitation, arguing that Indian cities' drive to be globally competitive and the demonstration that organizations of the poor can build and manage better and cheaper toilets than contractors have helped to change both policies and attitudes towards sanitation (2005: 228). Arjun Appadurai examines the work of the Indian Alliance and the wider international network, concluding that federations of the urban poor 'are, or can be, instruments of deep democracy, rooted in local context and able to mediate globalizing forces in ways that benefit the poor. In so doing, both within nations and globally, they are seeking to redefine what governance and governability mean' (2001: 23).

There are many other examples of critical engagement in our partners' work; such as the growing partnership between the Shack Dwellers' Federation of Namibia and the city of Windhoek described by Gold, Muller and Mitlin (2001: 51–54); and the Zimbabwe Homeless People's Federation engagement with local government despite an uncertain national political climate (Chitekwe and Mitlin 2001). As well as engagement at city and national level, SDI engages at regional level, for example, supporting younger federations in other countries in their work with city and national governments, and at international level, as described later in this chapter.

Box 9.4 The Indian Alliance and sanitation

The ideas for the Indian Alliance's early toilet projects emerged out of their discussions with women's groups, and enumerations were used to demonstrate the need (Burra et al. 2003: 15–16). In the early 1990s, Homeless International and others provided small amounts of grant funding for both this basic community organization process and for precedent-setting toilet construction projects. Around this time, the Indian Alliance received its first municipal contract to build a toilet in Mumbai. In 1999, the Municipal Commissioner of Pune started an ambitious toilet-construction programme. NGOs were asked to bid to construct blocks, with capital costs being paid by the Municipal Corporation, and NGOs and communities agreeing to maintain the blocks. Building on the Indian Alliance's existing work in Pune, SPARC submitted a bid and was one of eight NGOs to be awarded contracts in the first phase. The Alliance went on to build hundreds of toilet blocks in Pune, and in Mumbai under the Bombay Sewerage Disposal Project, benefiting millions of slum dwellers (see Chapters 2 and 7; Burra et al. 2003; Burra et al. 2005). The scaling up of the sanitation work required finance from a number of sources, including bridge finance from CLIFF (see Chapter 7) and a locally financed guarantee (see Chapter 6).

As a result of the Indian Alliance's toilet construction programmes in Mumbai and Pune, they were invited to make a presentation to the central government's Minister for Urban Development. The outcome of this engagement with national government was a new scheme offering a 50 per cent capital subsidy to sub-national (state) and local governments for construction of public sanitation facilities (Burra 2005: 83). Burra argues that 'pilot projects for community sanitation showed what could be done on a much larger scale. Pilot and precedent-setting projects can affect policies. They also leverage money for the poor, as in the case of the national policy on subsidies for slum sanitation that emerged directly from the Pune and Mumbai slum sanitation programmes.' At the time of writing, the Indian Alliance is implementing a city-wide sanitation programme in Tiruppur with the New Tiruppur Area Development Corporation Ltd, Tamil Nadu (Jack et al. 2005: 71) and is involved in training programmes for civil servants (see Chapter 7).

The Indian Alliance's engagement with government on sanitation issues has had wider impacts than even the scaling up, replication, and national policy change outlined above, it has also influenced the quality of governance:

'The community-designed, built and managed toilet blocks . . . developed new relationships between urban poor groups and government. In both Pune and Mumbai, the subject of sanitation entered the public domain, with municipal commissioners and other dignitaries 'inaugurating' public toilets. When these high-ranking officials visit slums and interact with the urban poor, a platform is created for dialogue on other issues that affect the urban poor. The community toilet blocks helped change the traditional patron–client relationship between elected representatives and slum dwellers. Whereas previously the provision of a public toilet in a slum was the gift of a local councillor, member of the legislative assembly or member of parliament, now, communities of the poor increasingly perceive it as a right' (Burra 2005: 84).

Challenges in engaging with local and national government

There are a number of challenges in dealing with local government and national government, some of which have been alluded to above. Local government may be weak, lacking the capacity or resources to implement policies, and governance may be poor. A study of PRSPs in seven Commonwealth countries found that problems with the implementation of decentralization policies were a common factor (ComHabitat 2005: 31–32). Local government may be hostile to slum upgrading. Alternatively local government 'may be strong and committed but have to deal with a hostile national government' (McLeod 2005b: 27). A particular slum upgrading or resettlement process can involve a multiplicity of agencies within government, making engagement difficult and complex. To give one example, the Indian Alliance's railway resettlement work in Mumbai involved engagement with agencies from national and sub-national government through to the World Bank (Patel *et al.* 2002).

Developing financial mechanisms, such as CLIFF, has helped partner organizations to engage with local and national governments by demonstrating community-led approaches in practice and achieving change at scale. However, these mechanisms need to be adapted to local contexts. CLIFF has taken different approaches in India and Kenya, whilst maintaining the loan criteria of supporting changes in policy and practice, because both the policy environment and levels of community capacity differed (see Chapter 7 and McLeod 2005a: 7–9). The key constraint in engaging with local and national government on slum upgrading is inadequate land: if government can find ways of creating land supply and providing bulk infrastructure, communities and civil society can manage onsite infrastructure and housing development, assuming they have access to finance. Cities Alliance have identified the essential ingredients for nationwide slum upgrading, highlighting action that local and national government need to take:

- demonstrate political will (nationally and locally);
- set targets (national and city level) and engage stakeholders in planning and monitoring;
- put slum upgrading in the budget – make it 'core business';
- implement policy reforms in areas of land, finance and institutional frameworks;
- ensure open and transparent land markets to tackle corruption and patronage;
- mobilize non-public sector resources, including slum dwellers' resources; and
- prevent the growth of new slums through planning realistically for future growth (2003: 37).

ENGAGING WITH DONORS AND INTERGOVERNMENTAL AGENCIES

Homeless International's role in working with donors and intergovernmental agencies on financing urban development has been more direct than with local and national governments, because of Homeless International's institutional location and core working practices, described in Chapter 2. Donors and intergovernmental agencies have provided funding for the financial mechanisms outlined in Chapters 3, 6 and 7; Homeless International has worked with these agencies to develop new financial mechanisms; and finally Homeless International has advocated policy ideas to these agencies to influence the financing of urban development. However, Homeless International's role in relation to donors and intergovernmental agencies has changed as its partner organizations have grown and developed, particularly with the establishment and development of the Shack/ Slum Dwellers International (SDI) network. A history of SDI's development describes how the network's international role has changed: 'Until 1999, international activity was mainly concerned with the capacity-building of federations, to better obtain local resources through local and national negotiations assisted by the SDI networks. Now this has extended to a dialogue with national and international agencies in global fora in order to increase the ability of grassroots groups to obtain resources and control local development' (Patel *et al.* 2001, 55). As so much of Homeless International's work is supporting SDI members, its engagement with donors and intergovernmental agencies must be sensitive and complementary to SDI's stated ambition of influencing development paradigms (Patel *et al.* 2001, 59).

Engaging with the UK Government

Homeless International is a niche agency rooted within UK civil society, particularly the UK social housing sector as described in Chapter 2. As such it makes sense to first examine Homeless International's engagement with the UK Government – in terms of funding, mechanism development and advocacy – before looking at other donors and international agencies. Homeless International has accessed funding from the UK Government, first through the Overseas Development Administration (ODA) and then through its successor, the Department for International Development (DFID), since 1987. ODA and DFID funding from competitive budget lines for NGOs, was an important element of Homeless International's support for the capacity building of organizations of the urban poor described in Chapter 3. Homeless International has packaged projects for DFID/ODA funding which have provided grants for several of the forms of financing outlined in Chapter 5:

- financing basic capacity – the economic and social base – for basic federation mobilization;
- developing small-scale pilot and demonstration (precedent-setting) projects (either direct grants or establishing revolving funds);
- core administration and operations of NGOs supporting federations; and
- financing learning, knowledge creation and capacity building, for example through exchanges.

Homeless International's funding relationship with ODA/DFID has evolved as both organizations have changed and at times our ability to raise funds for certain forms of financing, particularly for developing small-scale pilot and demonstration projects, has been limited. In addition to obtaining funding from DFID's general NGO budget lines, Homeless International has also obtained funding from thematic areas of DFID, such as the former Infrastructure and Urban Development Department (IUDD) and the United Nations and Commonwealth Department.

Homeless International has worked with DFID in our development of mechanisms for financing housing, infrastructure and urban development. DFID was one of the initial funders involved in establishing Homeless International's Guarantee Fund, as outlined in Chapters 2 and 6. More importantly, IUDD funded the 'Bridging the finance gap in housing and infrastructure' research project and worked with us to develop CLIFF as a DFID proposal to Cities Alliance (see Chapters 2 and 7). Finally, Homeless International supported DFID's development of mechanisms for financing urban development, when the Chief Executive, Ruth McLeod, was a consultant involved in the development of the C3 Challenge Fund.[6]

Homeless International has engaged with DFID to attempt to influence both its general policy, specific policies in our area of interest, and its NGO funding policies. In 1997, the newly elected Labour Government established DFID as a separate government department and produced a White Paper outlining a new poverty-focused approach to international development (Department for International Development 1997). Homeless International felt that the White Paper gave insufficient emphasis to the linkages between housing and infrastructure and poverty and so organized a lobby using its UK support base. A paper was produced outlining 'the significance of housing investment as a means of eliminating poverty' (McLeod and Satterthwaite 2000).[8] In recent years, DFID has consulted on two policy papers directly relevant to our area of work: the urban poverty 'target strategy paper' and an infrastructure paper (Department for International Development 2001; 2002). Homeless International produced responses to these consultations, in discussion with our partners, highlighting key issues, and also participated in the UK Urban Poverty Group's response[7]. We were able to track a number of changes in the final urban poverty 'target strategy paper' that were in line with the suggestions that we had made in our response, including stronger language on secure tenure, participation by the urban poor and some case studies of our partners' work.[9]

Involvement with other donors and intergovernmental agencies

Homeless International has been involved with a variety of other donors and intergovernmental agencies – including the Commonwealth, Cities Alliance, the European Commission, Sida, UN-Habitat and the World Bank – although the level of engagement has varied. The European Commission has been merely a funding partner, whereas we have worked collaboratively with, and been contracted by, both UN-Habitat and the Commonwealth. Cities Alliance and Sida, meanwhile, are key partners in CLIFF (see Chapter 7). Homeless International has been engaged with UN-Habitat to varying degrees since the International Year of Shelter for the Homeless (see Chapter 2). We were the UK platform for the Second United Nations Conference on Human Settlements (Habitat II) held in Istanbul in 1996, and staff members have been members of UK government delegations to numerous UN-Habitat meetings. In 2001, Homeless International's Chief Executive, Ruth McLeod, chaired the Habitat National Advisory Committee, which was responsible for producing the UK government's report to 'Istanbul plus 5', the UN meeting that reviewed progress on the Habitat Agenda since 1996. As the UK's national report brought together government action domestically and internationally, Homeless International's base in, and knowledge of, the UK social housing sector proved valuable.

Our engagement with the Commonwealth has been more recent. In 1999, the newly established Commonwealth Consultative Group (CCGHS) on Human Settlements agreed a goal of 'Demonstrated progress towards adequate shelter for all with secure tenure and access to essential services in every community by 2015'. The CCGHS is made up of Ministers responsible for implementing the Habitat Agenda, but the Commonwealth as a whole adopted the goal. In establishing this goal, the Commonwealth took the lead in the international development debate, as at that time the International Development Targets[10] did not include slums, water or sanitation. In June 2001, CCGHS presented the 'Commonwealth Input to Istanbul+5' to the UN General Assembly Special Session on the Habitat Agenda, which promoted the goal and discussed CCGHS activities towards its achievement. A mechanism to link the CCGHS to other agencies – including civil society, local government and the private sector – was established; it was later named ComHabitat. Homeless International was initially invited to be a member of the advisory group for ComHabitat in early 2002, and has hosted the ComHabitat partnership since May 2004. Since becoming involved in ComHabitat, Homeless International has co-authored a paper on partnerships in human settlements, water, sanitation and waste management, which was submitted to both CCGHS and the Commonwealth Environment Ministers, and written a paper on human settlements issues in PRSPs for the Commonwealth Finance Ministers Meeting (Commonwealth Secretariat 2004 and 2005; ComHabitat 2005). The PRSPs paper argued that there was a general lack of focus on urban poverty issues, which prevents governments and donors being able to take advantage of the opportunities within urban areas to address poverty and meet the MDGs. We are currently working with UN-Habitat to expand our research in this area.

Challenges in engaging with donors and intergovernmental agencies

Homeless International has faced a number of challenges in engaging with the UK Government, other donors and intergovernmental organizations. Having a distinct niche can be advantageous in terms of engagement with policy and programme development in our area of expertise. However, being a small niche agency also has its disadvantages in terms of engaging with large, complex and rapidly changing institutions. Our limited staff resources mean that we have to prioritize engagement in terms of processes where we perceive the greatest opportunities to make an impact. It is also more difficult for an organization such as Homeless International – which does not directly implement projects or have any field staff – to engage with the increasingly devolved decision-making process of the larger agencies. As discussed above, a final challenge is being clear about what is the most appropriate advocacy role for Homeless International, as our partners own advocacy work grows and develops.

CONCLUSIONS

Government policy and practice at all levels impacts on the affordability and desirability of formal housing and infrastructure for slum dwellers in various and complex ways. As Cities Alliance state:

> *Perhaps the greatest challenge still facing cities ... is that so few countries and development agencies have adopted policies and strategies to promote the positive aspects of urbanization. The need for this is both urgent and long term. Many cities suffer from the effects of genuinely bad national and local urban policies, including misguided incentives, little financial autonomy, and consistent exclusion of much of the population on which the cities depend (2004: 3).*

The core principles of Homeless International's work have remained unchanged, even as the sophistication of the financial mechanisms it has been involved in developing and supporting has grown. However, in Homeless International's dealings with donor and intergovernmental agencies, its articulation of the mechanisms and their impacts has changed as it has ridden the broader development trends. At particular times, or in dealings with particular agencies, we have described the work in terms of building the asset bases of the urban poor, in relation to a sustainable livelihoods framework (see McLeod 2001d), or in terms of helping the urban poor to realize their rights, through a rights-based approach. Most recently, with the international community's focus on the Millennium Development Goals (MDGs), Homeless International has developed an articulation of how tackling urban poverty through financing slum upgrading urban development is essential to not only the achievement of Target 11, but all eight MDGs.[11] Homeless International remains convinced that homelessness – defined as the lack of adequate, safe and secure shelter – is a characteristic feature of poverty, and that sustainable solutions can be created only if people have access to appropriate land, finance, information, organization and technology and the opportunity to play a lead role in designing solutions that work for them.[12] Homeless International's challenge, in engaging with government at all levels, from local to the United Nations, is not to compromise these beliefs, whatever the language used to articulate the work.

CHAPTER TEN

Reflections – Homing in on Homeless International

Malcolm Jack

This chapter attempts to bring together some of the lessons so far from our experiences in bridging the finance gap in housing and infrastructure. It also includes our own perceptions about the key features of Homeless International's operation that have enabled it to carry out the work described in previous chapters, as well as an analysis of how Homeless International, as a UK-based NGO, has positioned itself internationally to carry out this work most effectively.

The work of Homeless International's partner organizations, and the organizations of the poor with whom they are allied, has been well documented and analysed from a variety of perspectives. In addition to frequent evaluations of the impact of their work, a range of researchers, academics, students and other development practitioners have studied their experiences and sought to capture some of the insights emerging. Many of the individuals who have played integral parts in the evolution of the SDI, ACHR and Orangi Pilot Project networks (and the groups which form them) have also written extensively about their impressions and experiences (see, for example, Boonyabancha 2003; 2004; Burra, Patel and Kerr 2005; Makau 2005; Patel, Burra and D'Cruz 2001; Chitekwe and Mitlin 2001; Baumann and Bolnick 2001 and Gold and Muller with Mitlin 2001). The nature and characteristics of the organizational forms involved have also been examined, for example in terms of SDI's contribution to discussions about the role and nature of transnational networks in global civil society (see Batliwala 2002).

This chapter is not intended to repeat these analyses. Rather it is intended to add another dimension to the story. It tries to look at the nature of Homeless International as a northern NGO, and how it has operated to carry out the urban finance initiatives described in the preceding chapters. In the hope that our experiences have something to offer to the development field, the chapter seeks to consider the practicalities associated with a northern NGO's attempts to operationalize, over time, the strategies and principles described in Chapter 2.

We feel there are two dimensions to look at when considering the lessons described below. They are: Homeless International's institutional location and linkages in the development context, and Homeless International's internal structures, processes and procedures.

THE IMPORTANCE OF FLEXIBILITY WHEN 'LEARNING BY DOING'

The organizations of the poor, and their local support NGOs with whom Homeless International works, are committed to the concept of 'learning by doing'. In part this reflects an assumption borne out of their experiences to date – simply that it is better to test how ideas and strategies work in practice rather than to create policies, however well drafted, that never translate into meaningful change or significant progress as far as the poor themselves are concerned. In reality, tackling the issues of land, housing and infrastructure is institutionally complex and political in nature. For this reason it has also proved to be the case that institutional relationships are best evolved in practice. Roles, responsibilities and how agencies interact cannot be tested in the abstract.

Homeless International's approach has mirrored this ethos in the context of our own work. Like our partners, we have been clear about the non-negotiable principles and overarching aims of our work, but have sought to test out and refine the processes by which we put these into practice. Although we have strategic frameworks in place to ensure our work stays focused, we have tried to avoid pre-setting the approach we should use. We feel that innovation requires a more iterative process. Both the guarantee fund and CLIFF are good examples of this. Both were pre-dated by investigation, in close collaboration with partners, of the challenges that they sought to address, but both have also tested how agencies respond to new ideas and circumstances during design and implementation. As described in Chapter 7, it was only through the process of establishing and operating CLIFF that implementing agencies began to negotiate a balance between the need for 'formal' management systems to meet 'formal' expectations of what constituted accountability and transparency, and the need to avoid over-formalizing 'informal' community-based organizational structures and systems which have consistently produced the innovations and development opportunities which CLIFF was designed to support.

Homeless International's structure and systems have evolved to support the 'learning by doing' approach. The staff is relatively small (averaging about ten over the last few years) and is not organized into strictly defined departments, although there are three recognizable functional areas of work in which staff members anchor their individual roles:

- 'Root' functions – ensuring that the organization continues to run successfully (administration, finance, personnel and governance).
- 'Sustenance' functions – fundraising and liaison with the membership base in the UK social housing sector and other groups and individuals who contribute through voluntary fundraising activities.
- 'Branch' functions – developing and resourcing initiatives with international partners, which integrate grant-funded activities, financial services, research, advocacy and technical assistance.

Work is arranged on a team basis, with each staff member playing a variety of roles in different teams, whilst maintaining their anchor in one of the three function areas described above. These arrangements help ensure cross-skilling amongst staff (which in turn helps maintain continuity when staff members leave and new individuals are recruited); cross-fertilization of ideas between staff; and maintain a coherence across the portfolio of activities undertaken by the organization. Internal communication has improved within Homeless International as a result of arranging work in this fashion, which again helps to maintain coherence. In addition, team members check and balance each other's activities by feeding in knowledge of changes in the external context that could affect, or connect, different activities undertaken. Perhaps equally importantly, all financial information is shared between staff, and financial planning, budgeting and reporting are a collective responsibility.

The teams change according to the evolving portfolio of work determined through an annual strategic review and business planning process. The strategic review enables Homeless International's Council of Management, key advisers and staff to take a broad look at contextual factors affecting work, review the focal areas of existing work, question which areas of work Homeless International 'adds value' to partners' activities, and hence determine priorities and strategies to guide future work. The business planning process details the activities and milestones for the subsequent 12 months, and provides the framework within which staff members negotiate and allocate roles and responsibilities within teams. Subsequently the staff develop and balance the budget areas for which they are responsible. Throughout the year, Homeless International maintains significant flexibility guided by its statement of delegated authority, which provides for rapid decision-making by senior staff. Again, good internal communication underpins the effectiveness of these decision-making processes.

Homeless International's Council of Management is deliberately compact, and maintains a balance between experienced individuals from the UK social housing sector and individuals with knowledge and experience in the realm of international development. In keeping with the structure and spirit of delegation, the Council of Management plays an important role in supporting, reviewing and planning at the strategic level. Of more importance than the formal governance mechanisms within Homeless International, however, is the regular informal mentoring and advice with which the Council of Management support Homeless International's staff. This helps Homeless International maintain flexibility to make rapid, but well-informed, decisions and to take forward new ideas in practice without losing transparency and accountability to its UK constituency.

There are two other aspects that contribute to the degree to which Homeless International can maintain flexibility and the capacity to test, learn and refine in practice. Firstly, Homeless International has been fortunate to receive committed support, both financial and in-kind, from several of its key members and from some donor organizations. Homeless International's location in the UK housing sector has encouraged a number of members, both individuals and organizations, to take time to understand the nature of our work and that of our partners, and hence to commit resources for exploration and testing of new ideas. For example, several UK Housing Associations have, over time, provided grants for activities such as community exchanges, pilot community-led construction initiatives and exploratory work with organizations in countries where we had not previously worked, long before other forms of support could be found to mainstream such activities. UK Housing Associations also invested in the guarantee fund in its early stages, and key advisers helped examine how it worked and hence contributed to the research that led to the development of CLIFF.

Outside of our UK membership, various departments within DFID have provided different forms of funding to explore community capacity building initiatives, the guarantee fund, research into 'Bridging the finance gap in housing and infrastructure' and the CLIFF initiative which emerged. Comic Relief, uniquely amongst the European donor organizations with whom we have worked, has played an important role in providing relatively flexible grant funds to support the processes of community capacity building and establishing urban poor funds. It has also been one of the first donors to recognize the inter-relationship between capacity building and capital investments in precedent-setting initiatives, rather than focusing on capacity building in a vacuum as other donors have done in recent years. Comic Relief has supported Homeless International's work in Africa on a sustained basis for more than a decade, having gained an understanding of the nature of our work with African partners in some depth – a useful lesson for other donors who recognize the importance of the urban development and housing issues highlighted in Chapters 1 and 2.

Finally, and most importantly, Homeless International's ability to seek innovation and try new ideas in practice is grounded in the strength of its relationships with international partners and the organizations of the poor with whom they work The ability of our partner organizations, particularly those with whom we have worked for the longest periods, to contest our suggestions and negotiate mutually agreeable solutions provides important checks and balances in the 'learning by doing' process. This space for contentious discussion is protected by long-standing professional and personal relationships that exist across all levels of the organizations involved, from community activists to board members.

FINDING AN INSTITUTIONAL LOCATION TO IMPROVE PROVISION OF FINANCE

The importance of Homeless International's partnerships with NGOs who support networks of the urban poor has already been stressed. In order to add value, however, Homeless International has sought to explore and develop relationships with a range of other institutions, and to facilitate linkages between them. A recent study of Homeless International as an organizational example of 'social entrepreneurship' described Homeless International as both a 'knowledge broker' and a 'node' in a complex network of agencies within international development (Stevenson *et al.* 2005). Financial mechanisms such as the guarantee fund and CLIFF have developed as a result of investments by both Homeless International and partner organizations in these networks of relationships, but have also provided further opportunities to develop and strengthen institutional linkages that support community-driven housing and infrastructure development. In addition, our access to funding sources reserved for European NGOs has allowed partners to obtain funds that would otherwise be inaccessible.

Our location as the charity set up and supported by the UK's social housing movement is one feature of our institutional location. In addition to the sustained financial support they have provided, many organizations have provided, and facilitated access to, advisers who have helped shape our financial services. Their ability to help us understand the concepts and terminologies of the formal world of housing finance has helped us to articulate the financing processes that we sought to support. In certain circumstances, our location within the UK social housing sector has also lent credibility to our arguments and development concepts.

Another dimension to our institutional location concerns banks. As described in Chapters 6 and 7, Homeless International has by necessity engaged with local banks in countries where our partners work, as well as with international banks and UK branches. Other international banks have recently approached us with a view to developing our financial services work still further. The technical skills of the organization's staff are particularly important in this area of work. Financial modelling, feasibility assessment and larger contextual analysis are all needed if we are to be able to add real value to this area of our partners' work.

We have also endeavoured to build linkages with bi-lateral and multi-lateral agencies concerned with either urban development or financial innovation. The exchange of ideas, lessons and experiences has helped us to compare and contrast different approaches to the issues, and to identify and share the unique features of our work and that of our partners. UN-Habitat's Slum Upgrading Facility (SUF), although not yet operational, has drawn upon a great deal of the experiences garnered through the creation and implementation of CLIFF. The teams carrying out SUF feasibility studies are aiming to initiate work in collaboration with many of Homeless International's partners. Maintaining linkages with key donors provides a means of sharing information, accessing available funds and also influencing policy. Given the relatively low profile currently given to urban poverty in international development this collaborative approach is important in ensuring that the work we support becomes visible to institutions that have the resources to assist in potential scaling up.

Acting as a knowledge broker or node agency has compelled Homeless International to develop chameleon tendencies. As Stevenson *et al.* (2005: 8) point out:

> Building relationships as a node... is also one of [Homeless International's] greatest challenges because, as it is always bridging one stakeholder entity to the other, it can become invisible itself. It focuses on the capacity of communities, federations and NGO partners, which can lead to confusion or a lack of understanding as to what Homeless International actually does and how it adds value. Managerially, it requires that HI be very focused and customize its communications to each stakeholder to ensure that its theory of change rings true. Intermediaries all over the world struggle with similar challenges as their goals are primarily centred on creating or strengthening the infrastructure on which more visible social value can be created and sustained. This is, in itself, evidence that social entrepreneurship takes a great deal of patience and hard work. Not only are strong operations required, but also communication

on a limited budget... [Homeless International] faces a major marketing and brand challenge of how to refine the messages of [its] added value and reposition itself to stakeholders.

As the preceding chapters have tried to show, Homeless International has always sought to be small, flexible and focused. As we continue our work to bridge the finance gap in housing and infrastructure, we remain committed to building relationships with other organizations to scale up and diversify the forms of finance we can offer our international partners and the organizations of the poor with whom they work. Perhaps the best way then to finish this book is to urge other development organizations to recognize the growing challenges of urbanization, urban poverty and slums and work with us on scaling up solutions to complement the energy and determination of the urban poor themselves.

Glossary of technical terms

Asset Anything owned by an individual or organization having monetary value. This is a highly contentious and difficult concept as one of the main assets that the urban poor have is knowledge.

Asymmetric information Information that is known to some people but not to others. This definition will often be used in the context of this book to describe the different knowledge bases that banks and the urban poor and their support NGOs have.

Base rate The interest rate used as an index for pricing a bank loan or line of credit. This is often set by the Central Bank.

Bi-lateral Between two parties, usually two governments. For example an agreement for development assistance between the UK Government and India.

Bond An interest-bearing certificate of indebtedness that pays a fixed rate of interest over the lifetime of the obligation. The party that issues the bond, the issuer, is obligated by a written agreement (the bond indenture) to pay the holder a specific sum of money, usually semi-annually, and the face or 'par' value of the bond on maturity. Bond issues are one way in which municipalities in many countries can raise money for investment in urban infrastructure and service provision.

Bridge financing The capital that is required to get a project off the ground while other, more mainstream finance, is being negotiated. Bridge financing is used as a stopgap and is normally repaid once the formal loan financing is in place.

Bulk loan A single loan that is extended for 'on-lending' to multiple groups or individuals. Related term: on-lending.

Bullet repayment A loan arrangement in which the principal of the loan is repaid as a lump sum at the end of the loan period rather than over the lifetime of the loan. Interest is paid on a regular basis but having access to the full principal allows the organization to make maximum use of the loan. This is especially useful when NGOs borrow funds to capitalize a revolving loan fund, which may 'turn over' several times during the loan period (i.e. as soon as repayments are received from borrowers new loans are issued to others).

Buy forward To enter into agreement to buy something at a specified price at a specified point in the future (or within a specified time limit) whatever happens to the price in the meantime. One way of protecting against the risk that a local currency will devalue against a hard currency, such as the US dollar, during the period of a loan is to enter into an agreement to buy specified amounts and kinds of hard currency in the future at a fixed rate. Whatever happens to the actual exchange rate, the agreed rate is what you will buy the hard currency at. Related term: sell forward.

Cash-flow projection An overview of cash inflows (such as income and loan financing) and outflows (such as expenditure and loan repayments) to an entity (for example, a project or organization) over a specified period of time. A cash-flow projection provides an overview of the entity's financial status and can illustrate a need for additional financing.

Central bank Every country has a central bank, sometimes called a reserve bank, which is responsible for enforcing banking regulation within that country. For example the Reserve Bank of India specifies the terms and conditions under which NGOs can receive and use external hard currency loans.

Certificate of commencement A certificate issued by the Slum Rehabilitation Authority in Mumbai that indicates that all planning and regulatory requirements have been met with respect to a specific project. In effect, the green light for a project to proceed. In practice a certificate of commencement may only become available after construction has started.

Collateral An asset that is pledged as security to ensure repayment of a loan. This can take many forms ranging from a house or land, through to household assets, such as jewellery, televisions or goats. The main requirement is that the security can be taken away if the loan is not repaid, and will have a value to the lender that will at least partly compensate for the loss they will experience in the case of non-repayment.

Comfort factor A common term used by bankers. When they identify the 'comfort factor' it means that giving the loan 'feels right'. This intuitive judgement, made by credit managers in many different contexts, is often difficult to deal with because it is rarely articulated. It is however an extremely influential factor in deciding whether or not a loan will be given.

Compound interest An interest rate applied to the outstanding principal and any accumulated interest due (compared to simple interest).

Co-operative society A legal association of members organized on a mutual basis. Co-operative housing societies are a common form of organization used by the urban poor to obtain financing for the development of housing and infrastructure. Co-operatives are usually governed under special legislation in the form of national co-operative acts.

Credit line An agreement with a financial institution to provide loans up to a specified amount, and over a particular period, as the finance is needed, rather than in a lump sum.

Credit rating A lenders' assessment of a borrowers' creditworthiness. When the borrower is an individual, assessment is usually based on past history of borrowing and repayment, employment status, and other information supplied by the borrower in an application. When the borrower is an organization, assessment is usually based on key accounting information such as the balance sheet or the viability of the venture for which loan finance is being sought. Sometimes creditworthiness is assessed by a credit rating agency.

Deed A legal document certifying ownership of property that can be used as collateral.

Emergency loans Loans made available from community savings and loan schemes for use in emergency situations, for example when someone is sick and needs medicine.

Floor Space Index (FSI) A ratio that determines the allowable construction on a measured building plot, which has the effect of restricting the height of development.

Grace period A period after a loan is extended during which no repayment and/ or interest payments are required. This is often designed to accommodate the additional expenditure that families have when they move from their previous shelter into new homes.

Guarantee A legal agreement to provide security for a loan. If the loan is not repaid according to the terms and conditions agreed, the guarantor must give up the security that has been provided. Forms of security vary: collateral (see above) or cash deposits may be acceptable. Guarantees provide a lender with a level of security that makes lending easier either because it reduces actual credit risk, or because it helps a financial institution to comply with central banking regulations that require such security as a means of making lending more secure.

(Homeless International) guarantee fund A fund maintained with long-term deposits and donations, namely from UK Housing Associations, used to secure loans for low-income households in the countries where Homeless International has established partners.

Guarantor The individual or organization that provides the guarantee.

Hedging/Hedge funds A financial technique to offset the risk of losses from price fluctuations. In the area of community-led housing and infrastructure investment Hedge funds are sometimes established using deposits provided by members. When there are fluctuations in repayments, due to seasonal employment or sometimes in the case of unexpected events such as floods, the hedge funds are used to ensure repayments are kept up until borrowers catch up with repayments.

Informal settlement A settlement developed without legal planning permission and, normally, without access to financing from formal financial institutions.

Interest rate The price paid for borrowing money. It may be calculated on a daily, weekly, monthly or annual basis. Sometimes an up-front service fee is charged instead; this is particularly common among Muslim savings and loan groups.

Lien The right of a loan provider to take and hold or sell the collateral of a borrower as security or payment for a loan. If the loan provider holds a deposit under lien, it cannot be spent or withdrawn by the depositor until the loan it secures has been repaid.

Letter of guarantee A letter issued by a guarantor to a lender that gives irrevocable authority to the lender to draw down on guarantee deposits in the case of default and under terms and conditions that are clearly specified.

Letter of intent This is a legal document that declares an intention to finance a project or to provide a certificate of commencement once specified conditions are met.

Line of credit See credit line

Loan deposit A deposit made as security prior to a loan being extended.

Memorandum of understanding (MOU) A legal agreement between different individuals or organizations that specifies the roles that each will take responsibility for within a particular project. The MOU specifies terms and conditions and how disputes, if they occur, will be resolved.

Merry-go-round Rotation savings clubs in Kenya. Similar groups can be found in many other countries and are known by local vernacular names. Usually, members put an agreed amount of saving into the club each week and the collected amount is given to one of the members in a lump sum.

Microcredit Credit made available usually in the form of small short-term loans for the development of small businesses and microenterprises operating within the informal sector. Microcredit only entails making loans available, not taking savings or providing other financial services such as insurance (see related term: microfinance). Microcredit programmes are often managed by agencies that are not formally registered as financial institutions.

Microfinance Microfinance is the provision of a broad range of financial services (for example deposits, loans, payment services, money transfers and insurance) to low-income households. Formal or informal institutions may provide microfinance. Where savings are involved, microfinance institutions are increasingly subject to regulation by national bodies appointed by government. As with microcredit, the focus of microfinance is often short-term, high-interest individual loans for enterprises within the informal sector, rather than the medium- to long-term, collective loans that may be needed for housing, infrastructure and slum upgrading. Related term: microcredit.

Multi-lateral An agency or agreement that involves several (usually many) parties, usually countries. For example UN-Habitat, Cities Alliance.

On-lending The practice of lending money that is borrowed from another source in the form of a bulk loan (see above). This may be done in the context of supporting the poor through an intermediary, such as an NGO, because poor people are not able to access finance from another source directly themselves.

Peak exposure Also known as 'maximum exposure', this describes the biggest financial gap between the amount lent by a lender for a project, and the value of the recoverable assets created within the project, at any time throughout the life of the project. For example, the 'peak exposure' could emerge at the beginning of a housing project, when the bank has lent a large amount of money for the initial construction but few saleable physical assets (for example houses) have actually been constructed.

Pre-payment A loan repayment that is greater than required by the loan agreement.

Pre-purchasing Paying part of the entire price of an asset such as an apartment or structure before it is completed.

Principal The amount of capital that is being borrowed.

Project revenue/cost recovery/income to projects Income that is generated as a result of the implementation of a project. In the case of slum development projects, for example, this could be government subsidies and contract payments, community contributions, grant funds and sales of residential and commercial units.

Provisioning The retention of funds by the lender against potential losses associated with default. The level of provisioning usually varies with different kinds of loan and is generally specified in the national banking regulations governing the lender.

Re-financing The practice of an existing debt being either extended or increased, or taken over by an alternative debt provider. For example, when the development costs of a project such as the Rajiv Indira-Suryodaya scheme in Mumbai have been met, further arrangements may be negotiated so that units within the scheme can be paid for over a longer time period. Normally this is done as a mortgage loan with the long-term financing being provided by a commercial bank, a mutual fund or a building society. The financial institution covers the purchase cost of the individual units (so the project recoups its funds) and the unit owner then makes regular payments to the financial institution.

Repayment period The period during which a loan is repaid, following any grace period. Related term: term.

Repayment rate The amount of repayment received divided by the amount of repayment agreed, for a given period, expressed as a percentage.

Security See collateral

Sell forward To enter into agreement to sell something at a specified price at a specified point in the future (or within a specified time limit) irrespective of any changes to the market price in the meantime. Banks may sell forward foreign currency at a specified rate, or slum upgrading projects could sell forward any for-sale units or transferable development rights. Related term: buy forward.

Service charge Service charges are payments made when a loan is provided, sometimes instead of interest. The use of service charges is particularly common within Muslim communities where the Koran prohibits the charging of interest.

Simple interest The interest rate is applied to the original principal amount in calculating interest due.

Transferable Development Rights (TDR) The Slum Rehabilitation Authority in Mumbai uses transferable development rights (TDR) as an incentive to encourage developers to construct free housing for the city's slum dwellers under its slum development policy. Developers earn TDR at various stages of completion of approved developments for slum dwellers. Landowners who have released land for the construction of slum rehabilitation projects can also earn TDR. The Transferable Development Rights are issued in the form of a certificate which can either then be sold to another person or legal entity, or used by the developer to develop new or existing property elsewhere, within a given area and under specified conditions.

Term The period of time over which a loan will be provided.

Title See deed.

Top-slice A term that means taking the highest level of risk. For example, if a loan is issued for £100, a guarantor who provides a 20 per cent guarantee on a top-slice basis will pay for the first £20 of loss or default (the full guarantee would be called in for a default of only 20 per cent of the loan). This contrasts with a 20 per cent guarantee which is not top-sliced (effectively a 1:5 guarantee), where the guarantor would only cover 20 per cent of the first £20 of loss or default (i.e. £4), and then 20 per cent of all subsequent loss or default. Only if the entire loan of £100 is in default would a guarantor have to pay the full £20 in a '1:5' guarantee arrangement.

Variation agreement A clause within a loan agreement or construction contract that makes provision for unanticipated variations in costs and associated increases in the amount that can be borrowed as a result. This can be an important means of safeguarding cash flow in situations where costs are not certain.

Viability analysis or viability assessment A means of analysing what the financial returns on a project are projected to be and which includes development costs, construction costs as well as financing costs.

Wholesale borrowing or lending Taking out one large loan that can then be on-lent as smaller loans. Related term: bulk loan.

Working capital The cash that is available for investment in a scheme. This does not include cash held against current liabilities.

Notes

I INTRODUCTION

1   This book uses the term 'slum' because it has not only become widely used in the international development debate – not least because of the formulation of Millennium Development Goal 7, Target 11 and the Cities Without Slums Action Plan – but also is used by many of our partner organizations in Asia. We do however recognize that all the communities with whom our partners work might not be comfortable with this term and have used other terms where appropriate.

2   The authors would like to acknowledge the work done by Dave Hughes on a draft paper examining the arguments for investing in slum upgrading, and Malcolm Jack on a number of briefing papers produced by Homeless International, from which we have drawn material in writing the introduction.

3   The book also draws on collaborative research carried out with Shack Dwellers International, Intermediate Technology Development Group (now Practical Action) and Geoffrey Payne and Associates.

4   Knowledge and Research Contract Number: R7837.

2 HOMELESS INTERNATIONAL'S INVOLVEMENT IN URBAN DEVELOPMENT FINANCE

1   A Company Limited by Guarantee is a not-for-profit company that has members rather than shareholders.

2   In 2005, the National Housing Federation, which represents housing associations in England, had 1,400 members with a turnover of £7.5 billion, and collectively managing housing stock in excess of 2 million homes (Tickell 2005).

3   This later became the Rajiv Indira-Suryodaya project and is described in more detail in Chapter 6.

4   An excellent overview of these funds can be found in Asian Coalition for Housing Rights (2002)

3 BUILDING COMMUNITY FOUNDATIONS

1   http://www.worldbank.org/participation/participation/parthistory.htm

2   The achievements of Federations of the urban poor are outlined in 'A Home in the City: the report of the Task Force on Improving the Lives of Slum Dwellers' (UN Millennium Project 2005b) and a publication by D'Cruz and

Satterthwaite (2005) entitled 'Building Homes, Changing Official Approaches: The Work of Urban Poor Organizations and their Federations and their Contributions to Meeting the Millennium Development Goals in Urban Areas.'

3   More information on enumeration processes can be found in Asian Coalition for Housing Rights (2002; 2004), Weru (2004) and on the Shack/Slum Dwellers International website (*www.sdinet.org*).

4   TAKING RISKS

1   This can be a long saga in itself due to the number and complexity of the regulations that usually apply and the inability or unwillingness of the authorities to 'fit' community-driven design processes into their procedures. In the case of the Rajiv Indira-Suryodaya scheme it took nearly seven years for Citibank to release funds following initial agreement in principle.

2   This was an extremely complex situation. Loan repayments had been good until the seventh year of repayments when there were major policy changes at state level. The Youth Charitable Organization (YCO) entered into agreements with the state to carry out infrastructure work on a subcontractual basis and delays in payment by the state led to significant cash flow problems. At the same time it was reported that household incomes were badly affected by the fall of local market prices for rice possibly as a result of large-scale importation of rice from China. There were therefore a number of policy changes that had a significant impact on the programme. See Chapter 6.

3   Under the Maharashtran Slum Rehabilitation Act, development rights accrued in one location can be sold on the open market for use in other specified locations. The rights are known as Transferable Development Rights and their significance for community led slum upgrading in Mumbai is described in more detail in Chapter 6.

4   The use of funds centrally managed by Shack/Slum Dwellers International has been particularly important for this purpose.

5   See SPARC (2003)

6   I am grateful to Xavier Briggs of Harvard University for this insight, which emerged from email correspondence.

5   A CONTINUUM OF FINANCIAL SERVICES

1   Many of these institutions relied on compulsory deductions from wages and, in effect, ended up subsidizing better off families who could afford the stipulated building standards associated with 'completed' houses at the expense of poorer families who could only afford housing built incrementally over a considerable time frame.

2   It is interesting to note for example that a SEWA Bank (Shree Mahila Sewa Sahakari Bank Ltd) report to the Reserve Bank of India indicates that 50 per cent of the loans they had disbursed were for housing purposes although their dedicated housing loans comprised only 21 per cent of total loans. This

was possible because of the flexibility of use provided for general loans (Cities Alliance 2002: 10).

3 This is a complex and long standing issue that relates to the degree to which low-income settlement development should be subsidized and supported by government rather than being paid for completely by the poor.

4 For example what conditions are laid down regarding tendering construction contracts, hiring skilled labour, buying bulk material and so on.

5 This is an agreement to provide support should the borrower have difficulties in making repayments. No commitment to covering financial loss is made but a moral commitment to providing assistance of a more general kind is.

6 For example the sale of transferable development rights as explained in Chapter 6.

7 The resistance of the developer lobby to such approaches should not be underestimated, as illustrated by the successful attempts by developers in Pune in March 2004 to prevent physically members of Pune Mahila Milan delivering tender documents to city officials.

8 For example, the development of the Rajiv-Indira Suryodaya project in Mumbai, documented in Spicer and Hussock (2003)

9 For further information on this complex but very interesting approach see SPARC (2003) and Slum Rehabilitation Authority (1997).

6 GUARANTEES OF SUCCESS?

1 European NGOs such as Homeless International, SELAVIP, Misereor, Cordaid and the International Institute for Environment and Development (IIED).

2 Particularly Homeless International's Chief Executive Ruth McLeod, senior staff within partners organizations, community leaders, and key Homeless International advisers.

3 It should also be noted that exchange rates varied substantially from the time loans were negotiated (around £1=45 Indian Rupees) to the point at which the guarantees were called (around £1=70 Indian Rupees).

4 To learn more about Chagas disease, visit the Center for Disease control and Prevention website at *http://www.cdc.gov/ncidod/dpd/parasites/ chagasdisease/factsht_chagas_disease.htm.*

5 For more information about the programme, see Development Planning Unit (2001: 63) or Homeless International's website (*www.homeless-international.org*).

6 Following a drop in interest rates nation-wide, Homeless International, Fundación Pro Habitat and El Fondo later arranged for Homeless International to accept a lower rate of interest such that El Fondo agreed to lend at a lower rate, in turn allowing Fundación Pro Habitat to offer loans at a lower rate of interest to the low-income families participating.

7 Administration fees of US$2,000 were levied by El Fondo, meaning that the amount lent (US$ 48,000) was less than the amount of the guarantee (US$50,000).

8   See the 'CLIFF Annual Reviews' produced by Homeless International (2003; 2004; 2005) for further details about the wide range of community-led activities that paved the way for the Bharat Janata scheme to go ahead.

9   The not-for-profit construction and finance company set up by SPARC on behalf of the Indian Alliance of SPARC, NSDF and Mahila Milan – see Chapter 2.

10 The seven banks who have released loans underwritten by Homeless International's Guarantee Fund are SIDBI, HUDCO, HDFC, Bank of India, Citibank and National Housing Bank (NHB) in India, and *El Fondo de la Comunidad* in Bolivia.

11 For more details about the Indian Alliance's sanitation work in an increasing number of Indian towns and cities, see SPARC (2005a; 2005b) and Burra *et al.* (2003). For more information about the UTI Bank arrangements, see Jack *et al.* (2005)

12 As part of its tender process, the BMC required performance bonds (deposits returnable upon satisfactory completion of construction, equivalent to 10 per cent of the contract amount) and advance bonds (a deposit to show that the bidding agency has sufficient funds to begin construction prior to staged payments by the BMC for work completed – equivalent to between 15 and 25 per cent of the contract amount) from all organizations bidding for sanitation contracts.

7   THE COMMUNITY-LED INFRASTRUCTURE FINANCE FACILITY

1   The CLIFF project provides technical assistance grants and management grants to local CLIFFs until the point when it is expected to reach sustainability, at which time the associated costs can be borne by the projects themselves.

2   *Bidis* are hand-rolled Indian cigarettes. The workers who make the cigarettes have the right to access special subsidies for housing.

8   'THIS HOUSE BELIEVES THAT THE PRIVATE FINANCE MARKET WILL NEVER FUND MAJOR SLUM UPGRADING'

1   SPARC is referred to throughout this interview. In practice the working relationship is between ICICI and the Indian Alliance as a whole.

9   WORKING WITH GOVERNMENT

1   This is not to say that individual members of federations do not have personal political allegiances. The point is that federations as organizations do not align themselves with particular political parties.

2   Planning legislation may designate a minimum 'set back' from a road for house construction to allow for future road widening. Large set backs can increase the cost of development because plots may need to be larger, or the cost of installing services could be higher due to longer lengths of pipes required.

3   There are however other subsidies, for example subsidies for improving basic services through the Local Authority Service Delivery Action Programme and roads through the Roads 2000 programme (Hughes 2005: 19).

4   De Soto (2000) suggests that the value of real estate held, but not legally owned, by the poor in the developing world, is at least $9.3 trillion.

5   Extract from SPARC's Citywatch news website www.citywatchnews.net.

6   For further information about the C3 Challenge Fund see Jo Beall 2003.

7   The Urban Poverty Group is a network of NGOs, university departments and consultants in the UK with a shared commitment to addressing the challenges of urban poverty worldwide.

8   This paper was later produced as a booklet (McLeod and Satterthwaite, 2000) and has continued to be used in Homeless International's advocacy work.

9   For example paragraphs 2.2.7, 2.2.4, 3.1.20, and Lesson 1 (Department for International Development 2001).

10 The International Development Targets were a precursor to the MDGs first outlined by OECD's Development Assistance Committee.

11 See for example Homeless International and Intermediate Technology Development Group, 'CSD-13: issue briefing on human settlements', Homeless International, UK 2005.

12 See Homeless International's belief statement set out in Chapter 2.

References

Wherever possible, Homeless International has sought to provide web addresses to documents freely available from the internet in the hope that this will help readers to access information more easily. Although the web addresses were correct at the time of publishing, we cannot accept responsibility for any web addresses which may have subsequently changed. Many of the articles from *Environment and Urbanization* can be downloaded for free from *http://eau.sagepub.com*

African Population and Health Research Center, 'Population and Health Dynamics in Nairobi's Informal Settlements', Report of the Nairobi Cross-sectional Slums Survey (NCSS) 2000, African Population and Health Research Center, Nairobi, April (2002).

Alder, G., 'Tackling Poverty in Nairobi's Informal Settlements: Developing an Institutional Strategy', *Environment and Urbanization,* Volume 7, Number 1, (1995), pp.85–107.

Appadurai, A., 'Deep democracy: urban governmentality and the horizon of politics', *Environment and Urbanization,* Volume 13, Number 2, (2001), pp. 24–44.

Asian Coalition for Housing Rights, 'Face to Face, notes from the network on community exchange', Asian Coalition for Housing Rights, Thailand, January (2000).

Asian Coalition for Housing Rights, 'Housing by people in Asia', Issue 14, Special issue: Community Funds, February 2002, Asian Coalition for Housing Rights, Thailand, (2002). *www.achr.net*

Asian Coalition for Housing Rights, 'Housing by people in Asia', Issue 15, Special issue on how poor people deal with eviction, October 2003, Asian Coalition for Housing Rights, Thailand, (2003). *www.achr.net*

Asian Coalition for Housing Rights, 'Negotiating the right to stay in the city', *Environment and Urbanization,* Volume 16, Number 1, (2004), pp. 9–25.

Asian Coalition for Housing Rights, 'Understanding Asian Cities', Asian Coalition for Housing Rights, Thailand, (2005a). *www.achr.net*

Asian Coalition for Housing Rights, 'Housing by people in Asia', Issue 16, Special issue on how Asia's precarious coastal communities are coping after Tsunami, August 2005, Asian Coalition for Housing Rights, Thailand, (2005b). *www.achr.net*

Bartlett, S., 'An Alternative Model for Responding to Children in Poverty: The Work of the Alliance in Mumbai and Other Cities', *Children, Youth and Environments,* Volume 15, Number 2, (2005) pp. 342–355. *http://www.colorado.edu/journals/cye/15_2/15_2_20_AllianceInMumbai.pdf.*

Batliwala, S., 'Grassroots Movements as Transnational Actors: Implications for Global Civil Society', *International Journal of Voluntary and Nonprofit Organizations,* Volume 13, Number 4, December (2002), pp. 393–410.

Batliwala, S., 'Report of an assessment of the work of SPARC and its allies on resettlement and rehabilitation of the urban poor', Homeless International, Coventry, (2005).

Baumann, T. and Bolnick, J., 'Out of the frying pan into the fire; the limits of loan finance in a capital subsidy context', *Environment and Urbanization*, Volume 13, Number 2, (2001), pp. 103–116.

Beall, J, 'City–Community Challenge Fund (C3), Interim External Evaluation Report', commissioned by Infrastructure and Urban Development Division (IUDD), Department for International Development, United Kingdom, January (2003). *http://www.ucl.ac.uk/dpu-projects/drivers_urb_change/urb_economy/ pdf_innov_financ_mech/DFID_Beall_C3_Evaluation%20Report.pdf*

Bernstein, P.L., (1998), *Against the Gods, The Remarkable Story of Risk*, John Wiley and Sons, New York.

Boonyabancha, S., 'Savings and loans: drawing lessons from some experiences in Asia', *Environment and Urbanization*, Volume 13, Number 2, (2001), pp. 9–22.

Boonyabancha, S., 'A Decade of Change: From the Urban Community Development Office (UCDO) to the Community Organizations Development Institute (CODI) in Thailand', Poverty Reduction in Urban Areas Series, Working Paper 12, International Institute for Environment and Development, London, May (2003).

Boonyabancha, S., (2004), 'A decade of change: From the Urban Community Development Office to the Community Organisation Development Institute in Thailand', in *Empowering squatter citizen*, Satterthwaite, D. and Mitlin, D. (eds.), Earthscan, London, pp. 25–53.

Boonyabancha, S., 'Baan Mankong: going to scale with 'slum' and squatter upgrading in Thailand', *Environment and Urbanization*, Volume 17, Number 1, (2005), pp.21–46.

Burra, S., 'Guidelines for the revision of regulations for urban upgrading', paper produced as part of the Regulatory guidelines for urban upgrading research project co-ordinated by the Intermediate Technology Development Group, SPARC, Mumbai, (2004). *www.sparcindia.org.*

Burra, S., 'Towards a pro-poor framework for slum upgrading in Mumbai, India', *Environment and Urbanization*, Volume 17, Number 1, (2005), pp. 67–88. *www.sparcindia.org.*

Burra, S., Patel, S. and T. Kerr, 'Community-designed, built and managed toilet blocks in Indian cities', *Environment and Urbanization*, Volume 15, Number 2, (2003), pp. 11–32.

Burra, S., Patel, S. and T. Kerr, (2005), 'Community-designed, built and managed toilet blocks in Indian cities', *Reducing poverty and sustaining the environment – the politics of local engagement*, Bass, S., Reid, H., Satterthwaite, D. and P. Steele (ed.), Earthscan, London.

CGAP, 'Housing Microfinance', Donor Brief No 20, Helping to Improve Donor Effectiveness in Microfinance, CGAP, Washington, August (2004). www.cgap.org

Chitekwe, B. and D. Mitlin, 'The urban poor under threat and in struggle: options for urban development in Zimbabwe, 1995-2000', *Environment and Urbanization*, Volume 13, Number 2, (2001), pp. 85–102.

Cities Alliance, 'SEWA Bank's housing microfinance programme in India', Shelter Finance for the Poor Series, Cities Alliance, Washington, (2002).

Cities Alliance, '2003 Annual Report', Cities Alliance, Washington, (2003).

Cities Alliance, '2004 Annual Report', Cities Alliance, Washington, (2004).

ComHabitat, 'PRSPs, human settlements and urban poverty', paper prepared by Kim Mullard and Ruth McLeod and submitted to the Commonwealth Finance Ministers' Meeting, FMM(05)(INF)1, Commonwealth Secretariat, London, August (2005). *www.comhabitat.org*

Commonwealth Secretariat, 'Effective Partnerships in the Areas of Human Settlements, Water, Sanitation and Waste Management', Commonwealth Consultative Group on the Environment meeting paper, CCGE(04)1, Commonwealth Secretariat, London, February (2004).

Commonwealth Secretariat, 'Effective Partnerships in the Areas of Human Settlements, Water, Sanitation and Waste Management', Commonwealth Consultative Group on Human Settlements meeting paper, CCGHS(05)2, Commonwealth Secretariat, London, March (2005).

Cornia, G. A., Jolly, R. and F. Stewart, (1987), *Adjustment with a Human Face*, Oxford University Press, Oxford.

D'Cruz, C. and D. Satterthwaite, 'Building Homes, Changing Official Approaches: The Work of Urban Poor Organizations and their Federations and their Contributions to Meeting the Millennium Development Goals in Urban Areas', Poverty Reduction in Urban Areas Series, Working Paper 16, International Institute for Environment and Development, London, May (2005).

Datta, K. and G.A. Jones, (ed.), (1998), *Housing and Finance in Developing Countries*, Routledge, London.

de Soto, H., (2000), *The Mystery of Capital: why Capitalism Triumphs in the West and Fails Everywhere Else*, Basic Books, New York.

Department for International Development, 'Eliminating World Poverty: A Challenge for the 21st Century', White Paper on International Development, Presented to Parliament by the Secretary of State for International Development by Command of Her Majesty, CM3789, London, November (1997). *http://www.dfid.gov.uk/pubs/files/whitepaper1997.pdf.*

Department for International Development, 'Meeting the challenge of poverty in urban areas', Strategies for achieving the international development targets, Department for International Development, London, April (2001).

Department for International Development, 'Making connections, infrastructure for poverty reduction', Department for International Development, London, September (2002).

Development Planning Unit, 'Implementing the Habitat Agenda: in search of urban sustainability', Development Planning Unit, University College London, London (2001).

Gold, J. and Muller, A. with D. Mitlin, 'The principles of Local Agenda 21 in Windhoek: collective action and the urban poor', Urban Environmental Action Plans and Local Agenda 21 Series, Working Paper No. 9, International Institute for Environment and Development, London, December (2001).

Government of Kenya, 'Kenya Economic Survey 2003', Government of Kenya, Nairobi, (2003).

Government of Sri Lanka, 'Regaining Sri Lanka: Vision and Strategy for Accelerated Development', Government of Sri Lanka, December (2002).

Harvard University School of Graduate Design, 'Housing Microfinance Initiatives, Synthesis and Regional Summary: Asia, Latin America and Sub-Saharan Africa with selected case studies', Development Alternatives Inc., Bethesda, May (2000).

Hasan, A., Patel, S. and D. Satterthwaite, 'How to meet the Millennium Development Goals (MDGs) in urban areas', *Environment and Urbanization*, Volume 17, Number 1, (2005), pp. 3–19.

Homeless International, 'Homeless International', *Environment and Urbanization*, Volume 4, Number 2, (1992), pp.168–175.

Homeless International, 'International Guarantee Fund – YCO, India: evaluation report', Homeless International report to Department for International Development, Homeless International, Coventry, (1995).

Homeless International, 'The Habitat Agenda: progress since 1996', Homeless International Dialogue publication, Homeless International, Coventry, June (2001). *www.homeless-international.org*.

Homeless International, 'Community-Led Infrastructure Finance Facility (CLIFF) Development and Demonstration Project Implementation Plan', Implementation plan produced by Homeless International for CLIFF forming part of the partnership agreement with the World Bank, Homeless International, Coventry, (2002a).

Homeless International, 'Feeding back on the first UN World Urban Forum', Homeless International, Coventry, June (2002b) *www.homeless-international.org*.

Homeless International, 'Community-Led Infrastructure Finance Facility Annual Report to August 2003', Homeless International, Coventry, (2003) *www.homeless-international.org/cliff*.

Homeless International, 'Community-Led Infrastructure Finance Facility 2nd Annual Review to March 2004', Homeless International, Coventry, (2004) *www.homeless-international.org/cliff*.

Homeless International, 'An Interview with Anil Kumar, Assistant General Manager, ICICI Bank', Homeless International, Coventry, (2005c) *www.homeless-international.org/cliff*.

Homeless International, 'Community-Led Infrastructure Finance Facility (CLIFF) 3rd Annual Review to April 2005', Homeless International, Coventry, (2005d) *www.homeless-international.org/cliff*.

Homeless International and Intermediate Technology Development Group, 'CSD-13: issue briefing on human settlements', Homeless International, Coventry, (2005). *www.homeless-international.org*.

Hughes, D., 'First CLIFF Kenya monitoring report', Homeless International, Coventry, (2005). *www.homeless-international.org/cliff*.

Hughes, D. and G. Masimba, 'Feasibility studies for the application of Community-Led Infrastructure Finance Facility (CLIFF) operations in Zambia', paper produced by Homeless International as part of Homeless International's research into *Feasibility studies for the application of Community-Led Infrastructure Finance Facility (CLIFF) operations in Sub-Saharan African countries* for UN-Habitat's Urban Management Programme (UMP), Homeless International, Coventry, September (2004) *www.homeless-international.org/ump*.

Jack, M., 'Urbanisation, Sustainable Growth and Poverty Reduction in Asia', paper produced for the Department For International Development's Asia 2015 Conference, London, UK, March (2006) *http://www.asia2015conference.org/pdfs/Jack.pdf*.

Jack, M. and F.R. Braimah, 'Feasibility studies for the application of Community-Led Infrastructure Finance Facility (CLIFF) operations in Ghana', paper produced by Homeless International as part of Homeless International's research into *Feasibility studies for the application of Community-Led Infrastructure Finance Facility (CLIFF) operations in Sub-Saharan African countries* for UN-Habitat's Urban Management Programme (UMP), Homeless International, Coventry, September (2004) *www.homeless-international.org/ump*.

Jack, M., Morris, I. and R. McLeod, 'Third CLIFF India monitoring report', Homeless International, Coventry, (2005) *www.homeless-international.org/cliff*.

Levy, C. and D. Satterthwaite, 'Tracking a learning alliance to manage risks', CLIFF Monitoring Report', Homeless International, Coventry, August (2004) *www.homeless-international.org/cliff*.

Lupton, D. (ed.), (1999), *Risk and Socio-cultural Theory – New Directions and Perspectives*, Cambridge University Press, Cambridge.

McLeod, R., 'The Homeless International Guarantee Fund', Homeless International bulletin on housing finance, Volume 2, Homeless International, UK, (1994).

McLeod, R., 'Costs associated with accessing legal shelter for low-income groups in new urban developments', paper produced by Homeless International as part of the Regulatory frameworks for affordable shelter research project co-ordinated by Geoff Payne and Associates, Homeless International, Coventry, (2001a). *www.homeless-international.org/gpa*.

McLeod, R., 'Experiences of linking community based housing finance to formal finance mechanisms', paper produced for a meeting on Housing Finance held in Gavle (Sweden) on 28th March 2001, Homeless International, Coventry, (2001b) *www.homeless-international.org/bfg*.

McLeod, R., 'Humpty Dumpty, poverty and urban governance – an exploration of investment partnerships with the poor, insights from the Federation process', paper produced for the 2nd Regional Caribbean Meeting of UN-Habitat's Urban Management Programme (UMP) held in Dominica during September 2001, Homeless International, Coventry, (2001c). *www.homeless-international.org/bfg*

McLeod, R., 'The impact of regulations and procedures on the livelihoods and asset base of the urban poor – a financial perspective', paper produced by Homeless International as part of the 'Regulatory guidelines for urban upgrading' research project co-ordinated by the Intermediate Technology Development Group (ITDG), Homeless International, Coventry, (2001d). *www.homeless-international.org/itdg*.

McLeod, R., 'Paucity and capacity within city financing', paper produced as part of Homeless International's Bridging the finance gap in housing and infrastructure research project, Homeless International, Coventry, (2002a) *www.homeless-international.org/bfg*.

McLeod, R., 'Research on Bridging the Finance Gap in Housing and Infrastructure and the Development of CLIFF', paper produced by Homeless International as part of Homeless International's Bridging the finance gap in housing and infrastructure research project, UK, (2002b). *www.homeless-international.org/bfg*.

McLeod, R., 'Feasibility studies for the application of Community-Led Infrastructure Finance Facility (CLIFF) operations in Uganda', paper produced by Homeless International as part of Homeless International's research into *Feasibility studies for the application of Community-Led Infrastructure Finance Facility (CLIFF) operations in Sub-Saharan African countries* for UN-Habitat's Urban Management Programme (UMP), Homeless International, Coventry, (2004). *www.homeless-international.org/ump*.

McLeod, R., 'CLIFF – Achievements, learning and issues to be addressed', Homeless International, Coventry, (2005a) *www.homeless-international.org/cliff*.

McLeod, R., 'Feasibility studies for the application of Community-Led Infrastructure Finance Facility (CLIFF) operations in Sub-Saharan African countries', paper produced by Homeless International as part of Homeless International's research into *Feasibility studies for the application of Community-Led Infrastructure Finance Facility (CLIFF) operations in Sub-Saharan African countries* funded by UN-Habitat's Urban Management Programme (UMP), Homeless International, Coventry, (2005b). *www.homeless-international.org/ump*.

McLeod, R. and D. Satterthwaite, 'Why Housing? The Significance of Housing Investment as a Means of Eliminating Poverty', Homeless International, Coventry, (2000). *www.homeless-international.org*.

Makau, J., 'Building partnerships: local to global', in Homeless International with the Urban Poverty Group, 'Dialogue: Good urban governance, tackling urban poverty around the world', Homeless International Dialogue publication, Homeless International, Coventry, (2005), pp. 13–14. *www.homeless-international.org*.

Mitlin, D. 'Understanding Urban Poverty: What the Poverty Reduction Strategy Papers tell us', Poverty Reduction in Urban Areas Series, Working Paper, International Institute for Environment and Development, London, April (2004a).

Mitlin, D., 'Reshaping local democracy', *Environment and Urbanization*, Volume 16, Number 1, (2004b), pp. 3–8.

Mukhija, V., 'Enabling slum redevelopment in Mumbai: policy paradox in practice', *Housing Studies*, Volume 16, Number 6, (2001), pp. 791–806.

Nirman (2005), *SPARC Samudaya Nirman Sahayak Annual Report 2004–2005*, Nirman, Mumbai.

Overman, H. and A. Venables, 'Cities in the developing world', paper commissioned by Department for International development, London, (2005). *econ.lse.ac.uk/staff/ajv/difcit12.pdf*.

Pamoja Trust (2005), *Pamoja Trust Annual Report 2004*, Pamoja Trust, Nairobi.

Patel, S, Burra, S and C. D'Cruz, 'Slum/Shack Dwellers International – foundations to treetops', *Environment and Urbanization*, Volume 13, Number 2, (2001), pp. 45–59.

Patel, S, D'Cruz, C. and S. Burra, 'Beyond evictions in a global city: people managed resettlement in Mumbai', *Environment and Urbanization*, Volume 14, Number 1, (2002), pp. 159–172.

Payne, G., (2002), 'Introduction', *Land, Rights and Innovation, improving tenure security for the urban poor*, Payne, G. (ed.), ITDG Publishing, London, pp. 3–22.

Platt, R. (1997), 'Ensuring effective provision of low cost housing finance in India: an in-depth case analysis', University of Bradford Management Centre Working Paper Series, no. 9725, Bradford, November 1997.

Ravallion, M., 'On the Urbanization of Poverty', Development Research Group, World Bank, Washington, (2001).

Rojas, R., 'Bolivia: Fundación Pro Habitat – a Case Study', Paper produced for Homeless International as part of the Bridging the finance gap in housing and infrastructure research project, Homeless International, Coventry, (2000). *www.homeless-international.org/bfg.*

Sanyal, B. and V. Mukhija, 'Institutional pluralism and housing delivery – a case of unforeseen conflicts in Mumbai, India', Department of Urban Studies and Planning, Massachusetts Institute of Technology, USA, August (2000). *archidev.org/IMG/pdf/ Sanyal.pdf.*

Satterthwaite, D., Levy, C. and J. Benington, 'CLIFF monitoring and evaluation framework', produced for guiding the monitoring and evaluation of CLIFF, Homeless International, Coventry, (2004). *www.homeless-international.org/cliff.*

Satterthwaite, D., 'The Underestimation of Urban Poverty in Low- and Middle-Income Nations', Poverty Reduction in Urban Areas Series, Working Paper 14, International Institute for Environment and Development, London, April (2004).

Satterthwaite, D. (2005a), 'Meeting the MDGs in Urban Areas: The Forgotten Role of Local Organizations', in Bigg, T. and D. Satterthwaite, (ed.), *How to Make Poverty History: The Central Role of Local Organizations in Meeting the MDGs*, IIED, London, pp.99–128.

Satterthwaite, D., 'The scale of urban change worldwide 1950–2000 and its underpinnings', Human Settlements Discussion Paper (Urban-01), International Institute for Environment and Development, London, May (2005b). *www.iied.org/pubs/pdf/full/ 9531IIED.pdf.*

Shack/Slum Dwellers International, 'SDI Holds HIV/AIDS Dialogue', SDI Bulletin 15, Shack/Slum Dwellers International, Cape Town, September (2005). *www.sdinet.org.*

Sierra, K., 'Financing city infrastructure', *Villes en developpement*, Number 69, Bulletin de la coopération française pour le développement urbain, l'habitat et l'aménagement spatial, CitiesAlliance and Institut des Sciences et des Techniques de l'Equipement et de l'Environnement pour le Développement, September (2005) *http:// www.citiesalliance.org/doc/resources/financing/ved_no-69%20_eng.pdf.*

Slum Rehabilitation Authority, 'Guidelines for the Implementation of Slum Rehabilitation Schemes in Greater Mumbai', Slum Rehabilitation Authority, Housing and Special Assistance Department, Government of Maharashtra, Mumbai, December (1997)

Spicer, D.E. and H. Husock, 'Financing Slum Rehabilitation in Mumbai: A Non-Profit Caught in the Middle', Case Study 1688.0, The Kennedy School of Governance, Harvard University, USA, January (2003).

SPARC, 'Revised Report, Cities Alliance Project on Pro-Poor Slum Upgrading Framework For Mumbai, India', Submitted to Cities Alliance/United Nations Centre For Human Settlements (Habitat), June (2003).

SPARC, 'Citywatch India', a publication of the SPARC-NSDF-Mahila Milan Alliance, SPARC, Mumbai, June (2004).

SPARC, 'Citywatch India', a publication of the SPARC-NSDF-Mahila Milan Alliance, SPARC, Mumbai, June (2005a). *www.sparcindia.org*

SPARC, 'SPARC Annual Report 2004–2005', SPARC, Mumbai, (2005b) *www.sparcindia.org*

Stevenson, K. and MBA Students, 'Social Entrepreneurship – Innovation and New Business Models: Homeless International, an innovative social venture', case study produced by MBA students, Said Business School, Oxford University, Oxford, UK, unpublished, (2005).

Tickell, J., (2005), *Turning hopes into homes: a short history of affordable housing*, National Housing Federation, London.

Turner, J.F.C. and R. Fichter, (1972), *Freedom to Build: Dweller Control of the Housing Process*, New York, Macmillan.

UN-Habitat, (2003), *The Challenge of Slums: Global Report on Human Settlements 2003*, Earthscan, London.

UN-Habitat, 'Habitat Debate', Volume 10, Number 1, UN-Habitat, Nairobi, March (2004).

UN Millennium Project (2005a), *Investing in Development: A practical plan to achieve the millennium development goals*, New York. *www.unmillenniumproject.org/reports/fullreport.htm.*

UN Millennium Project (2005b), 'A Home in the City', Report of the Task Force on Improving the Lives of Slum Dwellers', Earthscan, London. *www.unmillenniumproject.org/documents/Slumdwellers-complete.pdf.*

Weru, J., 'Community federations and city upgrading: the work of Pamoja Trust and Muungano in Kenya', *Environment and Urbanization*, Volume 16, Number 1, (2004).

World Bank, 'The World Bank and Participation', The World Bank, Operations Policy Department, Washington, (1994).

World Bank and UNCHS, 'Cities Alliance for Cities Without Slum, Action Plan for Moving Slum Upgrading to Scale', special summary edition, (1999).

World Health Organization (1999) 'Creating Healthy Cities in the 21st Century', in Satterthwaite, D. (ed.) *The Earthscan Reader on Sustainable Cities*, Earthscan, London.

Index